THE Menorah

THE Menorah

FROM THE BIBLE TO MODERN ISRAEL

STEVEN FINE

HARVARD UNIVERSITY PRESS

Cambridge, Massachusetts, and London, England

2016

Printed in the United States of America
First printing

Library of Congress Cataloging-in-Publication Data

Names: Fine, Steven, author.
Title: The menorah : from the Bible to modern Israel / Steven Fine.
Description: Cambridge, Massachusetts : Harvard University Press, 2016. |
Includes bibliographical references and index.
Identifiers: LCCN 2016018189 | ISBN 9780674088795 (cloth)
Subjects: LCSH: Menorah—History. | Menorah in art.
Classification: LCC BM657.M35 F56 2016 | DDC 296.4/61—dc23 LC record
available at https://lccn.loc.gov/2016018189

Contents

NOTE ON TRANSLITERATION AND TRANSLATION

Transliterations of Hebrew and of Jewish Aramaic dialects follow the "general" system used by the *Encyclopedia Judaica* (Jerusalem: Keter, 1972, 1:71), with the exception that the letter *tsadi* is transliterated with "ts" and the letter *qof* with a "q." Hebrew and Greek nouns that appear in *The American Heritage Dictionary: Fifth Edition* (Boston: Houghton Mifflin Harcourt, 2016) are treated as English words. Names that appear in the Hebrew Bible or in the New Testament are spelled in standard English forms. *The Holy Bible: Revised Standard Version* (London: Nelson, 1965) served as the starting point for translations of the Hebrew Scriptures, the New Testament, and the Apocrypha. Unless otherwise noted, translations of classical authors are adapted from the Loeb Classical Library of the Harvard University Press, and translations of rabbinic literature are my own. All links were live as of January 1, 2016.

Preface

This historical reflection on the menorah has everything to do with my own biography and the ways that my interests have developed over an increasingly lengthy career. It is rooted in my childhood love of the festival of Hanukkah, with its ever-increasing yet flickering flames. I remember fondly my mother's shining chrome menorah with multicolored candles imported from Israel, their box gaudily decorated with the image of an Arch of Titus–like menorah that I now know was designed by the great Zionist artist Ze'ev Raban. It begins with the glow I felt as a nine-year-old American boy after the tears my mother shed in May 1967 as the prospect of yet another Jewish catastrophe turned to joy and laughter in six days at the start of June. This crisis was the beginning of my love affair with the seven-branched menorah, the symbol of the State of Israel, and thus of my cognizance of the Arch of Titus menorah.

From my first excursion to Israel as a high school junior through my most recent monograph, the menorah has never been far from me, whether as the subject of high school and college papers, the focus of my internship in the Judaica Department of the Israel Museum, my specialty as curator of an archaeological collection at the University of Southern California, the subject of my first academic article, the cover illustrations of most of my books, or an important part of my recent work on the polychromy of the Arch of Titus. My interest in the menorah peaked while I was Jewish Foundation Professor of Jewish Studies at the University of Cincinnati, when in 2002 the placement of a Chabad menorah in the city plaza, Fountain Square, provoked a truly disturbing—sometimes anti-Semitic—response. Supreme Court Justice John Paul Stevens intervened, overruling the city's decision to block the menorah display. To deepen the conversation, the following year I arranged a scholarly lecture series, "The Menorah: From Sinai to Cincinnati." The biblical lampstand, then, is an interest that has grown as I have developed—and I with it.

The book that you are reading is a piece of my larger Arch of Titus Project (www.yu.edu/cis), which is committed to exploring the arch and its reception from its construction in circa 81 CE to the present, here focusing upon just one element of that monument, the menorah. I write this diachronic study from within the disciplinary context of Judaic studies, even as I often reach beyond the traditional boundaries of that discipline. Happily, my first training included Jewish folklore under Dov Noy and Jewish art under Bezalel Narkiss and Stephen S. Kayser; religious studies at the University of California, Santa Barbara; and the history of Indian art under Pratapaditya Pal—fields that tend to focus upon themes and genre over time—the *longue durée.* My first formation in Jewish history as a disciplinary perspective took place under the late great Amos Funkenstein—perhaps the last "renaissance scholar" of Jewish history. Amos taught me not to fear boundaries of time or place, of scholarly "canon," "genre," or of simple prejudice—a legacy that I happily bear.

Institutions in the United States, Israel, and Europe have been most generous in support of this project. I thank Yeshiva University for providing me with a congenial home in which to write, think, and imagine; the Getty Research Institute for a productive stay in the spring of 2015 during which I was able to complete the first draft manuscript; and the International Catacomb Society for awarding me their Shohet Fellowship in support of this project. Librarians, curators, archivists and libraries, archives, and museums have been most gracious to me. I especially thank, in New York: Yeshiva University Libraries, Yeshiva University Museum, the New York Public Library, the Watson Library of the Metropolitan Museum of Art, the Library of the Jewish Theological Seminary, the American Numismatic Society, and the constituent organizations of the Center for Jewish History. In Los Angeles: The Getty Research Institute, UCLA's Young Research Library, American Jewish University's Ostrow Library, the Hebrew Union College's Francis-Henry Library, and Wilshire Boulevard Temple. In Washington, DC: The United States Holocaust Memorial Museum Library. In Rome: the Jewish Community of Rome, especially the Museo Ebraico di Roma; the Soprintendenza Speciale per i Beni Archeologici di Roma; Archivio di Stato di Roma; Archivio Storico Istituto Luce; and the Museo Pio Cristiano of the Vatican Museums. In Israel: Beit Hagdudim: The Jewish Legions Museum in Avihayil; the Center for Jewish Art, Jerusalem; the Central Zionist Archives, Jerusalem; the Gush Katif Museum, Jerusalem; the Hebrew University Archives, Jerusalem; the Israel Folklore Archive, Haifa; the Israel State Archives, Jerusalem; the Jabotinsky Institute, Tel Aviv; the Knesset Archives, Jerusalem; the archives of the Menachem Begin Heritage Center, Jerusalem; the Schatz Family Archive, Jerusalem; the Wolfson Museum of Jewish Art, Jerusalem; the archives of Yad Chaim Weizmann, Rehovot; and especially the National Library of Israel, Jerusalem. It is no understatement that this project, which cuts a very wide trench through Western culture, would have been far more difficult—if not impossible—were it not for the many fine Web resources developed even as I was writing. I especially thank the unsung people of Hebrewbooks.org, Historical Jewish Press of the Jewish National Library and Tel Aviv University, Ma'agarim: The Historical Dictionary Project of the Academy of the Hebrew Language, Perseus Digital Library, Rambi: The Index of Articles on Jewish Studies, Project Ben Yehuda, and Google Books.

Many individuals have helped me along the way—as primary sources, as scholarly interlocutors, and sometimes, unwittingly, as both. I am pleased to thank them here, in alphabetical order: Moti Benmelech, Shulamith Berger, Asher Biemann, Robert Bonfil, Ra'anan Boustan, Cinzia Conti, Jessica Dello Russo, Menachem Mendel Elishevitz, Helen Evans, Joseph Frager, Bernard Frischer, Isaiah Gafni, Matt Goldish, Nan Goldman, Galit Hasan-Rokem, Ena Heller, David Hendin, Elezar Hurvitz, Batsheva Goldman Ida, Joshua Karlip, Maya Balakirsky Katz, Sean Kingsley, Shulamit Laderman, Sean Leatherbury, Paolo Liverani, Carol Meyers, Eric Meyers, Alec Mishory, Ann Moffatt, R. Steven Notley, Jess Olson, Tomer Persico, Heinrich Piening, Umberto Piperno, Mark Podwal, Ira Robinson, Ben Zion Rosenfeld, Peter Schertz, Lawrence Schiffman, Marc Shapiro, Yonatan Shtencel, Jeffrey Spier, Ronit Steinberg, Michiel Klein Swormink, David Tartakover, Binyamim Tsedaka, Susan Walker, and Joe Zias. Ben Bowman, Akiba Covitz, Aiya Port, Abby Russell, and their team created my Coursera course, *The Arch of Titus: Rome and the Menorah* (https://www.coursera.org/learn/archoftitus), which was filmed and produced in Los Angeles, New York, Rome, and Jerusalem. This massive undertaking taught me much about filmmaking as well as ways to process my ideas—to the benefit of this volume. I thank my Yeshiva

University students—graduates and undergraduates—for helping me to sharpen my ideas and for always making me smile, even (or particularly) at times when my own results were not yet fully cooked. I especially thank my students Yitzchak Schwartz and Matt Williams for reading the entire manuscript. Sharmila Sen, my editor at Harvard University Press, encouraged me to try my hand at a book that would speak not only to scholars but also to students and to general readers. Writing with this challenge before me has been a glorious experience, and I thank Sharmila profusely for this. I thank the anonymous readers for their excellent suggestions. Heather M. Hughes and Annamarie McMahon Why; Deborah Grahame-Smith and her team at Westchester Publishing Services, especially Virginia Perrin, have made this a better book. For this I am grateful. My son, Yaakov Fine, now sixteen years old, has been my astonishingly able and dogged research assistant throughout this project. Elisha Fine is my nimble conversation partner, and also prepared the index. Leah Bierman Fine, who lived and proofread every word of this book, is my constant support and best friend. It was my late parents, Jane and Leonard Fine, who set the flames burning, however, and this study—like all of my work, is a memorial lamp to them.

The origins of this particular project date to the 1990s, when I became aware that radical elements within the Jewish world were taking ownership of the menorah, transforming it into a symbol for trends so worrisome that I—by then a scholar of the destruction of Jerusalem in 70 CE and the centuries that followed—first began to sense a slippage toward darkness that the reasonable middle might not be able to extinguish. Visions of the Jewish-Roman (or is it Roman-Jewish?) historian Josephus's Zealots dragging the Jewish nation into a catastrophic revolt against Rome, the destruction of the Jerusalem Temple, and the captivity of the menorah began to haunt me. These fears climaxed in the murder just over twenty years ago of the very general, then prime minister, Yitzhak Rabin, who had captured Jerusalem in 1967—unwittingly unleashing the darkness.

In the seven chapters that make up this volume—one for each branch of the menorah—I turn my scholarly lamp back on my beloved menorah, with the hope of illuminating what for me is good and interesting in this marvelous lampstand. While the theme is historical, this history is ever present and increasingly affects our—or at least my—present. I dedicate this book to the memory of Yitzhak Rabin, with the prayer and hope that "a new light will shine on Zion. . . ."

THE Menorah

Introduction

Standing before the Arch of Titus Menorah

The arch is now mouldering to its fall, & the imagery almost erased by a lapse of fifty generations. Beyond this obscure monument of our destruction is seen the monument of the power of our destroyer's family, now a mountain of ruins.

The Flavian Amphitheatre is become a habitation of owls and dragons. The power, of whose possession it was once the type, & of whose departure it is now the emblem, is become a dream and a memory. Rome is no more than Jerusalem.

—Percy Bysshe Shelley, "Arch of Titus," published in 1832

Shelley, the great British Romantic poet, places his reflection in the mouth of an imagined Jew, who, like him, is visiting the sacred center of classical Rome. This Jew stands before the Arch of Titus, looking back toward the nearby hulking ruin of the "Flavian Amphitheatre," what we now call the Colosseum. Such reflections were common among nineteenth-century visitors to Rome, first by European Romantics reflecting on the Jewish condition, and eventually by Jews themselves. As Freud put it on a postcard after a visit in 1913, "The Jew survives it." The arch and the theater together became a cipher for the complexities of Jewish integration into European society, a signpost in an imagined dichotomy between Judaism and Hellenism, between Rome and Jerusalem. These marble and brick ruins served, and continue to serve, as a stone emblem of a tortuous and, in the twentieth century, deadly process.

Romualdo Moscioni, the Arch of Titus, albumen print, latter nineteenth century, private collection, Wikimedia Commons

Unlike Shelley's imagined Jew, I am a flesh-and-blood one. At about eleven o'clock on June 5, 2012, I found myself face-to-face with the Arch of Titus menorah. I stood centimeters from this selfsame "monument of our destruction," nervously clinging to aluminum scaffolding some six or more meters above the pavement of the Via Sacra, the "Sacred Way" of ancient Rome. Here I was, beneath the triumphal arch of the Emperor Titus—a ruler who is referred to in classical Hebrew sources as *Teetuus ha-Rasha,* Titus the Evil. Built about 81 CE, this construction celebrates the triumphal entrance of Titus—together with the treasures of the Jerusalem Temple, prized slaves, and his triumphant troops—into Rome a decade or so earlier. There was another arch like it in Rome on the Circus Maximus (long ago destroyed), discovered in 2014. The Colosseum was off to my left. According to a recently deciphered inscription, "The Emperor Titus Caesar Vespasian Augustus ordered the new amphitheater to be made from the (proceeds from the sale of the) booty"—presumably of the Jewish War. A coin minted under one of the Flavian emperors—

The Arch of Titus, ca. 81 CE, photograph by Unocad, courtesy of the Arch of Titus Project

Vespasian and his sons Titus and Domitian—shows the Colosseum. There we see between the arches on the third-level symbols of that victory—including at the very center the palm tree of Judaea, a land famous for its dates (just as Florida today is known for its oranges). Just a few yards above my head, in a relief at the pinnacle of the arch, I could

Spolia Panel, bas-relief, Arch of Titus, ca. 81 CE, photograph by Unocad, courtesy of the Arch of Titus Project

look into Titus's eyes as his soul ascended on the back of an eagle to the heavens, to become a god. Here, there is none of the sardonic humor ascribed to Titus's father, Vespasian, as he died. According to the second-century Roman historian Suetonius, as Vespasian lay on his deathbed he exclaimed, *Vae, puto deus fio,* "Oh dear, I think I'm becoming a god," and expired.[1] The images on the arch, in contrast, are deadly serious in celebrating the deification of the Divine Titus and the rise of the dynasty that Vespasian had established out of the catastrophic "year of the four emperors," 69 CE, to restore the "peace" of Rome.

Directly across the arch, on its southern wall, I saw Titus riding his chariot in victory into Rome. I stood, imagining the parade before me, with triumphal Romans, Jewish slaves—their mangled bodies and festering wounds hidden beneath fine Roman garments, and "our" holy vessels passing by. Sometime over the last couple of millennia Titus's face was damaged. Someone had the good sense to knock off his head, I thought.

I was face-to-face with the Roman soldiers who carried the menorah, the table of the Divine Presence, a Torah scroll and other serving vessels

The Apotheosis of Titus Panel, Arch of Titus, ca. 81 CE, courtesy of the Arch of Titus Project

of the Jerusalem Temple as booty into Roman servitude. My eyes were fixated on the lampstand—so small from up close, at just eighty-two centimeters tall. In fact, I could not take my eyes off the menorah. Here I was, so close that I could touch it—but should I? I didn't—cognizant of the throngs of tourists watching me, the conservators observing from

The Triumph of Titus Panel, Arch of Titus, ca. 81 CE, courtesy of the Arch of Titus Project

below, and most of all, my own reticence to touch the holy object. The table, pictured within its original setting in the Jerusalem Temple, can still be seen on the coins minted during the Revolt of Bar Kokhba (called in Roman historiography the "Second Jewish Revolt," 132–136 CE), more than fifty years after the arch was built. At that time Jews still hoped to see the Temple rebuilt, as traditional Jews do to this day, and this messianic hope is interwoven throughout Jewish prayer and uttered many times in the course of each day (alas, Shimon Bar Kokhba was but one in a long line of failed messiahs).

I remembered the attempts of the Jerusalem Temple priests to protect the holy vessels from the throngs of well-meaning pilgrims who came to Jerusalem on each of the three Jewish pilgrimage festivals, Passover, Shavuot—Pentecost, and Sukkot—Tabernacles, so many that the city could barely support the influx; how the priests brought out the menorah and the table into the Temple compound to be seen by the throngs, much as a "pagan" cult object was displayed in pagan temples. According to the Mishnah in tractate Ḥagigah 3:8, these hereditary Temple servants stood by the vessels like museum guards in our own day and warned the pious "take care that you not touch the table and the menorah [and defile them]." I too didn't touch—though the temptation was huge.

Tetradrachm of the Bar Kokhba Revolt, 133/134 CE, courtesy of the American Numismatic Society

This time alone with the menorah was the culmination of my own pilgrimage from adolescent menorah-lover to scholar of Jewish history and visual culture. I kept looking and staring and trying to see some element that would surprise or suggest or explain some point that I had not understood or fully appreciated from the thousands of photographs and drawings I had studied. My eyes flashed up and down, left and right, as I moved from the menorah to the Roman garments, from the sandals of the conquerors to the silenced—now fossilized—silver trumpets of the Temple—and always back to the menorah. With each change of shadow, I saw something new. Every movement of the sun, which shines through the arch at something like a thirty-degree angle from a true east-west orientation, depending on the season, brought new revelations and sharpened the deep relief of the carving. It was as if the Romans marching forward, carrying the menorah and the other Temple vessels, were actually moving as the field of the relief moved deeper and deeper into the white marble—and the vessels of the Jerusalem Temple disappeared forever into the stone. How much more vivid—and ghastly—would this scene have been in full color, I thought.

I was in Rome as a scholar of antiquity, leading a team intent upon understanding the Arch of Titus in new ways through the marvels of technology. Our goal was to re-imagine the original colors of this once vibrant arch, to transform it from a shadowy—almost ghostly—white marble into a vibrant—almost living—polychrome drama. From June 5 to 7, 2012, our team of Americans, Italians, and Germans—Jews and Christians—undertook a pilot study of the arch. High-resolution three-dimensional scans of the menorah panel were made, and part of the menorah relief was examined to determine whether any traces of paint decoration were preserved. Happily, yellow ochre paint was preserved deep in the creases of the stone on the arms and base of the menorah. There was not much—just a few specks—but enough to prove that the menorah and, by extension, the entire panel, had been aglow in color. This discovery was all the more remarkable in that we used a noninvasive technique called ultraviolet–visible spectroscopy (UV-UVS), which means that the arch could be studied without touching it and with no risk of damage. This fabulous discovery follows upon nearly half a century of scholarship that has proven that classical art was not white, as most people—including scholars—had thought for so long. Rome was not white, as we often imagine it, but red and blue, green and white and golden. Roman art, including the Arch of Titus, was polychrome and vibrant. Using the newest technology, we changed how one of the world's most important monuments, and Judaism's most important menorah, would be viewed forever.

I am not a scientist, like my colleague Heinrich Piening, our mastermind of color-detection technology; nor a computer-modeling guru, like Bernie Frischer—the imagination behind "Rome Reborn," an online model of the eternal city.[2] I am, rather, a cultural historian—an eclectic scholar who pulls from ancient languages (Hebrew, Aramaic, Greek, Latin, and sometimes Persian), literature (like the Talmud, and the works of Jewish and Roman historian Flavius Josephus, Roman historian Tacitus, the New Testament, and the Church Fathers), archaeology from across the Mediterranean world, the newest theories, and even technology in my attempt to bring the past to life—or at least to present the past in a way that is historically plausible. My work is a kind of bridge between our culture and those in the past on the assumption that this knowledge can help us to understand ourselves better. In between antiquity and our time are generations that preserved, destroyed, loved, hated, ignored, restored, and lived with the texts and artifacts that I study. They are my conversation partners, interlocutors, and sometimes my subjects. In studying the menorah, the list of sources is very, very long—this being the longest

Above: The Menorah of the Arch of Titus Spolia Panel, 3-D scan, photograph by Unocad, courtesy of the Arch of Titus Project

Right: The Menorah of the Arch of Titus Spolia Panel, with the locations where yellow ochre pigment was discovered indicated, courtesy of the Arch of Titus Project

continuously used religious symbol in Western culture. This object, and the resultant "symbol," stretch back to the ancient Near East, more than a millennium before the Christian era (that is, more than three thousand years ago), and forward to our own time. The arch itself has been a part of the conversation for nearly 2,000 years. There are lots of people to talk to over that expanse of time, so the work is broad—and I am never alone—even when standing on scaffolding face-to-face with the Arch of Titus menorah.

I spend considerable time with images that are called today "symbols," or visual codes—"icons" in ancient Greek and in contemporary computer parlance—through which cultures try to express their complexities in simple forms that can be seen. The Christian cross is one religious symbol, the Islamic crescent another, and the menorah—the most ancient of the three—a third. Especially since the work of Swiss psychologist Carl Gustav Jung (d. 1961)—and even before—the study of symbols has been a preoccupation of scholars—particularly in a world transformed by photography, then video, and now computer imaging. Symbols have been seen as forms that preexist culture and religion, as primordial windows into all that is human. If only we could develop the right tools to unlock their meaning, the language of symbols, scholars thought, it would be possible to discover truths about our shared humanity that transcend the barriers set before us by modern notions of "religion," "race" and "nationalism."

This was a powerful draw in the years following World War I—when the European urge to find common humanity was great, particularly (though by no means exclusively) among some German speakers—and in the United States during the half century after the Second World War. Shared humanity—whether in terms of the United Nations or the European Union, the newly imagined "Judeo-Christian heritage," or the emphasis upon the universal in contemporary universities—required shared symbols. Scholars of religion in America, most notably the popularizer Joseph Campbell (who wrote about shared myths across cultures) and the University of Chicago's Mircea Eliade (with his influential studies of the "Sacred and the Profane") helped spread this gospel of the universal symbol as far as George Lucas's *Star Wars* (beginning in 1977) and Dan Brown's *The Da Vinci Code* (2003)—that is, everywhere. E. R. Goodenough, a giant of creative reflection on the past, sought to unlock the truths of a "mystical Judaism" of his own creation by assembling the entire corpus of ancient Jewish artifacts then known and interpreting them through the prism of

Jungian "archetypes." His thirteen-volume opus, *Jewish Symbols in the Greco-Roman Period* (New York, 1954–1967), was subsidized and published by the Bollingen Foundation as part of a series of books dedicated to Jung's interests.

Returning to my encounter with the greatest of all Jewish symbols, the menorah of the Arch of Titus, it became clear to me within minutes that my almost mystical ascent up the scaffolding—which I climbed in record time—was far more than a dispassionate academic trek. I found myself fidgeting and thinking about the humiliations that my ancestors had felt here, of the rabbis and simple Jews who came to peer up at the menorah from below, of early modern Jews humiliated here by the Church, of the Holocaust survivors who took the menorah symbolically "home" in a massive demonstration on December 2, 1947 supporting the United Nations Partition Plan for Palestine and the establishment of the Jewish State. I remembered these survivors marching through the arch in the opposite direction—survivors of Auschwitz, maimed for German amusement, all quite cognizant of the arches built by the labor of prisoners above the entrances of the death camps and their perverse slogan, *Arbeit Macht Frei,* "Work Makes You Free." In 1949 the Arch of Titus menorah became the symbol of the "renewed" State of Israel. I also empathized with those Jews who today passionately believe a new myth—one that suggests that the menorah is somehow hidden in the bowels of the Vatican (it isn't)—and even with those misguided and dangerous Jewish nationalists who hope to rebuild the Temple, and restore the menorah, with their own hands. This was a liminal moment, as anthropologist Victor Turner would call it—I was at the place in-between, suspended between myth and history, between reality and eternity—on a scaffolding within the Arch of Titus. Seldom before had I visualized my "imagined community" so vividly.

Was I acting out the kinds of searches that novelists imagine academics regularly set out on—and which we generally do not? Was this a kind of Jewish Indiana Jones moment, or perhaps a vicarious reenactment of Robert Langdon (the "Harvard symbologist" whom Dan Brown modeled on Campbell), who set out to uncover some deep hidden secret of the Da Vinci Code through his interpretation of symbols? The *New York Times* later called me "the Jewish Robert Langdon," which made me uncomfortable at the time. Indiana Jones and Robert Langdon are well grounded in the great scholarly explorers of the past, including the flamboyant nineteenth-century British explorer, military officer, and avid Freemason

Demonstration at the Arch of Titus, December 2, 1947, courtesy of the United States National Holocaust Museum

Charles Warren, who burrowed under Jerusalem in search of biblical treasures, and Yigael Yadin, who uncovered Masada and imagined it suspended somewhere between the Warsaw Ghetto uprising, Josephus, and modern Israel. Such explorers also include my friends Eric and Carol Meyers, who in 1981 discovered the broken pediment of the "lost ark" of a third-century Galilean synagogue, buried under the reading platform (the *bema*) in a place called Nabratein. This was the same year that Indiana Jones and his "lost ark" first appeared in theaters. In a press photograph Carol and Eric even posed as the film characters.

At the moment when I stood so close to the menorah panel, my scholarly self and my seeking self separated and merged and separated—at gyrating speed. Later in the day, I suspended the blue-and-white flag of Yeshiva University (intentionally reminiscent of the Israeli national flag, itself modeled on the Jewish prayer garment, the *tallit*) from the scaffolding, an event picked up by the press worldwide. I was—and am—an actor in the story and not just some dispassionate observer, if such a thing actually exists.

Long ago, I rejected the pietism of modern "symbology." I had encountered this field while a high school student, at a time in the late 1970s when the works of the modern symbologists were avant-garde. Jung's mystical contemplation on the mandala—originally a Hindu, and thus Buddhist, projection of the universe as a round sphere that Jung appropriated and transformed into an icon of personal centeredness—was all the rage. I was taken up in his *Man and His Symbols* (1964), and Goodenough was a bit of a hero to me. I became all the more caught up with them when I "met" these authors and their contemporary exponents as an undergraduate. At the time, religious studies often provided a kind of academic patina for this sort of scholarly universalizing. I soon realized that Eliade, the mythmaker, generalizes too much and that Campbell stirs a kind of secularizing stone soup of traditions and cultures into a broth that suits his own modernist predilections, which says little about the dead people whom he is ostensively studying and everything about his own spiritual search. Goodenough too, whose beautifully published opus was often collected by midcentury liberal rabbis as if they were holy books, creates an ancient, "mystical," nonlegal Judaism of whole cloth, with little connecting his theories to the actual artifacts and texts that he wove together with a thick dose of Jungian symbology. For many secularizing clergy and scholars these volumes were replacements for the writings of the ancient Rabbis and their Talmud. They were used by some late-twentieth-century historians, mainly Americans, as a sourcebook of "nonrabbinic" alternatives to the texts (and religious authorities) of late antique Judaism. My own study of symbols, as it has developed through the years, is based in the close study of texts and artifacts, in a real attempt to let these disparate forms "speak" to one another, knowing that the conversation changes almost from minute to minute. This transience reminds me of the light of the Roman sun as it passes over the menorah panel of the arch, giving the impression that the once-beautifully painted but now ghostly white Roman soldiers are moving forward—their garments fluttering in the breeze of imperial victory.

This book is as much about the past as the present, about my work as a scholar as much as my deep love for the menorah and for the Jewish people and its troubled land. It is a reflection on a beloved artifact, one whose significance has transformed and continues to transform in our own times, as Jews have taken on the yoke of modern nationalism with all of the frightening complexities that accompany modern national movements. Much of the impetus for the study of Jewish symbols over the past seventy or so years—especially the menorah—is their significance in modern Israel. Scholars—Israelis and concurrently Jews based in Europe and the United States—have been active in the national project, seeking out, or "recovering" roots for the Zionist enterprise. They have been very successful in this project, creating a vast literature. Still, most scholars have naturally focused on their own areas of specialization. Thus, biblical scholars have their literature, Roman historians theirs, and text scholars, archaeologists, art historians, and so on their own sources. Recent scholarship on symbols and themes in modern Israeli culture has quite naturally been carried out by experts in modern Jewish history and framed from within the contexts mainly of the Israeli secular—and generally socialist—culture of the last century. The pioneering works of Yael Zerubavel and Alec Mishory deserve special mention, though there are many others. Even within the context of modern Jewish history, however, the great significance of developments outside of Mandatory Palestine/Israel has not always been recognized. There is an underappreciation of the significance of previously marginalized groups within the Israeli body politic—notably Revisionist Zionists and a full array of Jewish traditionalist and traditionalizing groups. Dialogue across periods and places has been achieved only through an anthological, if telescoping, approach, with articles on earlier periods providing evidence for continuity from the Bible to contemporary Israel, and all roads leading to middle Israel. An excellent example is a 1999 Israel Museum exhibition catalog, *In the Light of the Menorah: Story of a Symbol,* a collection of eighteen articles brought together in celebration of the fiftieth anniversary of the State of Israel. This beautifully produced volume assembled much of the best scholarship carried out in Israel over a generation or so. In addition to international donors, this exhibition was funded by the Israel Ministry of Education, Culture, and Sport, the Central Office of Information. It is a consensus document—a fine statement of Israeli civil religion.

My background as a cultural historian, Talmudist, and art historian as well as an Ashkenazi Jewish-American (or is it American Jew?) educated in Southern California and equally in Jerusalem, with strong ties to Israel and equally strong opinions and deep roots within Judaism as a modern "religion," has inclined me toward a diachronic, object- and text-centered, comparativist and internationalist approach to interpreting the Jewish past. Here I tell a story of a living and transforming object of memory—beginning in antiquity and continuing through the medieval world to our own—in the belief that all of these contexts are necessary for understanding each context individually as well as the whole picture. I draw much from the work of French historian Pierre Nora and his studies of the continuing lives of "places of memory," aware that for the transnational and geographically displaced Jewish "virtual community," physical place has always been a precarious thing—and memory a vital activity. My work ultimately is focused on the present—or more correctly a series of "presents"—and the ways that each present has shaped the past. In this way, I hope to convey both continuity and rupture, appropriations and transformations. Imagined and embraced and illuminated by Jews, Samaritans, Christians, and, on occasion, Muslims for 3,000 years, the menorah is, I believe, an ideal artifact through which to reflect on all of these issues—from the age of the Bible to our own.

The Arch of Titus menorah is the starting point and focal point of this study. It is the most significant historical Temple menorah to "exist" beyond the written word—unlike the menorahs of Moses or the prophet Zechariah, or even the lampstands of the Maccabees and those of Herod himself. It is a tangible object—an ancient relic that has outlived the "real" menorahs of antiquity. Unlike the Ark of the Covenant and the Holy Grail—the most significant of the "lost" artifacts of Western culture—it can be touched and measured, and has been for centuries. In the end, however, the arch menorah is just an approximation—so close to the original, but not it. The Arch of Titus menorah provides a leitmotif for this entire study, beginning with the origins of the menorah in the biblical world, to the life of the menorah between the terrible destruction of Jerusalem in 70 CE and the dawn of the modern world, and continuing from there to the modern biography of this symbol, shaped by the choice of the Arch of Titus menorah as the "symbol" of the State of Israel in 1949. The arch menorah is poised between the ancient and the medieval, the modern and whatever comes next. With Shelley, we can indeed say that the menorah "is become a dream and a memory."

I

From Titus to Moses—and Back

The menorah of the Arch of Titus is a very imposing artifact. It is carved in the deepest relief into white marble by Domitian's workmen, and is carried by a group of handsome and triumphant Romans, likely soldiers, dressed perhaps in white with green laurel wreaths on their heads. The donning of wreaths was considered a great honor, reserved for the most worthy. The menorah-bearers—each approximately 140 centimeters tall (much shorter than actual Romans), bend under their burden. The artist thus expresses both the weight of this golden object, and its significance. Though only eighty-two centimeters tall, the menorah of the arch relief is nearly 60 percent the height of its bearers. The scene of Roman soldiers lugging the menorah and the table through the streets of Rome must have been all the more impressive as one looked up from the street to the relief above, brightly colored.

Once we "see" the immensity of this golden artifact, the next thing to notice is its unique form. This is the factor that clearly attracted Roman attention and is the reason that the menorah is featured so prominently in the relief. This image of the menorah overshadows all others that have survived from antiquity, in its fine deep carving, its prominence, and its continued significance. As we begin our study of the most ancient menorahs, we use the arch bas relief as a refracting lens through which to view all of the menorahs that came before it, from the earliest artifact—the Torah's description of the lampstand (the earliest manuscript evidence for which is preserved in the Dead Sea Scrolls)—through the biblical period, the early Second Temple period (after 516 BCE), and back to Herod's magnificent Temple, from which Josephus relates that two menorahs were taken by Titus in 70 CE.

Thankfully Josephus—who knew the menorah as a priest serving in the Jerusalem Temple, as a Roman informant at the fall of Jerusalem, as a viewer of Titus's triumphal parade, and who lived in Rome when the menorah too was there—has much to say on this count. He certainly examined the menorah in Vespasian's *Templum Pacis,* "Temple of Peace," built close by on the Roman Forum. There it stood within the temple's massive porticos, together with the table. Here the menorah was displayed among the booty of Rome's conquests. Was there anyone to warn the masses of Roman visitors not to touch it, as there had been in Jerusalem? The menorah and the other sacred objects brought from Jerusalem were more problematic than the other prized possessions, however. Roman polytheism was highly syncretistic. Typically, the gods of defeated nations were formally "invited" to inhabit new quarters in Rome, to join the Roman pantheon. So too, perhaps, the God of Israel, His "cult images" being the menorah, the table of the face of God (generally called the "showbread"), and the Torah scroll paraded in Titus's triumph. He too was escorted to Rome—and the Arch of Titus reliefs bespeak this pious invitation—one that the defeated God of Israel might hardly refuse.

Josephus provides more information about Roman triumphal parades than any other author. Regarding the Temple of Peace, which has been partially excavated, Josephus writes: "For, besides having prodigious resources of wealth on which to draw he [Vespasian] also embellished it with ancient masterworks of painting and sculpture; indeed, into that shrine were accumulated and stored all objects for the sight of which men had once wandered over the whole world, eager to see them severally while they lay in various countries. Here, too, he laid up the vessels of gold from the temple of the Jews, on which he prided himself."[1] The bases of some of the other artifacts in this museum to Roman greatness have been recovered by modern archaeologists, including the base of a sculpture labeled in Greek "Ganymede of Leachates of Athens," which once bore Leachates's now-lost sculpture of *Ganymede and the Eagle* (created ca. 350 BCE). We can imagine that the menorah stood on a similar base, duly curated as a trophy to Vespasian's greatness—and by extension, the greatness of Rome. Perhaps the base of the menorah was inscribed with a similarly understated label—one that needed no elaboration beyond "Lampstand of the Temple of the Jews"—or something like that.

Josephus's presentation of the triumphal parade is deadpan at best. It expresses none of the flamboyant joy and great pride that he brings to his depictions of Jerusalem. Josephus was in the employ of the emperor and his vast propaganda machine, intended to legitimize the Flavian peace, imposed at the end of the "year of the four emperors" in 69 CE, after the catastrophic reign of Nero and a deeply unsettling succession crisis. He clearly intended to both assert the greatness of Vespasian and Titus, his patrons, though Josephus's ambivalence at this event is palpable. He tarries on the beauty of the menorah, where he can negotiate his commitments to the Flavians and his allegiance to the Temple with equal measure. In book 7 of his *Jewish War* (completed in Rome around 75 CE), Josephus described what he saw in the triumphal parade to his Roman audience:

> The spoils in general were borne in promiscuous heaps; but conspicuous above all stood those captured in the temple at Jerusalem. These consisted of a golden table, many talents in weight, and a lampstand, likewise made of gold, but constructed on a different pattern than those which we use in ordinary life. Affixed to a pedestal was a central shaft, from which there extended slender branches, arranged trident-fashion, a wrought lamp being attached to the extremity of each branch, of these there were seven, indicating the honor paid to that number among the Jews. After these, and last of all the spoils, was carried a copy of the Jewish Law [a Torah scroll]. They followed a large party carrying images of victory, all made of ivory and gold. Behind them drove Vespasian, followed by Titus; while Domitian rode beside them, in magnificent apparel and mounted on a steed that was in itself a sight.[2]

Josephus's explanation here of the menorah is quite brief, providing just enough description without going into details of biblical origin, or reviewing an earlier description of it in *Jewish War,* book 5. His short gloss on the menorah here describes a cult object that is very different from the public objects of veneration that his Roman audience might easily imagine. This was no sculpture of a god or of a divine emperor in gold and ivory—the usual kind of trophy paraded in triumphal parades and which he tells us were well represented in Titus's celebration. This was a functional lampstand, though one in pure gold and created in huge proportions. All the fuss about a lampstand must have seemed unusual to Josephus's

Roman audience. A Roman viewer might have thought the notion of a lampstand as divinity—or even stand-in for a divinity—quite odd.

There is, however, literary precedent for this. Pliny the Elder, a contemporary of Josephus who died as a result of the eruption of Mt. Vesuvius in August 79 CE—an event that one Jewish author conceived as divine retribution for Jerusalem's destruction—presents a rather comical incident regarding a "divine" lampstand in Greece:

> Aegina [off Athens] specialized in producing only the upper parts of chandeliers, and similarly Taranto [in Apulia, in southern Italy] made only the stems, and consequently credit for manufacture is, in the matter of these articles, shared between these two localities. Nor are people ashamed to buy these at a price equal to the pay of a military tribune, although they clearly take even their name from the lighted candles they carry. At the sale of a chandelier of this sort by the instructions of the auctioneer (named Theon) selling it there was thrown in as part of the bargain the fuller Clesippus a humpback and also of a hideous appearance in other respects besides, the lot being bought by a woman named Gegania for 50,000 sesterces. This woman gave a party to show off her purchases, and for the mockery of the guests the man appeared with no clothes on: his mistress conceiving an outrageous passion for him admitted him to her bed and later gave him a place in her will. Thus becoming excessively rich he worshipped the lamp-stand in question as a divinity and so caused this story to be attached to Corinthian lampstands in general, though the claims of morality were vindicated by his erecting a noble tombstone to perpetuate throughout the living world for all time the memory of Gegania's shame. But although it is admitted that there are no lampstands made of Corinthian metal, yet this name specially is commonly attached to them, because although Mummius's victory destroyed Corinth, it caused the dispersal of bronzes from a number of the towns of Achaia at the same time.[3]

An aside to Pliny's story suggests just how rare golden lampstands must have been, and we can imagine that one made of a single piece would have impressed the technically minded. "Corinthian metal" was an alloy of bronze and gold that brings a patina of gold to the surface of the metal and made bronze artifacts appear to be golden. No examples of this technique have been discovered—owing undoubtedly to its still appreciable value, though this technology is well known from ancient literature.

Many Hellenistic and Roman lampstands have been discovered over the centuries. A group of five massive late Hellenistic marble lampstands, dated to the early first century BCE and recovered from a shipwreck near Mahdia, Tunisia, is particularly significant. These lampstands are 142 centimeters tall and replicate metal prototypes that were used in temples. The heavy stems of these lamps are well articulated in floral motifs and, together with their broad and heavy bases, are reminiscent of the arch menorah. Roman domestic lampstands were usually polished brass objects—the most common type showing a slender central stalk attached to a three-legged base, topped by a horizontal shelf to support oil lamps or from which to dangle lamps on chains. Silver and even gold lampstands are mentioned in literary sources. The menorah was a lampstand of a sort that Josephus's audience had never seen, of immense value. Roman lampstands generally did not have multiple "branches"—though some found in Pompeii are shaped like trees, and lampstands could be quite complex. Josephus described the paired branches of the Jewish lampstand not as a tree—as moderns are apt to do—but as looking like a sort of a trident, like the three-pronged spear of Neptune, god of the sea, a weapon used in gladiator fights. Two prongs of a trident, like the branches of the menorah, are set parallel to a central stalk and connect to it at an angle or in a slow arc. Each prong reaches the same height, like the branches of the menorah. My sense is that this is a formal comparison, not a conceptual equation of the Roman trident with the Jewish menorah. Josephus's language was intended to quickly make the unfamiliar familiar, within the context of what was, after all, a military parade. The truth is, every time I see a trident I can't help but recall that Josephus must have seen the form of the menorah held by a fighter in the games while the menorah itself was accessioned to the Temple of Peace.

Numerous less impressive and highly stylized images of the menorah have been discovered from the latter Second Temple period in Judaea that reflect this same basic pattern—all but one of them from the area of Jerusalem. The first use of the menorah as an icon appears on a bronze coin—a *lepton* in Greek, a *perutah* in Hebrew—minted in Jerusalem by the last Hasmonean king, Mattathias Antigonus. He used it to exemplify the Temple in his unsuccessful battle, with Parthian Persian support, to defend his kingdom against the Romans in 39 BCE against the usurper, Herod (later called "the Great"). On the other side of the coin is the showbread table, a Second Temple–period version of a biblical appurtenance. The image of the menorah was used more broadly in first-century Jerusalem. It has been discovered, scratched no less than five times, on the walls of an aristocratic tomb called today the "Tomb of Jason," decorating a sundial found near the Temple Mount, and etched in plaster that was discovered in a patrician villa. Art historian Bezalel Narkiss believed that this menorah graffito on plaster, discovered within view of the Temple in what is today the Jewish Quarter of Jerusalem's walled city, was used in the education of young priests—to show them the spatial relationship between the lampstand and the table. A single menorah appears in a relief from a synagogue in Magdala on the northwestern shore of the Sea of Galilee. It appears on one end of a large-footed limestone ashlar—the purpose of which is still a mystery—carved in shallow relief. The menorah is shown resting on a high, square, and decorated pedestal, roughly of the sort that I imagine was at the Temple of Peace. My guess is that this menorah was painted yellow, and the pedestal in other colors—though it has not yet been tested for residues of pigment, so this is conjecture. Menorahs appear in hundreds of images dating from late antiquity—the late third to seventh centuries CE—in virtually all cases with trident-like branches. The Second Temple–period images, taken together with the arch menorah, provide a real sense of what Josephus saw. The branches from lampstand to lampstand are virtually the same. The bases, however, vary widely—a theme to which we return later.

Philo of Alexandria, the great thinker and communal leader who lived a generation before Josephus, provides a less functional metaphor than the trident for the rounded branches of late Second Temple period menorahs. He relates their shape to the trajectory of the planets around the sun: "He says that the approach to them is from the side (and) the middle place is that of the sun. But to the other ["planets"] He distributed three positions on the two sides; in the superior [group] are Saturn, Jupiter and Mars, while in the inner [group] are Mercury, Venus and the moon."[4] Philo is the earliest author known to explain the rounded branches, associating them with his larger astral concerns. As we will soon see, this approach hearkens back to an association of the lamps with the planets that first appears in the

Above: Lepton of Mattathias Antigonus, showing the menorah, 37 BCE, Shlomo Moussaieff Collection, Ardon Bar Hama, photographer, courtesy of George Blumenthal

Below: Lepton of Mattathias Antigonus, showing the table of the showbread, 37 BCE, Shlomo Moussaieff Collection, Ardon Bar Hama, photographer, courtesy of George Blumenthal

Relief of a menorah on a base, on a footed ashlar, Magdala, first century CE, courtesy of R. Steven Notley

prophet Zechariah during the sixth century BCE. In *The Life of Moses,* Philo goes further in associating the menorah with the cosmos:

> The candlestick he [Moses] placed at the south [of the Tabernacle] figuring thereby the movements of the luminaries above; for the sun and the moon and the others run their courses in the south far away from the north. And therefore six branches, three on each side, issue from the central candlestick, bringing up the number to seven, and on all these are set seven lamps and candle bearers, symbols of what the men of science call planets. For the sun, like the candlestick, has the fourth place in the middle of the six and gives light to the three above and the three below it, so tuning to harmony an instrument of music truly divine.[5]

The rounded branches thus give expression to this "music truly divine," supporting the planets in their paths, even as they support the lights of this rather awkward artifact. Philo makes another association regarding the relationship between the central lamp and the others, through the metaphor of the matriarch Sarah, comparing her virtue to the light emanating from the central shaft of the menorah, "which is the brightest of all and geared to God's eyes."[6] Our author was not the first to associate the strong spine of the menorah with a woman. He was preceded by Joshua Ben Sira, a priest of the last half of the second century BCE, whose works are preserved in the Orthodox and Catholic Old Testaments, in the Protestant Apocrypha, and partially among the Dead Sea Scrolls and in the Cairo Genizah:

> The sun shines in the heights of God,
> And the beauty of a good woman adorns the home.
> A lamp shines on the holy menorah,
> And a beautiful face on an upright figure.[7]

The association between the "good woman" of Ben Sira and then of the ultimate "good woman," Sarah, by Philo may relate to the fact that the Hebrew word menorah is a feminine noun. I wonder, though, whether the rounded top-heaviness of both the menorah and the typical physique of a mature woman lurk behind this metaphor. Whatever the case, we have now seen three very different metaphors applied to the lampstand: the trident, the planetary motions, and the upright woman.

Someone who had read, or heard a reading of, Josephus's *Jewish War* consecutively would have been well prepared for the pathos of the triumphal procession in book 7. In book 5, Josephus describes the Herodian Temple to his audience in all of its glory, explaining that the menorah, the showbread table, and the altar of incense of Herod's Temple were "three most wonderful works of art, universally renowned." This renown drew attention to the Temple and led to the reproduction of these images in first-century Jerusalem, to their prominence in Titus's triumph, their placement in the Temple of Peace, and their immortalization in the arch bas-reliefs. It was a mixed renown, one held both by initiates and the empire, like other art and cult objects taken by Rome. In this case, however, we can listen in to the voices of both the captor and the captive, both the Roman and those defeated by Rome—a unique situation in the study of Roman culture. As did Philo, Josephus in book 5 already states that "the seven lamps (such being the number of lamps [*luchnoi*]) from the lampstand represent the planets."[8] He returned to this theme around 90 CE in his magnum opus, *Antiquities of the Jews,* where Josephus ostensibly describes the menorah of the Tabernacle:

> Facing the table, near the south wall, stood a candelabrum of cast gold, hollow, and of the weight of a hundred minae; this (weight) the Hebrews call *kinchares,* a word which, translated into Greek, denotes a talent. It was made up of globules and lilies, along with pomegranates, and little bowls, numbering seventy in all; of these it was composed from a single base right up to the top, having been made to consist of as many portions as assigned to the planets with the sun. It terminated in seven branches [*kefalas*] regularly disposed in a row. Each branch [literally, head] bore one lamp, recalling the number of planets; the seven lamps faced southwest, and the candelabrum being placed crosswise.[9]

The richness of Josephus's portrayal in *Antiquities* is far more expansive than anything he had written about the menorah before. Perhaps this is in part because the *Antiquities* menorah is that of the Tabernacle menorah, with "globules and lilies, along with pomegranates" that evoke the book of Exodus. Such detail does not appear, however, in the Titus arch menorah—though it does include "globules" on the branches—nor in images from Judaea—though the Jewish Quarter graffito does seem to evoke "globules" and some repetitive floral decoration. Josephus's description of the menorah in *Antiquities,* then, is an amalgam of the Exodus menorah and what Josephus knew of Temple menorahs in his own day. He filled in textual lapses with the known, and explained the current object in light of scripture.

Explaining the seven branches as a Jewish idiosyncrasy, Josephus in book 7 of *Jewish War* briefly notes that they represent "the honor paid to that number among the Jews"—though he doesn't examine why Jews like the number seven, nor does he mention the planetary explanation of book 5. In fact, this fascination with seven has biblical origins, seven having been described by one modern author as Judaism's "most sacred number."[10] It is no coincidence that Josephus composed *Jewish War* in seven books. Perhaps he was trying to associate the menorah with the general Roman interest in special numbers. Within the context of this grand parade, a vague theological explanation was apparently sufficient. In a similar way, Josephus does not remind his readers at this point in *Jewish War* that the menorah—like the table—is a Temple implement of biblical origin and Divine design. That could certainly have made the parade all the more painful for a man as furiously complex as Josephus, and the lingering sense that the defeated God of Israel was being escorted into Roman captivity all the more evident.

The Biblical Origins of the Lampstand

What I have detailed here is as much as we can know about the lampstand that was taken to Rome from Jerusalem, based upon Josephus, Philo, and a few other scattered sources. Before each of these authors, of course, stood the prolonged biblical descriptions of lampstands, principally the description of the Tabernacle menorah in Exodus 25:31–40. The menorah is described two times in the extant Hebrew book of Exodus: once when Moses is commanded to make the biblical Tabernacle and its implements, including the lamp, and once after the great biblical artisan, Bezalel, son of Uri, carried out the fabrication.[11] The Greek version of the Torah, the Septuagint (and likely its Hebrew predecessor), however, does not contain the repetition, sufficing with the initial Divine command alone. As a well-educated Jerusalem aristocrat, Josephus knew these biblical texts well—a fact demonstrated in his *Jewish Antiquities,* where he retells the entire history of Israel from Abraham to his own day. In Exodus 25:31–40 we read:

> And you shall make a lampstand of pure gold. The base and the shaft of the lampstand shall be made of hammered work; its cups, its bulbs, and its flowers shall be of one piece with it; and there shall be six branches [or, "stalks," *qanim*] going out of its sides, three branches of the lampstand out of one side of it and three branches of the lampstand out of the other side of it; three cups made like almonds, each with bulb and flower, on one stalk, and three cups made like almonds, each with bulb and flower, on the other stalk—so for the six branches going out of the lampstand; and on the lampstand itself four cups made like almonds, with their bulbs and flowers, and a bulb of one piece with it under each pair of the six branches going out from the lampstand. Their bulbs and their branches shall be of one piece

with it, the whole of it one piece of hammered work of pure gold. And you shall make the seven lamps for it; and the lamps shall be set up so as to give light upon the space in front of it. Its snuffers and their trays shall be of pure gold. Of a talent of pure gold shall it be made, with all these utensils. And see that you make them after the pattern for them, which is being shown you on the mountain.

This compulsive word picture is one confusing text, whether in translation or in the original Hebrew. When I have asked students to draw what they read—or listen carefully when it is read aloud—it is virtually impossible to imagine what is being described. Most students agree that the menorah is a kind of overgrown plant, complete with branches, bulbs, and flowers.

Ancient rabbis were cognizant of this conundrum as they read the biblical text, imagining that God was forced to show Moses a fiery prototype of the lampstand, and that even that was too difficult for him, until the divinely gifted artisan, Bezalel ben Uri (literally "in the shadow of God, son of light"), "filled with the Spirit of God, with ability and intelligence, with knowledge and all craftsmanship, to devise artistic designs, to work in gold, silver, and bronze, in cutting stones for setting, and in carving wood, for work in every craft" proved up to the task. Moses, son of Nahman, known as Nahmanides (d. 1270), as much as threw up his hands at the futility of reconstructing the intricacies of the menorah. Commenting on Exodus 25:30, he writes, "the wisdom of the menorah, of its cups and calyxes and flowers, from whence will you find it, as it is well hidden"—that is, it is a sort of lost cause (*me-ain timtsa ve-ne'elmah me'od*). Nahmanides here references Job 28:20–21—"Whence (*me-ain*) then comes wisdom? And where is the place of understanding? It is hidden (*ve-ne'elmah*) from the eyes of all living, and concealed from the birds of the air." Figuring out where to place the cups, bulbs, and flowers; the branches; and the base is no easy matter for those of us who did not live during the biblical period, when the technical denotations of the various artifacts might have been clearer. It is like asking a contemporary teen to imagine a samovar without ever having seen one or having been served tea from one.

Even the branches of the menorah are nearly impossible—we do not want the rounded branches of Second Temple–period menorahs to predetermine our reading of scripture. The Hebrew of Exodus 25 describes the "branches" as *qanim.* We habitually translate *qanim* as "branches" on the assumption that the menorah looked like a plant, a kind of Near Eastern "tree of life." Generally, however, *qanim* refers to "reeds" in biblical Hebrew, hollow, tubelike plants that grow near bodies of water. For this reason, the Septuagint came up with *kalamiskos,* "tubes," to translate *qanim*—imagining, as we will see, something like reeds. There are no biblical instructions as to how to fashion the *qanim*—a point that may have been caught by the twelfth-century scholar Moses Maimonides (d. 1204), who, as we see in the Chapter 2, must have thought that the *qanim* emanated from the central stalk as a straight angle and not as an arc. Round branches were an interpretative decision, which assumes a connection between the menorah lamps and the heavenly planets that is first expressed during the Second Temple period.

It is hard to know what scripture means when it refers to the *qanim* of the Tabernacle menorah. The association of the *qanim* of the menorah with branches appears in the King James Version of 1611 and was maintained by the first English translation of Josephus, produced by William Whiston in 1737, which translates the "seven *kefalas*" of Josephus in *Antiquities of the Jews* as "seven branches." This rendering has been followed by all subsequent translations. Sensing a difficulty in this approach, in 1930 H. St. J. Thackeray notes in a footnote that in fact the Greek reads "heads" and not branches.[12] With some discomfort, he has forced Josephus to conform to standard translations of scripture. In fact, a *kefaleh* is a "head," perhaps best translated here as a finial, or more colloquially as a "top." This choice by Josephus is all the more surprising since the Greek Septuagint did not use *kefaleh* in reference to the branches, but *kalamiskos,* "tubes"—an attempt to reproduce the Hebrew *qaneh,* "reed" (a decision shared with St. Jerome in his Latin translation). This association with reeds likely rests behind Josephus's comment that the menorah was "hollow." I have often chosen to translate *qanim* as "branches," but only because this term is conventional. Josephus maintained the botanical descriptions of other parts of the menorah, even comparing its bulbs to "pomegranates" (an approach found in later Jewish art, but not in literary sources). My sense is that he used what must have been a standard term for the finials of lampstands to describe the branches of the menorah.

Carol Meyers has shown that the workmanship described by the Torah in the making of the menorah resonates with the kind of metalwork that was carried out in Egypt around the thirteenth century BCE or so. There is deep and long memory encoded in this very wordy description. The biblical text seems to assume that more words might lead to more comprehension, rather than the kind of disconnect that my students have felt when actually confronting the physicality of this description. For anyone not from the thirteenth century BCE, or there about, there is just not enough cultural information embedded here to allow us to imagine what is described—and so we tend to read the arch and other contemporaneous and later portrayals between the words of the stark biblical text. The kinds of denotations for each word and artifact that would have been obvious to ancient craftsmen are just not available to us. Thus, the commandment to make it "after the pattern, which is being shown you on the mountain." For those who listen to this text (which, after all, was meant to be heard as much as it was written down), whether they were people who were not craftsmen in antiquity, or simply members of every generation since the Torah's compulsive compounding of words upon words to describe every aspect of the Tabernacle, repeated twice, it is still not enough to help one to imagine this object—which, according to scripture, followed a heavenly model. This notion of a heavenly model for temples and temple appurtenances has a very long history in the ancient Near East. The menorah is indeed a part of this tradition.

Scripture makes no mention of any sort of base on the Tabernacle menorah—even though a lampstand of this size and complexity had to have one. This led scholars to suggest instead that the lampstand had a thickened central "stem." Such a thickened central stalk was rather common to lampstands throughout the Near East and the Mediterranean Basin during biblical antiquity. One can imagine such a lampstand, often decorated with arboreal patterns, with six *qanim* added, three branches on each side. Scripture knows nothing of a "pedestal" of the sort mentioned by Josephus in *Jewish War* that supported the menorah paraded in Titus's triumph, nor—the wedding-cake-like construction of the Arch of Titus with a "single base" (*miâs báseōs*) that Josephus mentions in his description in *Jewish Antiquities* 3.146.

These are distinctly Greco-Roman-period solutions. In fact, images from Second Temple Palestine are very consistent in their portrayals of the menorah branches and lamps, but not of the base. Late antique Jews chose a different Roman solution, beginning the production of their menorahs as typical Roman lampstands, which have three-legged bases, and then adding the distinct branches (a tactic used by Jews in the modern period as well). During the late Second Temple period, we find a wide variety of bases: triangles and squares and semicircles, and sometimes menorahs without bases. The earliest example, on the coin of Mattathias Antigonus of 39 BCE, has what looks like a triangular base that is almost as wide as the branches. Similarly, the relief from the Magdala synagogue shows a menorah with a triangular base or perhaps three legs (it is unclear), sitting on its large decorated pedestal. Menorahs scratched as graffiti in the tomb of Jason in western Jerusalem either have no bases or stand on squares—perhaps also pedestals. The form of this object seems to have been well known to Jews at this time—at least the branches. Mishnah Ḥagigah 3:8 and parallel texts suggest that pilgrims to the Jerusalem Temple could view a Temple menorah on festivals. In addition, priests like Josephus and Levites from throughout the country—and beyond—could see it while serving in the holy place.

The variety of menorah base types preserved in the archaeological record, first among them the Arch of Titus, has disturbed scholars for generations—many wondering what *the* base of *the* menorah actually looked like. My own sense is that a singular answer to this question is not necessary. Mishnah Ḥagigah 3:8 suggests that "two or three" duplicate menorahs were kept in the Temple, lest one become defiled. Similarly, Josephus mentions that two menorahs were handed over to Titus, though only one is illustrated on the arch, and apparently only one was displayed in the Temple of Peace.[13] There could well have been more.

While fashioned after the Exodus description, the menorahs of the later Second Temple were objects of their own age and not themselves "biblical." It is likely that the menorahs of the Herodian Temple date no earlier than the Hasmoneans. After all, according to Josephus, the Temple was ransacked by the Seleucid Greeks under Antiochus Epiphanes IV in 166 BCE and its artifacts taken back to Antioch.[14] No lamp that predates that event is likely to have survived in the Temple (though Josephus relates that Antiochus's successors deposited brass objects from the Temple in an Antioch synagogue). The earliest menorah that could have existed in Herod's Temple was first made by the Hasmoneans when they reentered the Temple in the Jewish month of Kislev (December) 164 BCE. More menorahs were likely added over time as part of a general process of expansion and beautification of the Temple that was redoubled under Herod and his successors. The rabbis later on remember a process of menorah production that seems generally plausible: "The Hasmoneans [at first used] iron skewers and they covered them with lead. When they grew richer, they made them of silver, and when they became still richer, they made them [the branches of the menorah] of gold."[15]

This kind of incremental upgrading took place with other aspects of the Temple. A wealthy first-century Jew from Alexandria in Egypt named Nicanor, for example, donated doors of Corinthian bronze to the Temple. These doors must have been quite impressive, as they are mentioned by Josephus, discussed later by the ancient Rabbis (who developed a folk tradition about them), and commemorated in the tomb of Nicanor's sons—which overlooked the Temple from Jerusalem's Mt. Scopus. Inscribed in Hebrew (or perhaps Aramaic) and in Greek, the inscription on a limestone burial box, an ossuary, found there reads: "Sons of Nicanor, who gave the doors." Rabbinic literature remembers that these doors "shone like gold."[16] At some point, the Rabbis suggest, the other doors of the Temple were upgraded and replaced with gates of pure gold. Only the Corinthian doors of Nicanor, with their gold patina, were retained. The process whereby Jews and Romans lavished gifts—both individual donations and public benefaction—on the Temple continued throughout antiquity and included gifts from the Emperor Augustus himself. While certain characteristics of the Temple vessels must have been maintained with each "upgrade" or addition, slavish copying was unlikely. While certain telltale elements were surely kept fastidiously, other stylistic and formal parts of the vessels were likely left to the discretion of the donor. It certainly was not necessary for all of the Temple menorahs to be exactly the same, when scripture does not prescribe so many elements (despite the Torah's multiplication of words in describing the biblical/heavenly prototype). The base is a case in point; scripture simply does not suggest what the base should look like.

Unlike the other extant menorah bases, the face of the arch menorah base is decorated with a mythical animal, a hippocamp (a sea horse or sea monster with the tail of a fish); a dragon; a sea lion; and, in the upper center, two eagles holding a garland. This base provoked great discussion beginning in the seventeenth century, when the Great Dutch Protestant scholar Adriaan Reelant (d. 1718) asserted that the base was inauthentic, since Jews would never have tolerated such imagery. Reelant assumes that Judaism has a strict abhorrence to religious imagery based upon a rigorous interpretation of the Second Commandment of the Decalogue that was current in Protestant circles. In the modern world, this notion of an "aniconic" Judaism and of Jews as a "Nation without Art" took on a life of its own and came to be seen as a determining characteristic of Judaism by both Christians and Jews in nineteenth- and twentieth-century Europe and America. This trope says little, however, about actual Jewish visual culture, which historically has negotiated biblical and rabbinic concerns about visual idolatry in a wide range of ways. This was the case even in Reelant's world. While human or animal images would certainly not be allowed in synagogue decoration in eighteenth-century Holland, many animals, even mythological ones, appear in the synagogue decoration of the time farther to the east—especially in southern Germany and Ukraine. In some synagogues we find entire bestiaries, including rabbits, bears, and even mythological creatures like two-headed eagles, dragons, and unicorns. Even in Reelant's Holland, some Jews in the complex cultural mix of Sephardi Amsterdam of this period decorated their tombstones with images of biblical heroes and, in one case, even a personification of God. The tombstone of Samuel Senior Teixeira (d. 1717) in the Sephardic cemetery at Ouderkerk near Amsterdam is the premiere example. This relief shows the divine vision of God to Samuel in the Tabernacle at Shilo. In the background is the Ark of the Covenant and, behind the biblical Samuel himself, a large seven-branched menorah, its branches reminiscent of the Arch of Titus menorah (its base is shielded by the reclining Samuel). Nonetheless, rabbis of his age—not to mention Protestant thinkers—agreed with Reelant in their discomfort with the Arch of Titus menorah base.

Israeli archaeologist Maximilian Kon, writing in 1950/51, pointed to a parallel to this base in a group of massive column bases from the ancient temple at Didyma in Asia Minor. Kon thought that the Didyma bases were dated to the second century BCE, treating them as models for the arch menorah base. This association itself has been used by scholars to "discredit" the base, one historian even asserting—without basis—that Vespasian passed through Didyma en route back to Rome from the Judaean War, intentionally using imagery from this temple to Apollo to assert victory over the Jews. In fact, recent scholarship places the column bases nearly four hundred years later, to the early second century CE—making the menorah base a precursor to the Didyma column bases. At Didyma creatures also appear on panels of the base, though in that case the creatures include a dragon as well as the god Triton with a nude goddess, a nereid.

The Arch of Titus base is far more conservative than the Didyma bases, and the creatures that appear there are very common in Roman decorative arts of the first century. The arch base includes nothing that Jews could

Column base, Didyma in Asia Minor, second century CE, Musée du Louvre, Paris, photograph by Steven Fine

consider to be "idolatrous" deities, but as Adrienne Mayor has so nicely shown, only animals that everyone in those days believed could be found somewhere in the world, if only we knew where to look. They were the equivalent of the brontosauruses that early-twentieth-century people believed lived near Lake Victoria—everyone "knew" the classical creatures that we consider to be "mythological" could be found somewhere. They were rare creatures, to be sure, but not idolatrous ones. It is fascinating to remember that Roman rulers, including Emperor Augustus, maintained collections of fossil bones that some of the best Roman scholars reasonably (though incorrectly) identified as cyclopes and other animals that today we call mythological. This menorah base is decorated with images of such animals, which is enticing.

Troubled by its imagery, though, some moderns have claimed that this menorah base was created in Rome by Titus. It encloses, they suppose, the original triangular base inside the "wedding cake" construction made in Rome for the purpose. Were the poles shown beneath the menorah in the bas reliefs simply set below the broad base of the Jerusalem menorah as an ad hoc *ferculum,* or do they perhaps provide evidence of a specially made *ferculum* that was not intrinsic to the artifact? This latter position has been taken by interpreters troubled with the base and its "idolatrous" imagery. The discovery by our team of the same yellow ochre pigment on both the branches and the base would suggest, however, that they were the same color, apparently made of the same material. This discovery tilts the balance in favor of those who consider the base to be integral to the arch menorah.

It is clear, at least to me, that questions of idolatry—or deviance from later tradition—cannot serve as evidence to disqualify the base of the Titus menorah as original. Just to broaden the context and problematize the "aniconic Judaism" argument, I point out that a similar claim was made regarding the human and "idolatrous" imagery that was found in late antique synagogues in the Galilee and published beginning during the mid-nineteenth century. Explorers of the Palestine Exploration Society, finding winged angels and even a medusa, surmised that these synagogues were built by the Roman overlords and given to local communities to use—against their own aniconic instincts. This attempt to distance—and even absolve—Jews of responsibility for "idolatrous" imagery is wrong in both cases. This synagogue iconography—like the painted synagogues of Eastern Europe—was clearly created by Jews, who absorbed it from the imagery of the wider culture. Clearly, they didn't think it was "idolatrous."

If the imagery on the menorah base was made by Romans in Rome, we might expect iconography that is explicit in expressing Flavian ambitions. The eagles point in that direction. The images on the Arch of Titus menorah were very conservative in that Jewish way (like the beautiful reliefs of the Tobias family palace in Jordan, which dates to the third century BCE, with its images of leopards and she-wolves)—no gods or goddesses here. In a similar way, the Hasmonean royal tombs in their hometown of Modi'in—a town in Judaea—were described in the First Book of Maccabees, (another book of the Catholic and Orthodox Old Testament and the Protestant Apocrypha, originally written in Hebrew and preserved in Greek) as having been decorated with images of ships and weapons and armor—almost human figures, but not quite.[17] I could imagine that such a menorah base stood in the Temple of Jerusalem under the latter Hasmonean kings or certainly under Herod and his successors. Reflecting back on first-century Jerusalem, the Rabbis were very clear that animal images were not a religious problem. Tosefta Avodah Zarah 5:2 cites a first-century sage: "Said Rabbi Eliezer son of Tsadok: All sorts of [animal] faces could be found in Jerusalem, but not the face of a person." This insight seems to be basically correct.

Josephus nonetheless points to a level of complexity that needs to be acknowledged. An extensive apologetic runs through all of his works to the effect that Jews do not tolerate the images of humans or of animals, an overstatement that serves to explain to his Roman audience the peculiarity of Jewish practice, even as the realities were far more complex. He has pointedly transformed the "lions, oxen, and cherubim" that 1 Kings 7:29 says Solomon decorated the brazen laver of his Temple into "reliefs of a lion, a bull and an eagle."[18] These animals were imaginable to our author (though later he faults Solomon for the bronze bulls of the laver and lions of his throne).[19] The image of a cherub—a "winged creature" that Josephus was careful to note was "unlike to any that a man's eyes [other than Moses] have seen"—was not.[20] While I could see Josephus not liking the base of the arch menorah, I can also imagine others who were not so closely tied to the "anti-idolic" apologetic that runs throughout Josephus's writings being more comfortable. I recall, for example, that a gate of Herod's Temple (we do not know which) was decorated with the image of an eagle, which according to Josephus was disliked by Jewish extremists near the end of Herod's life, but does not seem to have been generally scorned.[21] Archaeology has proved Rabbi Eliezer son of Zadok right. No human images have been discovered from Herod's Jerusalem, though animals occasionally appear in wall paintings and carved in relief on stone furniture discovered in the villas of the rich. Even the Rabbis, who are usually wrongly imagined to have had difficulties with the sorts of images that appear on the base of the Titus menorah, were more nuanced than that. An early rabbinic work, the Tosefta (edited ca. 250 CE) describes exactly which dragon images might be forbidden, and under which circumstances. While the Rabbis may not have liked such imagery, particularly in the Temple, they certainly had the resources to accept it if they had no other good options.

Other Biblical "Menorahs"

Other biblical texts describe menorahs, which later Jewish tradition assimilated to the Exodus account. Solomon's Temple is said to have had ten menorahs, though the form of these objects is not described in any detail in 1 Kings 7:4: "the lampstands of pure gold, five on the south side and five on the north, before the inner sanctuary; the flowers, the lamps, and the tongs, of gold." An early Second Temple–period retelling of the Davidic history written in fifth-century Palestine and that appears in 2 Chronicles 4:7 provides even less information: "And he made ten golden lampstands as prescribed, and set them in the temple, five on the south side and five on the north." A later Jewish tradition that seems to begin with this 2 Chronicles passage assumes that these lampstands were designed after the model of the Tabernacle menorah. Apparently realizing a discrepancy between the ten lampstands of the Solomonic Temple and the one of the Tabernacle, and knowing of the significance of the single lampstand of the postexilic temple that is imagined by the prophet Zechariah during the early sixth century BCE, the Chronicler has it that, in defending the uniqueness of the Jerusalem Temple cult, Abijah, king of Judah, created a single lamp. Thus, 2 Chronicles 13:11 has it that the Temple priests, "sons of Aaron," array "the golden lampstand, and its lamps to burn every evening." The Rabbis later took a different synthesizing approach, describing the menorah of Moses standing at the "center," with five of Solomon's lamps flanking at the right, five to the left.[22]

The problem of identifying the ways that the biblical menorahs were constructed and deployed within the Tabernacle/Temple is one of denotation. Nouns change meaning over time, and religious traditions, particularly Judaism, generally prefer to assert continuity. I recall that the English word "car," to choose an example, has referred variously to a late antique carriage, an eighteenth-century horse-drawn wagon, a train, a Model T, or my own vehicle driving down the freeway. Similarly, an "icebox" was a very different contraption when my mother used the term to refer to her refrigerator well into the twentieth century than it was when my grandmother bought ice during the Depression. The modern Hebrew noun *menorah* refers to the Tabernacle lampstand, to all other biblical cultic lampstands, to simple oil lamps, and today to all sorts of electric lighting fixtures. The Rabbis went so far as to use biblical terminology—the only terminology they had in Hebrew for such things—to describe standard Roman lampstand parts. They thus created, likely unintentionally, a kind of interpretive circle between lamps in their homes and the parts of the biblical lamp. Mishnah Kelim 11:7 describes the *qanim,* the "branches," the "cups," and the "base" of the menorah as objects of current daily use. On the other hand, Hanukkah lamps—eight lamps attached in a row—came to be called "menorahs" in Jewish tradition, creating an intentional connection between the menorah of the Hasmoneans and the domestic lamp. This connection was broken in modern Hebrew in 1897 when Hemda Ben Yehuda, the wife of linguist and early Hebrew speaker Eliezer Ben

Yehuda, sought to differentiate the Hanukkah lamp from the increasingly present seven-branched lampstand of modern Jewish culture and from modern lighting fixtures. There was an increasing need for nouns in modern Hebrew for these fixtures, especially with the advent of the electric light bulb. Ben Yehuda drew on a rather obscure noun developed by Jews in the Balkan lands, *ḥanukkiah,* in order to distinguish the Hanukkah lamp (*menorat ha-Ḥanukkah*) from other sorts of menorahs. The range of possible denotations for the noun menorah is thus broad and elastic, as it is for most nouns that have been used for generations (and for this one, for millennia).

The prophet Zechariah provides the most extensive postexilic reflection on the menorah, describing in detail a lampstand that is very different from the Tabernacle menorah. In Zechariah, chapter 4, the menorah takes center stage:

> And the angel who talked with me came again, and waked me, like a man that is wakened out of his sleep. And he said to me, "What do you see?" I said, "I see, and behold, a lampstand all of gold, with a bowl on the top of it, and seven lamps on it, with seven lips on each of the lamps which are on the top of it. And there are two olive trees by it, one on the right of the bowl and the other on its left." And I said to the angel who talked with me, "What are these, my lord?" Then the angel who talked with me answered me, "Do you not know what these are?" I said, "No, my lord." Then he said to me, "This is the word of the Lord to Zerubbabel: Not by might, nor by power, but by my Spirit, says the Lord of hosts. What are you, O great mountain? Before Zerubbabel you shall become a plain; and he shall bring forward the top stone amid shouts of 'Grace, grace to it.' " Moreover the word of the Lord came to me, saying, "The hands of Zerubbabel have laid the foundation of this house; his hands shall also complete it. Then you will know that the Lord of hosts has sent me to you. For whoever has despised the day of small things shall rejoice, and shall see them plummet in the hand of Zerubbabel. "These seven are the eyes of the Lord, which range through the whole earth." Then I said to him, "What are these two olive trees on the right and the left of the lampstand?" And a second time I said to him, "What are these two branches of the olive trees, which are beside the two golden pipes from which the oil is poured out?" He said to me, "Do you not know

what these are?" I said, "No, my lord." Then he said, "These are the two anointed who stand by the Lord of the whole earth."[23]

The book of Zechariah was composed around 520–518 BCE, soon after the call by King Cyrus for Jews to return and rebuild the Jerusalem Temple (540 BCE), reflecting the social conditions in the Persian *satrap* of *Yehud*—the province of Judah—just as the Babylonian Exile was coming to an end. It is a prophecy that works to sort out the complex relationship between Judaism and its Persian overlords and benefactors, and to reformulate the traditions of Israel for a new age and a restored—if rather modest—Temple to the God of Israel. Zechariah's vision is one of the last of the prophetic books of the Hebrew Bible, a genre of literature that assumes direct communication with the Divine, somewhat rationalized by Abraham Joshua Heschel as "divine pathos." Zechariah, our book tells us, received a heavenly messenger, an "angel," who instructs Zerubbabel, a descendant of the Davidic family and a Persian government employee, in the complexities of this relationship. Though Zerubbabel is a functionary of Persia, Zechariah claims Zerubbabel is doing the work of the God of Israel.

The symbol of this realignment between Jews and Persians was a menorah. According to Zechariah, this lighted lamp is the "eyes of God," its seven lamps corresponding to the seven visible "planets." This is the source of the metaphor used by Philo and Josephus during the first century, and by rabbis later on. For these authors, this astral association provided meaning for the lampstand, but also an explanation of the rounded branches. For those of us who, like me, live under a dome of light pollution, we must struggle to remember that in places without skyscrapers, the stars and constellations seem to follow a similar rotation around our world. For this reason, Aristotle believed that they encircled us on a dome, and the book of Genesis sees a hard "firmament" of heaven. Beneath these "planets" are the Sun, the Moon, and the five visible planets—objects of varying shape and color even to the naked eye (hence, red Mars) that flash across the sky at irregular intervals when compared with the utter predictability of the stars above. This notion of the "planets" as God's "eyes" has continued in Judaism, even appearing as an Aramaic curse inscription found in a late antique synagogue floor mosaic of Ein Gedi (a town on the Dead Sea), which dates to the sixth century, more or less. This inscription warns any trespassers against the communal code that "He whose eyes range through the whole earth and who sees hidden things, will set his face against that man and his seed and will uproot him from under the heavens. And all the people shall say [literally, "said"]: Amen, Amen, Selah."[24] The roughly contemporary synagogue poet Yannai puts it this way:

> The seven lamps of the menorah below
> Are like the seven constellations [planets] above.[25]

Ancients had a profound awareness that "God is watching us from a distance." The menorah was intimately associated with this notion.

On a physical level, however, the description of the lampstand in Zechariah yields a very different artifact from the one that we have seen in Exodus, and certainly an object that was very different from the arch menorah. Above the lamps of the Zechariah menorah is a *golah,* a bowl that served as a kind of reservoir for oil, with a "lip" for each of the seven flames. This lampstand does not seem to have "branches," curved or otherwise, like the Exodus menorah—though Jewish tradition has asserted continuity from one to the next. In order to maintain this continuity, medieval illustrators imagine a *golah* suspended above the branches, each with a pipe or a similar contrivance that brings the oil to each lamp. Carol and Eric Meyers suggest that the Zechariah lampstand is a golden version of a terracotta lamp that is well known from the Persian period, which is likely.

To conclude—from the Bible to the Arch of Titus the menorah is among the best-known artifacts of Jewish antiquity, a fact that in no way instills confidence that we know much about it. The distance from scripture to first-century Jerusalem was a long one, passing from the late Middle Bronze period through the Persian Empire, from Bezalel son of Uri to Solomon's artisans to the prophet Zechariah, from the Maccabees to Herod the Great and on to Titus's artisans. It is a history written in texts and in artifacts, with many, many holes in our knowledge along the way. It is a rather messy history, the lamps unified as a group by the noun used to describe them, by their descriptions as appurtenances of the Jewish Tabernacle/Temple, and by the number seven. We have seen that interpreters beginning with Zechariah associated these lamps with the seven visible "planets" as the "eyes of God," and that Philo of Alexandria and Josephus interpreted the rounded branches of menorahs of their age with the rounded paths of those "planets" around the sun. By the first century BCE, and probably considerably earlier, the sort of menorah that we see on the arch and in Jewish portrayals beginning with the last of the Hasmonean kings, Mattathias Antigonus, represent the artifacts that stood aglow in the Jerusalem Temple. The many extant images are actually very similar across Jewish art, including the arch—except for the bases (the one part of this artifact not described by scripture). We need not choose one menorah as the original or most significant menorah, with the original base, over the others. Numerous menorahs were used in the service of the Second Temple over its long history. One of these, perhaps the most ornate of all, was reproduced on the arch and displayed as booty in Vespasian's Temple of Peace for the glory of Vespasian, Titus, and, above all, Rome.

2

Flavian Rome to the Nineteenth Century

Yannai, a virtuoso of Hebrew liturgical poetry (*piyyut*)—likely in the Galilee during the century or so before the Islamic invasion of Palestine in 636 CE—writes:

> The lamps of Edom [Rome] strengthened and increased.
> The lamps of Zion were swallowed up and destroyed.
> The lamps of Edom prevailed and glittered.
> The lamps of Zion were crushed and extinguished.
> The lamps of Edom prance over every pitfall.
> The lamps of Zion receded.
> The lamps of Edom their brightness shines.
> The lamps of Zion were darker than soot.
> The lamps of Edom were filled and they dripped [oil].
> The lamps of Zion were lowered and broken.
> The lamps of Edom were honored and adorned.
> The lamps of Zion were seized and turned asunder.
> The lamps of Edom shine over the dead.
> The lamps of Zion are forgotten like the dead.[1]

This prolific poet performed in the synagogues of Galilee some fifteen hundred or so years ago. Yannai laments the destroyed "lamps of Zion," identifying Rome here with the biblical enemy of Israel, Edom. The "lamps of Edom their brightness shines." This brilliance is expressed in a map of the Holy Land set in a sixth-century CE floor mosaic of a church at Madaba, near Mount Nebo in modern Jordan. From this isolated site Christian pilgrims could look down into the Holy Land and see, through the eyes of this map, a land filled with churches commemorating the life of Christ and of the Old Testament, a land that was the birthplace of the city of David, David's son Solomon, and their descendant, Jesus Christ. No Jews appear in the Madaba map—they were erased by Edom triumphant, just as many "Indian reservations" were erased in maps of the United States until just a few years ago. In Yannai's lament, the extinguished menorah represented far more than just the extinguished lamp of the Temple. It symbolized the Jews themselves.

For some centuries after Jerusalem was destroyed in 70 CE, it was still possible to "visit" the menorah of the Herodian Temple in Vespasian's Temple of Peace—just as Jews occasionally "visited" the site of the destroyed Temple in Jerusalem. The artifacts of the Temple were available for all to see in Rome, not far from the Forum—and it is likely that Jews and others, locals and visitors to Rome, went to view them there, even as they could see images of the final procession of the Menorah and the Table into Rome in bright color nearby on the Arch of Titus (and I would imagine elsewhere as well, since there were many monuments to the Flavian victory in Rome, including another—now lost—Titus arch where the victory was explicitly lauded). It is likely that early Christians visiting the Temple of Peace or viewing the Arch of Titus were fascinated by the traces of the Temple and especially the menorah, even as they saw in both the vindication of Jesus's prophecy in all three of the Synoptic gospels that "There will not be left here one stone upon another."[2] During the mid-second century, a rabbi from Palestine, Shimon bar Yoḥai, is said to have seen the menorah in Rome, presumably at this temple, and described the arrangement of the lamps upon its branches: "Said Rabbi Shimon: When I went to Rome there I saw the menorah. All of the lamps were pointed toward the middle lamp."[3]

According to rabbinic testimony, the oil lamps on the six outer branches were all inclined toward the central stalk—an arrangement well known from images of the menorah in the Galilee, Asia Minor, and Rome from the fourth and fifth centuries. Other rabbis of this same generation are said to have "seen" the purple curtain of the Temple, the *parokhet,* and the golden priestly headpiece, the *tsits.* This sparse testimony, which is part of a group of rabbinic sources that describes mid-second-century rabbis seeing the Temple vessels in Rome, says nothing about where sages like Rabbi Simeon may have gone to see the vessels, nor does it provide details of such visits. The fact that the facade of the Temple, the table of show-bread, and the silver horns are portrayed on coins of the Bar Kokhba Revolt (132–136 CE); that many of the Bar Kokhba coins are inscribed "for the freedom of Jerusalem"; and that Shimon bar Yoḥai was a student of Rabbi Aqiva—executed by Rome for his support of the revolt—adds a level of poignancy to this group of legends, and may have in antiquity as well. Jews could "see" their holy vessels in the Temple on these coins, knowing that the originals could only be "seen" in captivity in Rome.

As an aside, I note that scholars have long been puzzled by an element of First Revolt and Bar Kokhba coinage that *does not* appear. The menorah is nowhere to be seen, while the table and horns are prominent. Shulamith Laderman's recent discussion of this issue in regard to Bar Kokhba's issues reflects a consensus position:

> It is interesting that the design he developed did not include the menorah. Possibly, the highly visible presence of the seven-branched menorah on the Arch of Titus, which commemorated the Roman victory and was at the same time the symbol of Jewish defeat, dissuaded him from using it on the coins. It is also possible that as the menorah was associated with the priestly functions in the temple it did not fit in with Bar Kokhba's plan to portray the temple as a religious symbol to unite the entire nation—priests, levites, and commoners.[4]

My own sense is somewhat less sure. The Arch of Titus and its menorah were well known in the city of Rome, but likely not so well known beyond—images of the menorah do not appear on the wide array of coins minted by the Flavian emperors to celebrate their victory, the *Judaea Capta* coin issues. For Romans in other parts of the empire, Judaean palm trees and their dates were far more evocative of Judaea than the Temple artifacts. Knowledge of these artifacts must at some level have been tied to the city of Rome—thus the reported visit of Aqiva's student Shimon bar Yoḥai to Rome and his report on the form of the menorah. We cannot know why the menorah did not appear on the coins of either revolt, though Bar Kokhba's minters seem to have chosen the table over the lampstand in their portrayals of the Temple facade. The choice might have been as simple as the fact that the rectangular table "fit" into the rectangular portal and angular facade less obtrusively than the menorah might have—though this is a very formal explanation. Perhaps the Mishnah in Ḥagigah 3:8 provides a clue. This text, we have seen, warns pilgrims not to touch "the table and the menorah."[5] This text follows the biblical order of these artifacts, which is followed by Josephus in his description of the Tabernacle and even by the Arch of Titus's triumphal parade.[6] The commissioning of the table begins in Exodus 25:23 and the menorah after it in Exodus 25:31. Perhaps this ordering affected actual ways that people thought about these artifacts, and so the added prominence of the table. This is all guessing and grasping at small morsels of evidence. The prominence of the table may be counterintuitive to us, with our modern focus on the menorah, but this does not seem to have been the case in antiquity.

Rabbinic sources vigorously assert the continued significance of the vessels of the Jerusalem Temple after 70 CE—and a deep rabbinic interest in describing, and thereby "owning" the Tabernacle, the Temples, and their service. A large portion of the Mishnah (redacted ca. 200 CE) is dedicated to reflection on the Temple, and a collection from roughly the same period, the *Baraita de-Melekhet ha-Mishkan,* the "Traditions on the building of the Tabernacle," (ca. 250 CE), explores the Tabernacle in depth. Synagogue art as well, beginning at Dura-Europos sometime before 244–245 CE and particularly in the fifth and sixth centuries, shows real interest in the Temple and its cult, including the menorah. This interest was not antiquarian, but rather based on an active and oft-prayed for hope and belief that the Temple would be rebuilt sooner rather than later. Earlier sources suggest a more active anticipation that this restorative memory would be activated soon, while later *Amoraic* sources, reflecting the late third to fifth centuries and beyond (e.g., the Jerusalem Talmud, homiletical *midrashim,* liturgical texts, and, farther afield in Sasanian Persia, the Babylonian Talmud), seem more resigned that rebuilding might take more time.

Jews across a hostile border in Sasanian Babylonia, modern Iraq and Iran, imagined that the vessels had been hidden away in Rome, and were not on public display. According to Babylonian Talmud Meilah 17a–b, the Temple curtain, the *parokhet,* is stored in the house of an unidentified emperor in his "treasury" (*genizah*) in Rome itself, where it was seen by Rabbi Shimon bar Yoḥai thanks to the intervention of a demon. In fact, during the "Age of Transition" between Byzantium and Islam, *The Fathers According to Rabbi Nathan* reports to its audience that "the grinding tool of the house of Avtimas [used for making incense] and the table and the menorah and the curtain and the headpiece are still stored [*munaḥim*] in Rome."[7] An apocalyptic text called *Otot ha-Meshiaḥ*, "Signs of the Messiah," imagines that Temple vessels were stored in Rome in the house of "Yulianus Caesar."[8] According to *Otot ha-Meshiaḥ,* the "Messiah son of Joseph" will kill the king of "Edom," Rome, "destroy the city of Rome and remove some of the vessels of the Temple which are stored [*genuzin*] in the house of Emperor Julianus and bring them to Jerusalem." In messianic times, *Otot ha-Meshiaḥ* has it, these vessels will be returned in a violent conflagration—settling a score with Rome.

The menorah is not specifically mentioned among the artifacts saved after a fire in the Temple of Peace in 192 CE—which may only mean that the Roman author of this list did not consider it notable enough among the treasures of Vespasian's ancient museum to mention. Alternately, it could mean that the menorah was lost in the fire. The Byzantine historian Procopius of Caesarea (d. ca. 565) makes no mention of Jerusalem Temple vessels among the famous sculptures of the Temple of Peace.[9] Rather, he has it that vessels from the Temple were taken by the Visigoths during their sack of Rome during the fifth century—an idea that is unknown to the Rabbis, or to any other ancient authors. This author preserves two traditions of what happened next. The first tradition is that the vessels may have been placed on a boat and taken either to the city of Gallia Narbonensis, today called Carcassonne, by Alaric in 410:

> And the Germans, gaining the upper hand in the engagement, killed the most of the Visigoths and their ruler Alaric. They took possession of the greater part of Gaul and held it; and they laid siege to Carasiana with great enthusiasm because they had learned that the royal treasure was there, which Alaric the elder in earlier times had taken booty when he captured Rome. Among these also were the treasures of Solomon, the king of the Hebrews, a most noteworthy sight. For they most of them were adorned with emeralds; and they had been taken from Jerusalem by the Romans in ancient times.[10]

Alternately—and more famously—the second tradition is that they were pillaged from Rome by the Vandal Gaiseric in 455, who shipped the items to Carthage in North Africa. They were then taken by the Byzantine general Belisarius as booty back to the Emperor Justinian in Constantinople and on to Jerusalem:

> Belisarius, upon reaching Byzantium with Gelimer and the Vandals, was counted worthy to receive such honors as in former times were assigned to those generals of the Romans who had won the greatest and most noteworthy victories. And a period of about 600 years had now passed since anyone had attained these honors, except, indeed, Titus and Trajan, and such other emperors as had led armies against some barbarian nation and had been victorious. For he displayed the spoils and slaves from the war in the midst of the city and led a procession which the Romans call a "triumph," not, however, in the ancient manner, but going on foot from his own house to the hippodrome and then again from the barriers until he reached the place where the imperial throne is. And there was booty—first of all, whatever articles were wont to be set apart for the royal service—thrones of gold and carriages in which it is customary for a king's consort to ride, and much jewelry made of precious stones, and golden drinking cups, and all the other things which are useful for the royal table. And there was also silver weighing many thousands of talents and all the royal treasure amounting to an exceedingly great sum (for Geiseric had despoiled the Palatium in Rome, as has been said in the preceding narrative). And among these were the treasures of the Jews, which Titus the son of Vespasian, together with certain others, had brought to Rome after the capture of Jerusalem. And one of the Jews, seeing these things, approached one of those known to the Emperor and said: "These treasures I think it inexpedient to carry into the palace in Byzantium. Indeed, it is not possible for them to be elsewhere than in the place where Solomon, the king of the Jews, formerly placed them. For it is because of these that Geiseric captured the palace of the Romans, and that now the Roman army has captured that of the Vandals." When this had been brought to the attention of the Emperor, he became afraid and quickly sent everything to the sanctuaries of the Christians in Jerusalem.[11]

Improbably, this legend suggests, a Jew in Constantinople convinced the emperor—known from his legal enactments to have treated Judaism quite harshly and even forbidding the study of rabbinic tradition—that it would be bad luck to keep the Jerusalem treasures in his capital, and so Justinian sent them on to a church in Jerusalem. This is quite a fanciful legend, clearly building upon Josephus's triumph in its assertion that the glory of both

Rome and Jerusalem are transferred to the Christian emperor in Constantinople. It is noteworthy that Procopius, who was born in Caesarea Maritima on the coast of Palestine and wrote extensively about Justinian's benefaction of churches in the Holy Land, could well be conveying a local legend. Nonetheless, he makes no specific mention of the menorah, which is perhaps (though not necessarily) subsumed among the "treasures of the Jews." Procopius makes no reference to these Temple treasures in his descriptions of Justinian's church construction in Jerusalem.[12] "Jews" often serve as a literary trope in Byzantine literature, portrayed as theological troublemakers with a biblical pedigree who cause such things as Byzantine destruction of religious images—iconoclasm—during the eighth century by convincing Christians to forsake their holy icons. David Olster has shown that this deployment had nothing to do with "real live" Jews, but rather are a construction of the Christian theological imagination. The "usable Jew," so well known in Christian sources, is similarly deployed mischievously convincing Justinian, to whom he somehow has personal access, to transfer the menorah to Jerusalem. Through his story, Procopius "explains" why the Temple vessels were not maintained at the seat of empire.

An association of Justinian with the Temple treasures is perhaps inevitable, as the center of Christian Rome passed to "New Rome," to Constantinople. Temple imagery was rife in sixth-century Constantinople. The Church of St. Polyeuctus (ca. 523–527) was built, the designers believed, on the proportions of Solomon's Temple and was donated by members of the old aristocracy, who looked unkindly toward the rising Justinian. The donor, a woman named Anicia Juliana, compares her beneficence in an epigram that has survived to the emperors Constantine and Theodosius II. She even claims to have surpassed Solomon. According to legend, upon completion of the Hagia Sophia in Constantinople, Justinian exclaimed, "Solomon, I have outdone you." This association was so well known that a rabbinic poem from southern Italy that describes Jewish life there during the ninth century, "The Scroll of Aḥimaaz," treated this claim with scorn. Be that as it may, this association well fits Justinian's intentions. Possession of the Temple vessels would up the ante for Justinian. He could claim to have "outdone" Solomon, taking possession of the Temple vessels and piously sending them on to Jerusalem. No Christian, Jewish, or Moslem source mentions the menorah in Jerusalem during late antiquity. If it were there, the stirrings would surely have left ripples in the extant sources. We really do not know what happened to the menorah and other "treasures of the Jews." Rome was in turmoil, and precious metals of all sorts were apparently taken away en masse. The path runs dry.

Since the eighteenth century, European historians have cited the two stories in Procopius as if they were transparently historical documents, their main task being to reconcile the two very different accounts. No less a scholar than Reelant cited him believingly, as have most scholars since. The great historian of medieval Rome, Ferdinand Gregorovius (d. 1891), wrote that while Alaric took some vessels from "Solomon's Temple" to Carcassonne, other Jewish objects "he must have left unheeded, since, together with the spoils acquired from the churches, some of the sacred vessels of the Temple, brought by Titus from Jerusalem, were shipped by Genseric to Carthage."[13] A German scholar of the 1848 generation with considerable sympathy for the Jews of Rome and their eventual emancipation, Gregorovius even imagines the Jewish treasure and the treasures of Rome shipped off from the Eternal City in shared ignominy. This vision was later adopted by Stefan Zweig in his Zionist novella, *Der begrabene Leuchter,* published in Vienna in 1936 and translated almost immediately into English (Zweig was already in England) as *The Buried Candelabrum* in 1937. Gregorovius writes: "It is possible that on board the same vessel that sailed to Carthage, laden with the spoils of Rome, the Lychnuchus [menorah] of Solomon and the statue of the Capitoline Zeus, symbols of the oldest religions of the East and West, may have rested side by side."[14] It is not surprising that Gregorovius's writings on Jews were republished in a generally available format in 1935 in the *Schocken Bucherei,* the Schocken Library, a collection of short books published in Nazi Germany by department store magnate and cultural Zionist Salman Schocken as an act of cultural resistance against the Nazis. Gregorovius's German volume closes with a poem glorifying the eternal existence of the Jews, as exemplified through the menorah.

Even Hans Lewy (in Hebrew, Yoḥanan), a renowned Berlin-trained German-Jewish classicist and member of the Hebrew University faculty, cited Procopius as historical truth. He did this in a short, though highly influential, Hebrew article, "A Note on the Fate of the Sacred Vessels of the Second Temple." With an air of classical German philological surety typical of his age, Lewy went so far as to suggest—based upon the precarious Jewish and Byzantine sources that we have discussed, that each of Procopius's legends represents different Temple objects. Some of these found their way to Constantinople, the rest to Jerusalem. Evidence for the Constantinople assemblage is derived from *Otot ha-Meshiaḥ.* A generation before, the great Hungarian scholar Samuel Krauss fashioned this source to correspond to the legend in Procopius. Krauss identifies "Julianus," the spelling of which is inconsistent in early versions of this text, with Emperor Justinian, asserting through the magic of philology the presence of Jewish artifacts in Constantinople. Lewy rejects this emendation, while still identifying "the House of Julianus" very concretely with a library built by the Emperor Julian "the Apostate" in the palace in Constantinople.

Lewy claimed that the menorah remained in Constantinople until the First Crusade, after which the path finally ran dry. His approach goes back to Krauss's teacher David Kaufmann, as early as 1886. It is based upon what is now known to be a precarious marginal gloss to the only complete manuscript of the Byzantine *Book of Ceremonies* composed under the Emperor Constantine VII Porphyrogennetos (d. 959 CE). This rubbed and poorly preserved note mentions that a *heptaka[ndelos]*, a lighting fixture with seven candles, stood in the palace in Constantinople.[15] It nowhere mentions *the* menorah, but just a fixture with seven lamps. The gloss does not use the slightly different ancient Greek term used by Jews for the menorah in antiquity, *heptaluxion* (literally, "seven lamps"), nor the terms used in the eleventh-century Florence manuscript of Kosmas Indikopleustes's sixth-century *Christian Topography,* which contains the image of the Tabernacle menorah and glosses it "seven-light candelabrum" (*luxnia heptamussos*), which a later scribe corrected to *heptamuxos.* These terms make the identification of the *heptaka[ndelos]* as a menorah all the more suspect, as this is not a standard term for the menorah in roughly contemporary sources. As we will see, seven-branched Christian lampstands became increasingly popular during the Middle Ages. To top it off, John Wortley notes that the menorah was not listed among the relics carried away by the Crusaders—though the tablets of the Ten Commandments and the Ark of the Covenant were. The association of this obscure gloss with the Jewish menorah is a modern one—quite a historical burden for a short marginal gloss to bear.

Lewy here departs from the kind of objectivity for which he is still renowned. In the body of the essay, Lewy suggests that the menorah found its way to Constantinople, while other unidentified Temple artifacts were sent to Justinian's Nea Church in Jerusalem. In a footnote, however, he suggests, based upon Josephus's mention of two menorahs, that "it is possible that both of them were brought from Rome to Carthage, and from there to Constantinople, and that one was sent by Justinian to Jerusalem, while the second he left in Constantinople."[16]

This deeply committed Zionist author is clearly responding to contemporary questions by fellow Jews who hoped for the imminent restoration of the menorah. This concern was in the air, popularized by Zweig's novella—a book which, to my surprise, was never translated into Hebrew and so is largely unknown to contemporary Israeli readers. Zweig built upon the Procopius legend in surprising ways, claiming that Jews in Constantinople had tricked Justinian, leaving him with a fake menorah, while spiriting away the original. In his telling, the biblical menorah was buried by Jews near the road between Jaffa and Jerusalem—in this case, awaiting their eventual return to the Holy Land:

> Like all God's mysteries, it rests in the darkness through the ages. Nor can anyone tell whether it will remain thus for ever and ever, hidden away and lost to its people, who still know no peace in their wanderings through the lands of the Gentiles, or whether, at length, someone will dig up the Menorah on that day when the Jews come once more into their own. Only then will the Seven-Branched Lampstand diffuse its gentle light in the Temple of Peace.[17]

Oddly, Lewy accepts Procopius's claim that Temple vessels were sent to a Jerusalem church by Justinian most uncritically and even extrapolates, like Zweig, that some are buried today somewhere in Palestine, wondering out loud, "Who knows if the temple vessels aren't buried under the ruins of that church?" [that is, Justinian's Nea Church]. This, despite the fact that Procopius makes no such claim. Lewy's conclusion expresses the laden moment between the end of World War II and the establishment of Israel in 1948. He writes that: "It is apparent from this that some of the holy vessels were returned to Jerusalem and were kept there more than two hundred years opposite the destroyed Temple Mount, and perhaps they are buried there under the soil to this very day; and the golden menorah was kept in Constantinople more than a thousand years after the destruction of the Temple."[18]

Lewy's essay was first published in *Kedem: Studies in Jewish Archaeology*, a publication of the Hebrew University's then Museum of Jewish Archaeology in 1945, the year of his untimely fatal heart attack. The issue was edited by E. L. Sukenik, and the heaviness of the hour permeates Sukenik's introduction to this volume. The small and insular (though deeply self-important) Jerusalem community for this Hebrew-language journal included archaeologists more than ready to "redeem" Jewish archaeological remains through scientific methodologies. In fact, Sukenik and other Zionist archaeologists had already found many astonishing things—from biblical cities to coins and tombs of the Second Temple period, late antique synagogues across Judaea and the Galilee, a usable stone menorah from Tiberias—and soon (beginning in 1947) the Dead Sea Scrolls. Why not, the cultural logic surely went, the Temple menorah?

This hope of finding *the* menorah has not been a subject of Israeli scholarship since then, though to this day every discovery of an ancient menorah seems to warrant press coverage and even celebration. Scholars have mostly relied on Lewy's essay to discuss the whereabouts of the Temple menorah. Even during the excavations of Justinian's Nea Church in Jerusalem during the 1970s, this hope was not voiced by archaeologists—at least in print. In 2006, however, a British scholar renewed the search, based on Procopius. In that year archaeologist Sean Kingsley, known for his fascinating work in marine archaeology, turned his attention to the ultimate lost treasure, the menorah. Kingsley has extensive experience in the recovery of treasure from shipwrecks, setting the context for his menorah search. In a trade volume called *God's Gold: A Quest for the Lost Temple Treasures of Jerusalem* Kingsley accepted Procopius's stories at face value. He asserted that at the Sasanian capture of Jerusalem, the Temple vessels were hidden away by the Byzantines. This assertion rests on the fact that they are not mentioned among the booty taken by the Sasanians. Kingsley does not entertain the possibility that perhaps they were not in Jerusalem because the Temple booty never was sent to Jerusalem, and that Procopius is not a viable historical source in this regard. Based upon this tale, Kingsley asserts that the menorah is actually beneath the ruins of the Monastery of Saint Theodosius, near al-Ubeidiyaa—a town six kilometers east of Bethlehem. As proof, he provides images of the monastery and in an image label asserts with certainty, "Disturbed soil and the entrance to an underground cave on the grounds of the Monastery of Saint Theodosius. The Temple treasure of Jerusalem ended up concealed in just such a place."[19] In a thrilling narrative, Kingsley describes how he was rebuffed by the keepers of the monastery when he arrived, according to the text, unannounced, and without, I point out, the requisite introductions from the Greek Orthodox Patriarchate in Jerusalem. He concludes this volume without irony, reflecting that: "The gold menorah, precious Table of the Divine Presence, and silver trumpets ended up in a 'city of saints,' hidden in the grounds of the monastery of Saint Theodosius in the wilderness of Judea. As I bade my farewell to Jerusalem, I stared one last time at the Temple Mount, and offered up a little prayer that the treasures remain hidden for all time, sealed beneath swirling desert sands, far from the treacherous clutches of man."[20] Alas, this search did not end with the success of many of Kingsley's underwater studies. He laments that he has not been allowed to prove his theory, because the Greek-speaking caretaker of the monastery will not let him enter.[21] In this way, his narrative ends like many of the searches for the menorah at the Vatican associated with rabbis in Jewish folk traditions of the latter twentieth century that I discuss later on. At the last minute, Kingsley was barred from reaching the treasure.

Few authors have questioned Procopius's tale. Two who did are particularly noteworthy, though their caution has generally been forgotten. Novelist Robert Graves wrote a fascinating, though today seldom read, novel based on Procopius's account that focuses in on the Jerusalem vessels incidents. This volume is called *Count Belisarius* after Justinian's general. Published in 1938, shortly after Zweig's story appeared, Graves was clearly suspicious of Procopius's more audacious claims throughout his *History*, particularly regarding Jews. Publishing as Nazi propaganda against Jews was in full swing, Graves pointedly did not attribute the decision to move the menorah from Constantinople to Jerusalem to a doom-saying Jew. Graves was well aware that Procopius was an internally focused Byzantine court historian. Rather, he asserts that the supposed movement of the Temple vessels (including, errantly, the "golden Mercy Seat") was an internal Christian decision—a blatant attempt by churchmen to build Jerusalem's treasury of relics. Had the artifacts actually reached Jerusalem, this explanation of Procopius would be far more satisfactory than the Jewish influence assumed by most scholars. Graves places memory of the event into the mouth of Belisarius:

> As for the golden Mercy Seat and the golden seven-branched candlestick and the shew-table and the other Jewish treasures, Justinian was persuaded by the Bishop of Jerusalem to return them to the city. The Bishop argued that they had brought no luck to the men of Rome, whose dominion had passed to the barbarians, nor to the Vandals, whom Justinian himself had defeated. They plainly carried a curse with them. Justinian sent them back to Jerusalem, to the very building where they had once been stored for a thousand years—the

> Temple of Solomon, which was now a Christian church. What a grand source of profit for the clergy there. The Jews lamented that they were still deprived of their holy instruments of worship, and prophesied that the Christians would before long be cast out of Jerusalem; but this did not come to pass in my lifetime.[22]

The other skeptic was a German-Israeli art historian named Heinrich Strauss. Strauss was a bit of a maverick among scholars of Jewish visual culture during the 1950s and 1960s. While others were determined to construct and imagine a national "Jewish art," Strauss saw Judaism as an international minority culture, its "art" defined by content rather than form. Among his most significant articles was a study of the history of the menorah in antiquity, which he published in Hebrew in 1956, in English in the *Journal of the Warburg and Courtauld Institutes* in London in the same year, and in abbreviated form in German in 1962. Here this classically trained scholar—who never achieved an academic position in the new state of Israel and is all but forgotten (I have had great difficulty finding even basic information about his biography)—set what little was known about the menorah in antiquity in context. Strauss provided a far more nuanced if deferential (and unfortunately, less read) approach to Procopius than Lewy before him. Strauss's most stringent caution appears in his later article on the menorah in the *Encyclopaedia Judaica* (1970). There Strauss writes quite unequivocally regarding Procopius's accounts of the Temple vessels and their travels: "This story has little credibility; no other source, such as the reports of the pilgrims, can be adduced in its support, nor is the menorah mentioned explicitly in this story."[23] Happily, in a recent series of articles, Ra'anan Boustan of UCLA unpacked this tradition for the folklore that it is, in ways similar to my own position. Folklore it is—a transfer of power and authority from Rome and Constantinople, then with Christian imperial piety back to Jerusalem.

The poet Yannai, writing sometime after Procopius, assumed a very different history even as he too was considering the whereabouts of the menorah. He suggested a far more extreme and dishearteningly simple answer:

> They were broken in anger, the branches of the menorah.
> And the city that was a light to all [Jerusalem], is now more ugly than all others.[24]

This paean to the menorah is a reflection on the lost menorah, refracting the lampstands of Moses, Zechariah, and perhaps the Herodian Temple. Beyond any single historic menorah, Yannai's shattered "lamps of Zion," as I discussed in the opening to this chapter, represent the current fate of the Jewish people—by his time living under the unrelenting theological pressure of Christian Rome. Christian destruction of synagogues and Jewish institutions was well established in his world and recorded in the writings of the Church Fathers, rabbinic sources, Roman law, and archaeological discoveries. Synagogue buildings in Elche, ancient Ilici in Spain, Apamea in Syria, and at Gerasa (modern Jerash in Jordan) were replaced with churches—erased and superseded all at once. Other synagogues, at Ein Gedi, Huseifa, and Caesarea Maritima in Israel, show evidence of having been burned. The "lamps of Zion" were indeed darkened. The most vibrant archaeological evidence appears on a column drum from far away Laodicea in Asia Minor. There we see the image of a typical menorah, a palm frond (*lulav*) to its left, a shofar to its right, decorating what must have been a column of a Jewish building, perhaps a synagogue. At some point, a Christian took control of this column, haphazardly inscribing a large and deep cross over the menorah. This manner of Christianization was common in the newly Christian empire. Statues of emperors were Christianized through the addition of baptismal crosses on their foreheads, and religious sites "cleansed" through the addition of crosses. The Laodicean stone is unique, however, for its visceral expression of the power of Edom and, for Christian leaders, perhaps the worrying attractiveness of Judaism.

Yannai's lament cited in our chapter opening that "the lamps of Edom shine over the dead" refers to the bright lamps set above the ever-increasing number of shrines of the saints in the churches of his native Palestine. In comparison with the churches of Jerusalem, Bethlehem, Nazareth—or the many, many other brightly lit and exorbitantly decorated pilgrimage churches of the Christian Holy Land—the small synagogues built by Jews—no matter how beautifully decorated—must surely have paled. These synagogues were often decorated with images of the menorah—on mosaic floors, wall paintings, lintels, "chancel" screens, oil lamps, and fixtures for hanging glass lamps. The same can be said of Jewish tombs, Jewish jewelry, and even household goods. Seven-branched menorahs were everywhere. This reality did not cease at the borders of the Holy Land. Synagogue buildings across the Roman Empire (and if the

Column barrel inscribed with a menorah and a cross, Laodicea, Turkey, fourth to sixth century CE, courtesy of Carl Rasmussen, www.HolyLandPhotos.org

Dura-Europos synagogue is any indication, likely beyond in Sasanian Persia) show the same basic iconographic vocabulary. When even broken fragments are discovered, it is often easy to identify the remains of this unique form. It is an excellent branding image on the order of the Christian cross, the Muslim crescent, and the golden arches of McDonald's. The branches of late antique menorahs were amazingly uniform—just as we would expect from a branding symbol of this power—though a wide variety of bases are still shown. Most, though, look like typical Roman lampstands of the period, constructed to rest on a tripod of three small legs. "The lamps of Zion" may have been "lowered and broken," but they were anything but "forgotten like the dead."

Yannai wrote and performed within a culture fully ablaze with the light of the menorah—in wall paintings and mosaics; on amulets and jewelry; and in synagogues, tombs, and private homes. He wrote two major poems that were paeans to the menorah, and homiletical sources—midrashim—of the late Byzantine and early Islamic periods are also expansive in their portrayals of the lampstand. Menorahs were essential to the marking off and development of Jewish space across the Roman Empire and in the

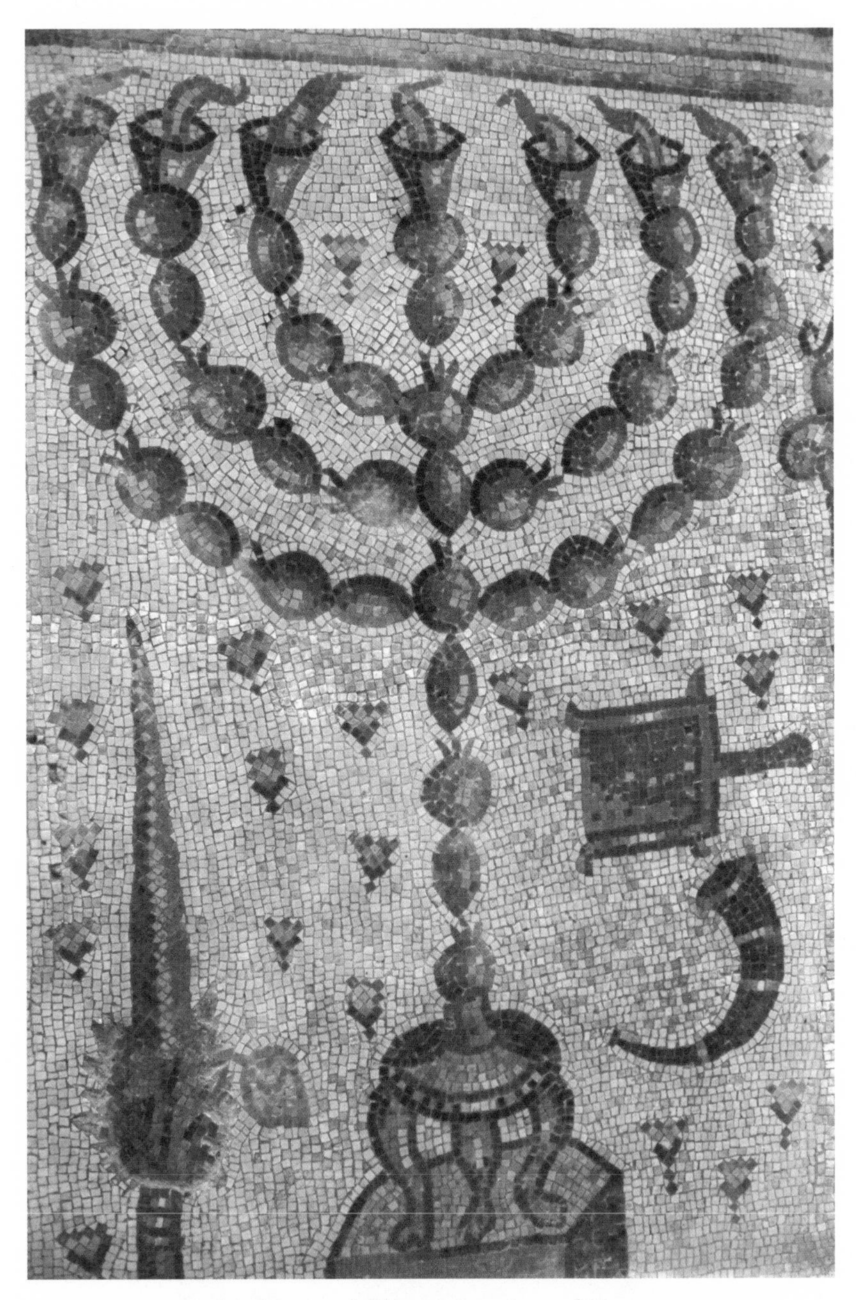

Mosaic pavement of the Hammath Tiberias Synagogue, fifth century CE, courtesy of Photography Department, Government Press Office, Israel National Photo Collection

Synagogue screen, fragment, Ashkelon, fifth to sixth century CE, photograph by Steven Fine

Sasanian realm as well, beginning in the third century and increasingly more so as late antiquity progressed. No less than four images of the menorah appear in the wall paintings of the Dura-Europos synagogue, completed ca. 244–245. These paintings, preserved in the sands of the Syrian desert in a city built on a bluff above the Euphrates River, glow even today with the vibrant colors with which they were painted nearly 1,800 years ago—and we can only hope that this will continue to be the case, as the synagogue has been reconstructed in the National Museum in Damascus. Of the four menorahs, one appears on the face of the Torah shrine, one in an image of the Tabernacle, one set before the Tabernacle in an image of the Israelite camp, and one inscribed in the tympanum of an image of the Ark of the Covenant, and each one is somewhat different in styling. The oldest image of this group, which appears on the Torah shrine, has arms formed as bulbs that are more vertical than rounded, certainly designed such so that the branches would fit on the rather cramped surface of the Ark facade. Oil lamps rest atop each branch, their flames directed toward the right. In the two images of the Tabernacle, nearly identical unlit menorahs are set before the Ark, a candlestick placed to each side of the menorah—apparently for additional light. This multiplication of menorahs—and the absence of a showbread table—suggests the growing significance of the lampstand. Beyond that, the focus on the menorahs fits well with the many oil lamps that undoubtedly provided light within the hall, and whose light flickered before these two-dimensional lampstands.

At the focal point of many of the synagogues in Palestine of the Byzantine period were large Torah arks, set within deep apses and sometimes separated from the nave of the synagogue by low screens. To either side of the ark was a menorah, ablaze—each of the seven lamps providing large quantities of twinkling yet golden light—wicks burning within translucent glass goblets with olive oil floating above crystal-like water below. Sometimes additional lamps were suspended from the menorah's lowest branches, with other lamps dangling from the gable of the Torah ark. We know this not only because remains of Torah arks, lamps, menorahs, and screens have been discovered, but because mosaic pavements set before some of the arks reflect the actual furnishings of the synagogue—much as a reflecting pool reflects an impressive building in our own day. This was the holiest area of the synagogue, called in dedicatory inscriptions, the

Tabernacle panel, Dura Europos synagogue, Syria, 244/245 CE, photograph by Fred Anderegg, in E. R. Goodenough, *Jewish Symbols in the Greco-Roman Period* (New York: Pantheon, 1964), 11, pl. XIV

writings of the Rabbis, and even (grudgingly) by the Church Fathers, a "holy place."

The menorahs of these synagogues were often bronze—as depicted in floor mosaics and other media. They were essentially standard Roman lampstands with branches added to create menorahs. These were certainly brightly polished. Bronze Roman lampstands were often decorated with spots of silver, which enhanced the yellow bronze of the stands and must have created a kind of twinkle that cannot easily be reproduced in painted representations but is evident in the glow of menorah images that appear on Jewish gold glasses found in the catacombs of Rome, which served as reflectors within those dark and dank underground mausoleums. Occasionally synagogue mosaics in Israel attempt to reproduce the glow using glass tesserae set within the branches of their menorah representations—as at

Maon (Nirim) near Gaza. In Rome, images of menorahs were sometimes gold and studded with colorful jewels. We see this both on gold glasses from the catacombs and in the decoration of the Torah shrine of the synagogue at Ostia Antica, the port of Rome. Bronze free-standing menorahs were closely related to free-standing branched candelabra of the same period, except that Christian lamps were assembled all around the stem, and the Jewish branches were set on a single plane. A marvelous example of this from the sixth century is in the collection of the Metropolitan Museum of Art. Like the images of menorahs in most synagogue mosaics, it too held glass lamps at the pinnacles of each of its branches. This Christian candelabrum also has hooks to suspend lamps below it, a characteristic of the menorahs depicted in the mosaic of the Na'aran synagogue near Jericho, and from the study house in Beit Shean/Scythopolis. In Rome, Asia Minor, and in a mosaic recently discovered on the northern shore of the Sea of Galilee, clay oil lamps rather than glass cups are depicted—clearly reflecting a pre-fourth-century usage.

Most of the three-dimensional menorahs that have been discovered are made of stone. These were likely colored, though we cannot know how brightly without testing. The idea that ancient art was polychrome is a new one, and scholars have "discovered" polychromy in stones once believed to have been white just in the last few decades. This polychromy was not restricted to the kind of yellow ochre we discovered at the Arch of Titus. Yannai imagines a colored menorah of the sort that might have existed in our synagogue. He writes:

> One gold was as in the vision, and the image of three [different] golds was seen.
> The calyxes were formed in green gold, the bulbs in red and the flowers in white.[25]

Based upon this text, I fantasized finding evidence of a multicolored menorah at the arch. Roman craftsmen were well skilled in adding colored patinas to metals and to making mixtures of gold with other metals that yield differing shades of color. I had hoped that this shading existed even on the Temple menorah, which was not the case. No brightly colored menorahs have been discovered from ancient synagogues either, though lots of color has been found in ancient synagogues. In a recent article, I

Jewish gold glass, Rome, from the collection of Dr. David and Jemima Jeselsohn, Zurich. Currently on long-term loan with the Israel Museum, Jerusalem

described how I even played with crayons to imagine what Yannai is talking about, using a limestone menorah from Hammath Tiberias as my "guinea pig" and applying colors that appear on artifacts of the period. Happily, the illuminator of a medieval manuscript in the Rhineland, circa 1300 CE, had a tradition like that of Yannai, and he preceded me in coloring his menorah in blue, gold, green, and red. Some of the most important evidence for menorahs in color comes from Rome, where a wall painting of the Jewish catacomb below the Villa Torlonia—Mussolini's villa for a time—shows a menorah in shades of green and black. In the synagogue of Ostia, two reliefs of menorahs found on the Torah ark are decorated with square, round, and diamond-shaped jewels that were likely colored—like similar imagery in Christian mosaics from the Eternal City. In fact, the excavator suggests that evidence of glue used to affix gold foil may have been found on these corbels.

The upper parts of menorahs from Rome generally bear an uncanny similarity to one another, to menorahs in other parts of the Mediterranean world and the Near East, and to the Arch of Titus relief. There is fascinating evidence of local types—in Asia Minor, for example, the space between stone branches of a menorah from the Great Synagogue of Sardis is supported with curls, and curls are shown beneath the bottom set of branches—apparently for support—on menorahs reliefs from Sardis, Nicaea, Priene, and elsewhere. Bases are generally three-legged, if they are shown at all—even in Rome. It is clear that the base of the Arch of Titus menorah never caught on in Jewish iconography. This is partially because the menorah was a lampstand, and in the Roman world most lampstands had three legs. In fact, some images of the menorah reflect this practical reality clearly. The image of a menorah from Iznik in Turkey, the ancient Christian city of Nicaea, shows a typical Roman lampstand, well-designed and reflecting affluence. Rather plain undecorated branches are shown attached to this lampstand, the design suggesting the transformation of a Roman lamp into a menorah. Jews in Europe during the early modern period did the same, transforming large candlesticks into Hanukkah menorahs with the addition of branches. I wonder also if Jews in Rome and elsewhere "knew" that the arch menorah did not fit with their own memory of the lamp (expressed by the Rabbis and in synagogue art going back to the third century CE) or that the arch menorah was not the biblical menorah. Perhaps, simply, the consistency of design across the Roman world reflects a deeply conservative visual culture that was reticent to change—an instinctive wish by an international virtual community to assert relationship. This Jewish predilection continued through the Middle Ages and until the 1880s. Jews never reproduced the Arch of Titus menorah base, even in Rome.

Jewish discussions of the menorah during late antiquity not only asserted the specialness of this biblical artifact, but also reflect a coming together of the lampstand with Byzantine religious iconography and craftsmanship. The biblical artisan Bezalel son of Uri is focused upon in Byzantine period

Ashlar with the image of a menorah, Nicaea (Iznik), Turkey, fifth to sixth century CE, photograph by Marvin Labinger, collection of Leah and Steven Fine

sources in ways unknown in earlier rabbinic sources, but consonant with the increased stature of artisans and artists in Jewish and Christian sources during this period. Thus, the artisans of the sixth-century Beit Alpha synagogue are mentioned by name, and liturgical poets—Yose ben Yose, Yannai, Eleazar ha-Qallir, and others, actually sign their works in acrostics set within their poems (*piyyutim*). *Midrash Tanḥuma,* a Hebrew-language midrashic collection of this transitional period, affirms the heavenly source of the menorah form. This delightful and playful text confronts the complexities of imagining the biblical menorah as it resolves a perceived tension between Moses's role as builder/patron of the Tabernacle and Bezalel's status as a divinely gifted artisan. This is an issue of long duration between Roman benefactors and their artists. The midrash centers around the very translation of Bezalel son of Uri's most auspicious name, "In the shadow of God, son of Light":

> Rabbi Levi son of Rabbi says: A pure menorah came down from heaven. For the Holy One, blessed be He, said to Moses, "And you will make a menorah of pure gold" (Exodus 25:31).
>
> Moses said to Him: "How shall we make it?"
>
> He said to him: "Of beaten work [shall the menorah be made]" (Ibid.)
>
> Nevertheless, Moses still found difficulty with it, and when he came down he forgot its construction.
>
> He went up and said: "Master of the Universe, I have forgotten how to make it!"
>
> The Holy One, blessed be He, showed Moses again, but he still had difficulty.
>
> He [God] said to him: "Look and Make [it]," and finally He took a piece of gold and showed him its construction.
>
> Still, he [Moses] found its construction difficult.
>
> So He said to him: "See it and make it" (Exodus 25:40) and finally He took a menorah of fire and showed him its construction.
>
> Yet, in spite of all this, it caused Moses difficulty.
>
> Said the Holy One, blessed be He, to him: "Go to Bezalel and he will make it."
>
> He went down to Bezalel, and the latter immediately constructed it.
>
> Immediately Moses began to wonder, saying: "To me it was shown many times by the Holy One, blessed be He, yet I found it hard to

> make, and you who did not see it constructed it with your own intelligence! Bezalel, you stood in the shadow of God [*be-tsel El*] when the Holy One, blessed be He, showed me its construction![26]

The centrality to this playful tête-à-tête of the menorah, rather than the showbread table or other Tabernacle implements, is clearly related to the increased significance of the menorah in Jewish iconography during late antiquity. One can only imagine the storyteller—or a synagogue poet like Yannai—extolling the menorah in a Galilean synagogue or study house. In my mind's eye, he and his community are surrounded by images of the lampstand on the floors, walls, lintels, chandeliers, and on the glass jewelry worn by the women. The apse housing the Torah shrine is set behind a low marble screen decorated with colorful images of the menorah. The ark is illuminated by a single glass lamp suspended from its gable, and shining three-dimensional polished brass or polychrome menorahs—golden olive oil glistening within their seven glass cups—stand to either side.

The lavishness of the Byzantine context is expressed in a text known as *Tractate Kelim,* recently dubbed "The Tractate of the Vessels," which dates to the very end of the Byzantine period, or perhaps even the early Islamic period. Describing the menorahs "hidden" together with the rest of the Temple vessels when Nebuchadnezzar destroyed Jerusalem in 586 BCE, this author imagines that "Ten myriad lampstands of fine gold and seven lamps on every single one; twenty-six fine stones were on every single lampstand. As for each one of the pearls, its value was unknown. And between every single stone were two hundred stones, likewise their value unknown."[27] While no menorahs covered with "fine stones" appear in Palestine, the jeweled menorahs of Ostia and Rome—together with surviving jeweled crosses and images of crosses and furniture in contemporaneous church mosaics—provide fine parallels.

An Aramaic-language midrash that dates to the same period, known as the *Targum Sheni le-Esther* (the *Second Targum to Esther*), provides a rather unique image of a menorah, one that is repeated nowhere else. This menorah appears attached to the fantastic "Throne of Solomon," a literary description of a Byzantine automaton, a device where animals bray, birds fly, and the king appears in his glory. Such devices are known from the Byzantine court and found their way to rabbinic fantasies of Solomon's incomparable throne:

> Now at the top of the throne was located a golden lampstand set in proper order in its arrangement of its lamps with pomegranates, with its ornaments, with its snuffers/ash pans [and] with its cups and with its lilies. Now at one side of the lampstand were standing seven golden branches, upon which were portrayed [*metsayrin*] the seven Patriarchs of the world, and these are their names: Adam, Noah and the great Shem, Abraham, Isaac and Jacob and Job among them. Now at the other side of the lampstand were standing seven other branches, upon which were portrayed the seven pious ones of the world and these are their names: Levi, Qehat, Amram, Moses, Aaron, Eldad and Medad, as well as the prophet Haggai among them. Now at the top of the lampstand was a golden vessel filled with pure olive oil, whose light supplied the lights of the lampstand, and upon it were portrayed the high priest.[28]

This Aramaic midrash goes a step further than previous interpreters. *Targum Sheni*'s approach builds on the verb *metsayrin,* "drawn," or in this case, "engraved," which was first applied to the Tabernacle menorah in the Aramaic *Targum Onkelos* to Exodus 25:33 and which supplies a verb otherwise missing from this verse. That text imagines that the blossoms were cups, their surfaces inscribed in a decorative manner. In *Targum Sheni, metsayrin* is used far more expansively. Here it is used to justify two-dimensional representations of human figures on the lampstand. Our author imagines a lampstand holding the images of Jewish heroes in the same way that an iconostasis might function in later churches or that images of saints and biblical heroes decorated Gospel books in his own day. While strange for a rabbinic source, I point out that *Targum Sheni* has achieved an almost canonical status, so it is a text that has been well known for a millennium. In fact, some manuscript traditions "erase" the portrayals and simply list the biblical heroes—a typical approach in the history of Hebrew manuscript transmission to once-acceptable positions that are no longer favored. Nothing like this depiction existed again in Jewish sources or art before German-born Jewish British artist Beno Elkin's 1956 bronze Knesset menorah (see Chapter 4).

Jews were not the only ones to portray menorahs in their religious art—likely to the dismay of people like Yannai. Samaritans, Christians, and even Muslims adopted the menorah. In Roman antiquity, the Samaritans were a major community in the cultural mix of Palestine, numbering, by some educated guesses, up to a million people. Samaritans identify themselves as the descendants of the ten northern tribes of Israel, and Samaritanism is the second lobe of Israelite religion to have survived to the present. Like Jews, Samaritans await a kind of messianic redemption, when the Tabernacle will be revealed and the *rehutah,* the "time of favor," instituted. Their Yom Kippur liturgy includes prayers for forgiveness and the accompanying restoration of the Tabernacle:

> We cry with bloody tears, for days of favor and mercy;
> Days of goodness and blessings, of pardon and forgiveness;
> Days of the urim and thummim, days of the incense offering;
> Days of the illuminated menorah [*menorat ha-meor*], days of the pure table [of showbread; *ha-shulkhan ha-tahor*];
> Days of the holy of holies, and of holy priests;
> Ah, for our days wholeness, and for the days of our kingdom;
> And for the Tabernacle and its greatness, and the glory of the Lord that filled it;
> Ah, for its glory and its majesty, and for the days that have past.[29]

The significance and richness of Samaritan visual culture in Greco-Roman antiquity became evident only in the 1990s, with the excavation of the Samaritan sacrificial compound on Mount Gerizim and significant synagogue sites in the West Bank. We now know that the menorah is ubiquitous in Samaritan visual culture of this period, to no less a degree than it is in Jewish art. Menorahs appear on oil lamps that bear Samaritan inscriptions from Deuteronomy 33:26, "There is none like the God of Jeshurun," in the ancient Hebrew script still used by Samaritans today. Menorahs are inscribed on a basalt millstone and on the floor mosaics of Samaritan synagogues. It is often difficult to identify artifacts with menorahs as Samaritan rather than Jewish, based both upon scholarly predilection and because Jewish examples are far more numerous. Context is everything.

The first Samaritan mosaic uncovered—in 1949—was found at Salbit, today Shaalvim, in the southern coastal plain of modern Israel. This mosaic, dating to the fifth century, shows two menorahs flanking a stepped pyramid-like structure that scholars have identified—probably correctly—with Mount Gerizim. Another was discovered in the mixed city of Scythopolis, in Hebrew, Beit Shean, and Aramaic, Beisan, a city in the eastern Jezreel Valley near the Jordan River. A synagogue mosaic discovered there was identified as Jewish owing to its iconographic connections to the synagogue at Beit Alpha and the fact that at least part of both floors was made by named craftsmen who also worked at the nearby Jewish synagogue of Beit Alpha. A Samaritan inscription was found in one of the side rooms. Before the Torah ark was a beautiful mosaic depiction of an ark, flanked by two metal menorahs topped with glass lamps. You would think that this floor is Jewish, except that it is likely not. While the iconography is consistent with Jewish iconography, one small distinction supports this identification. Our Samaritan mosaic lacks the image of a palm frond bunch (*lulav*) and citron (*etrog*), so common to Jewish ritual and depictions, but not used in Samaritan ritual. Jews and Samaritans in this city of the Decapolis used the same imagery on their floors, with the Samaritans distinguishing their synagogue floor through use of Samaritan script and by not using the image of the *lulav*. These are relatively subtle differences. No doubt, other signs of Samaritan-ness could be seen by sixth-century visitors to this synagogue on the walls and in the furnishings of the synagogue that are lost to us. All we have to judge by is the floor pavement, which hints at these distinctions. Another fine Samaritan mosaic is from a site referred to as El-Hirbe, literally "the ruin." The menorah is carefully crafted in shades of white- and ivory-colored stone, depicting in detail the "bulbs and flowers" of the biblical lampstand, with seven oil lamps set atop the branches. Were this array discovered in a Jewish synagogue, it would not raise eyebrows.

The development of a rich Christian iconographic vocabulary from the fourth century onward occasionally included the menorah as well. Beyond the "Old Testament" sources that we have discussed, Christian interest in the menorah can be found as early as the Book of Revelation. There the narrator recalls that "on turning I saw seven golden lampstands" (Revelation 1:12) and later on in Revelation 1:20 are identified with the seven churches of Asia Minor. An association between church architecture and the Jerusalem Temple appears first in a letter written by Eusebius of Caesarea to one Paulinus of Tyre, circa 313 CE. Eusebius wrote in praise of the benefactor of a new church in Tyre, the bishop Paulinus, whom he called a "new and excellent Zerubbabel"—comparing the rebuilder of the church to the rebuilder of the Jerusalem Temple after the Babylonian captivity.[30] Temple imagery derived from scripture and from Josephus is rife in Eusebius's panegyric. While Eusebius does not describe a seven-branched lampstand within the church, he calls Paulinus a new Bezalel, who modeled

Samaritan synagogue mosaic, el-Hirbe, West Bank, fifth century CE, photograph by Steven Fine

the church "after heavenly types given in symbols." In Rome, a grouping of seven lampstands appears above the apse of the Church of Saints Cosmas and Damian, which dates to the reign of Pope Felix IV, 526–530 CE. What is strange is that the artist portrayed a full seven lamps, unaesthetically placing four on one side of the Lamb of God, three on the other. Usually six symmetrically arranged lamps would suffice, as they do on many church altars today, flanking a large cross. Here, however, the number seven was important enough to break symmetry. Could it be, as John Osborne has postulated, that the Church of Saints Cosmas and Damian was intentionally consecrated atop the ruins of the Temple of Peace—the church literally building on the ruins of the last known location of the seven-branched menorah? Osborne wonders whether there is an opaque reference to the Temple lamp in Felix's Latin dedicatory inscription, "God's residence radiates brilliantly in shining materials, the precious light of faith in it glows *even more* [*plus*]." "Even more," than what? Does "even more" light refer back to the lost menorah? Our author is justifiably cautious: "It is certainly tempting to read the verses as an allusion to the site having borne some prior importance in a Christian context. The former presence of the Temple treasure would provide an obvious explanation for such thinking."[31]

The Venerable Bede, an English monk of the eighth century (d. 735 CE), included the lampstand in his spiritual interpretation of the Tabernacle. This very extensive typological interpretation follows the order of verses and gives a real sense of what one very influential Christian thinker "saw" when he thought about the menorah. I cite some significant sections, to give a sense of how Bede read this text:

> "You shall also make a lampstand of beaten work of the purest gold" (Exodus 25:31).
>
> Like the table, the lampstand in the tabernacle also designates the Church universal of the present time. . . .
>
> "Its shaft, and the branches, the cups and the bowls, and the lilies proceeding from it" (Ibid.).
>
> The shaft of the lampstand ought to be understood as "the one who is the head of the Church, the Mediator between God and humankind, the man Christ Jesus" (Colossians 1:8, 1 Timothy 2:5). It is as though the Apostle were speaking of branches proceeding from a shaft when he says of [Christ's] body (which we are) that "from him the whole body, nourished and knit together by its joints and ligaments,

> grows in the increase of God" (Colossians 2:19). . . . Doubtless this is because Almighty God our Redeemer, who in himself does not make progress in anything, still has increase daily through his members. Therefore the branches proceeding from the shaft are the preachers established in the world. The branches are the children of the Church to whom the prophet says "Sing to the Lord a new song, his praise from the ends of the earth" (Isaiah 42:10); they willingly comply resounding with praise to the Lord and saying "He directed my steps and put a new song in my mouth, a hymn to our God" (Psalm 40:3).[32]

Bede's commentary goes on for pages. He compares the two groups of three branches to the trinity. The "three cups, bowls and lilies for every branch" for him "signifies the three divisions of time in which the elect lived devoted for God, both before and after the Lord's incarnation."[33] I cite this section, however, specifically because it reminds me of a midrash that similarly interpreted the body of the menorah—there as the Jewish people and their rabbis:

> And thusly was it shown to Moses, "And you shall make a menorah of pure gold" (Exodus 25:31).
>
> This is the congregation of Israel:
>
> "And you shall make the menorah of pure gold; of hammered work shall you make the menorah, its base and its shaft, its cups, its bulbs, and its flowers shall be of one piece with it" (Ibid.).
>
> What is "its base"? This is the patriarch.
>
> "and its shaft"? This is the head of the court.
>
> "[its] cup[s]"? These are the Sages.
>
> "its bulbs"? These are the students.
>
> "and its flowers"? These are the young children who study at school.
>
> [All of these] "shall be of one piece with it."
>
> [Hence], "Thou art all fair, my love" (Song of Songs 4:7).
>
> "I see, and behold, a lampstand all of gold, with a bowl on the top of it."[34]

In other words, when Christians "saw" the menorah, they too saw themselves in it. Where rabbis (and likely others) looked at the lampstand and saw themselves and their congregation, churchmen (and likely others) saw Christ and his people. Significantly, the lampstand is described as Christ.

Rabbis never made such a claim directly for the God of Israel, though for them, Torah, personified in the Sages, is light.

For Bede, the lampstand—like the other elements of the Tabernacle—was a metaphor for the truths of the church. Doctrine read into the very body of the lampstand. So, in his concluding section, our author comments on Exodus 25:40, "'Look, and make [these things] according to the pattern that was shown you on the mountain.' The mystery of the commandment is quite readily apparent from the things that have been set forth above. For surely the pattern of the lampstand that he was to make was shown to Moses on the mountain because it was on the height of most sacred contemplation that he openly learned the manifest sacraments of Christ and the Church."[35] The seven-branched lampstand was thus a distinctly Christian symbol, a symbol of Christ and his church. The fact that it had begun with biblical Israel is, of course, acknowledged by this author. That truth provides roots for the eternal truth of Christ.

In fact, the use of biblical imagery by late antique Jews was an irritant to many a churchman—the most verbal being Saint John Chrysostom (d. 407), who delivered a series of homilies before the Jewish fall holidays in 387 CE to a congregation that included Christians attracted to Judaism in Antioch on the Orontes on the Syrian coast (today southern Turkey). Chrysostom, whose writings have been widely influential, polemicizes against Jewish associations of the Torah shrine with the "Ark of the Covenant": "What sort of ark is it that the Jews now have, where we find no propitiatory, no tablets of the law, no Holy of Holies, no veil, no high priests, no incense, no holocaust, no sacrifice, none of the things that made the ark of old holy and august?"[36]

One can only imagine what John might have said about lighted menorahs within synagogues, of the sort found to the south of Antioch in the Galilee or to the northwest in Sardis. Images of the menorah as a Jewish symbol were common in Syria, as they were across the empire, by John's time. Truth said, Jews would likely have been aghast at Christian appropriation of biblical imagery as well—though the power differential between these communities from the fifth century onward would have rendered Jewish opinion less relevant—while Christian positions could actually become hazardous to Jews.

Actual seven-branched menorahs, in no way different from those portrayed by Jews and Samaritans, appear occasionally in Christian art. A menorah flanked by crosses is seen on a sixth-century tombstone of a monk at Avdat in the Negev Desert, for example, and menorahs appear together with Christian symbols occasionally. A group of glass flasks from sixth-century Jerusalem show images of the menorah. What is perhaps most fascinating about these jugs is that they were made in the same workshops where Christian pilgrim flasks were manufactured, though with "Jewish" rather than intrinsically Christian imagery. Many scholars suggest that these bottles were used by Jewish pilgrims to Byzantine Jerusalem to carry holy water or oil home, just as Christians did. The problem is that we have no real evidence for such a practice among Jews. I wonder, then, whether these bottles were actually intended for Christian pilgrims—who did carry holy water and oil home with them. For them, the menorah would be a Christian symbol, derived from the Bible and representing the light of Christ. Large seven-branched menorahs illuminated the new temple, the church, as early as the eighth century—albeit only in the West and only as evidenced from written sources, in Aniane (in southern France, around 779) and in Fulda (after 822). While the Aniane menorah is associated with Bezalel in Carolingian sources, the Fulda menorah is described as a gilded candelabrum set among a grouping that included other furnishings of the Tabernacle, including the Ark of the Covenant and the cherubim.[37] In the Byzantine realm, later images of the biblical menorah appear in medieval illuminated manuscripts of the first eight books of the Old Testament, called Octateuchs (the earliest dating to the eleventh century). These menorahs are quite similar to those on our bottles—not to mention Jewish and Samaritan depictions. Do these bottles represent an actual menorah in Jerusalem? I could well imagine the fabrication of a seven-branched lampstand and the placement of such a lamp in a Jerusalem church. As we will soon see, such lampstands stood in churches in the Latin west as early as the ninth century. Though we cannot know what kinds of lampstands Christians might have built, images of freestanding seven-branched menorahs appear in tenth- and eleventh-century Byzantine manuscripts of the Bible. These bear a clear resemblance to synagogue lamps and look like those on the Jerusalem glass flasks. Perhaps more interesting than any Jerusalem connection, these lamps sometimes show a broad lip or support just below the lowest set of branches not unlike the spirals below the branches of menorahs from Asia Minor. Like the supports of these Jewish menorahs, the Christian lampstands illustrated reference an attempt to stabilize the branches on the lampstand.

Umayyad bronze coin with a lampstand, after 696/697, Shlomo Moussaieff Collection, Ardon Bar Hama, photographer, courtesy of George Blumenthal

Muslim coin designers made use of the menorah on one occasion, early in the history of Islam. They followed Byzantine and Sasanian models, borrowing their basic iconography while adapting it to the developing aesthetic of Islam. A group of bronze coin issues bears the image of a seven- and then five-branched menorah, topped with a crosspiece like those that appear on many Jewish menorahs, but with the Arabic legend: "There is no god but Allah alone, and Muhammad is Allah's messenger," which appears uniquely on both faces of the coin. This short-lived currency coincided with the Islamization of Jerusalem and its folklore, with a particular interest in the Temple of David and Solomon. In fact, under the Umayyads, the city of Jerusalem was often referred to in Arabic as *Madinat*

Bayt al-Maqdis, "city of the Temple," *Bayt al-Maqdis* being an Arabic version of the Hebrew *Beit ha-Miqdash.* As the Temple has been rebuilt, then, for one brief moment, the coins of Jerusalem suggest that the menorah of the Temple has become a possession of Islam. This responds to Jewish and then Christian claims to own this object. The coin iconography parallels continued Jewish use of this image under the Islamic Empire. This is expressed in a postconquest synagogue in Jerusalem and in synagogue mosaics at Jericho. This experiment in visual supersession was unique.

Medieval Reflections: Churchmen and Rabbis on the Menorah

Medieval rabbis, churchmen, and artists continued to be fascinated with the menorah. Christian authors wrote commentaries of various sorts. Some of them were within the homiletical tradition of the Venerable Bede, while Byzantine authors interpreted the menorah, with the rest of the Tabernacle—as a metaphor for the cosmos. In the West, artisans created seven-branched lampstands to illuminate churches that sometimes are so similar to Jewish conceptions as to be striking. Nicholas of Lyra (d. 1349), a Franciscan scholar of considerable importance for medieval and later Christian thought on the menorah, made extensive use of the most important Jewish commentary of the age, that of Rabbi Shlomo son of Yitzḥak (known by the acronym Rashi, d. 1105). Numerous medieval illustrated manuscripts of Nicholas's work are extant. Each manuscript provides paired images of the menorah that follow both the positions of "Rabbi Isaac" (as Rashi is called in the manuscripts) and his own slightly different ordering of the knobs and calyxes. The images portrayed are all in agreement regarding the essentials of the menorah—and both fit well with the many and rather consistent images of the menorah that illustrated Hebrew manuscripts produced in Europe. The image of the Tabernacle menorah was very well established among both Jews and Christians during this period.

Rashi discussed the form of the menorah, exploring each and every detail of the biblical text in his attempt to visualize what was "shown to you on the mountain." His commentary provides a kind of baseline for Jewish commentaries in subsequent centuries. Rashi describes the shape of the menorah branches as *alkason,* a Greek loanword that appears already in the

Mishnah and means, roughly, "diagonal." He is almost certainly trying to explain and make specific the opaque language applied to the branches in classical rabbinic sources. *Baraitha de-Melekhet ha-Mishkan*, a third-century CE text, has it that "two branches go [*eilekh*] from it [from the central stalk]."[38] The Babylonian Talmud, Menaḥot 28b, adds more words, but is little more successful. Regarding each pair of branches, "one goes out [*eilekh*] from it [from the central stalk] and the other goes out [from the central stalk] and they continue and rise up [*nimshakhin ve-olin*] to the height of the menorah." The denotation of *alkason* itself is not transparent. The usual definition of *alkason,* simply "diagonal," is how some recent interpreters have understood Rashi. It can refer, however, to a line that ascends at an angle, and need not necessarily be straight. In fact, manuscript illustrations from medieval Ashkenaz generally assume arced and not straight diagonal branches. A manuscript of Rashi's commentary copied in France during the early thirteenth century—now in the Bodleian Libraries in Oxford—shows an image of the menorah, its branches rounded. Mayer Gruber believes that illustrations within this manuscript are copies of those prepared by Rashi himself. This roundness was obvious to this visually aware commentator. Medieval biblical commentators (Joseph ben Isaac Bekhor Shor of Orleans, a student of Rashi's grandsons [twelfth century], and Levi ben Gershon [d. 1344], better known as Gersonides), responding to Rashi, looked for still clearer language.[39] They each described that the branches looked like the "branches of a tree"—a metaphor for branches that are both paired and naturally curved. While a strict interpretation of "diagonal" as angular may be a reasonable—if somewhat mechanical—lexical explanation, the larger context of Rashi's manuscripts, Nicholas of Lyra's manuscripts, and almost all Jewish manuscript illustrations of menorahs from medieval Europe suggests that Rashi's use of this geometric term was an attempt to approximate the shape.[40] Again, we have run into the problem of denotation, Rashi's attempt to specify rabbinic language creating yet another problem.

Rashi's most interesting discussion of the menorah revolves around Exodus 25:33, "three cups made like almonds, each with bulb and flower." His discussion is an excellent example of how a later reader of scripture marshaled the technology of his own day to imagine the ancient lampstand—making it his own. More than that, it is an excellent locus to examine ways that Jewish and Christian thinking about a biblical artifact

Rashi's Commentary to Exodus 25:31–40, France, early thirteenth century, MS., Opp. Add. Fol. 69, fol. 40a, courtesy of the Bodleian Libraries, University of Oxford

intersected in high medieval northern Europe. Rashi began by quoting the ancient Aramaic translation of scripture ascribed to Onkelos that I discussed earlier, *Targum Onkelos,* a book frequently used as a commentary by medieval (and modern) readers. He notes that, according to Onkelos, "They were engraved, as is done to silver and gold objects." It is not hard to imagine the kinds of surface engraving of precious metals that this ancient text refers to. Engraved artifacts, both from the Roman and Sasanian Persian empires, are well known. In his commentary to Menaḥot 28b, Rashi describes the flowers of the menorah as being like those "drawn as on columns," likely comparing this element of the menorah to Corinthian capitals, with their floral patterning. This kind of "engraving" was particularly prevalent in Rashi's world, where the deep carving of classical Corinthian capitals was reduced to simple linear surface decoration—as in the capitals of the medieval synagogue at Worms. This notion of an engraved surface allows for the decoration of the gold with floral motifs. It fulfills the biblical command to make the bulbs and flowers of the menorah "of one piece with it" in a reasonably simple way. Rashi goes further than Onkelos, however. He writes that this kind of engraving "is called *nieller*" in the French of his day—a denotation that was presumably obvious to his medieval readers, but has not been clear to most readers since.

In 1942 Mordecai Narkiss, the most profound historian of Jewish art of the last century, identified Rashi's *nieller* with niello work—that is, a form of delicate and minute decoration of a polished metal surface through the use of incised lines that are filled with a black metallic amalgam. During the eleventh century this method was used, for example, on the capitals of the Benedictine abbey church of Cluny, which were covered with silver plates and decorated with niello in various patterns. This notion of menorahs with surface decoration in niello is expressed in our manuscript of Rashi's commentary at Oxford. The artist of this rather primitive drawing made a menorah with round branches—as we would expect—and included an example of *nieller,* which he placed on the central stem in a kind of twisted rope pattern. This approach to decorating the menorah was not Rashi's invention, however.

While Jews did not fabricate menorahs for use in synagogues during this period, seven-branched lampstands within church contexts were more common. These lampstands were assembled by German Jewish art historian Peter Bloch in a 1961 compendium and illustrated in the catalog of *Monumenta Judaica. 2000 Jahre Geschichte und Kultur der Juden am*

Rhein, a major exhibition on Jewish culture in the Rhineland held in Cologne in 1964—at a delicate point in the postwar German rapprochement with Jews and Judaism. The finest extant example is the lampstand of the Convent of the Holy Trinity in Essen, commissioned by Abbess Matilda—granddaughter of Emperor Otto the Great—circa 1000. This lampstand measures a full 3.30 meters tall. It falls well within the tradition of lampstands that appear in late antique and contemporaneous Byzantine contexts, and later in the commentary of Nicholas of Lyra. While Rashi and Jewish artists were working from literary and two-dimensional illustrations, Christians like Nicholas may well have had three-dimensional models in mind as well. What is unique for our purpose, however, is the workmanship of the bulbs of the menorah branches. Each of these is cast, with a floral pattern incised on its surface. In other words, the solution that Rashi suggests to show the floral characteristics of the bulbs and that he imagines as niello work had already been achieved in a slightly different medium by Christians in church menorahs shortly before his birth.

The square base of the Essen lampstand originally contained anthropomorphic images of the four winds, one on each corner of the base, and are identified as such in inscriptions. Bianca Kühnel suggests, drawing upon Old and New Testament traditions, that this base "places the candelabrum at the center of the universe and lends it eschatological significance," especially since the lampstand stood at the center of the church. Kühnel goes further with the Essen lampstand, suggesting that Christian interest in the menorah at this time continues a Carolingian conception of empire and the church, the Carolingians—like Justinian before them—drawing authority through iconographic transfer of Temple themes. Thus, for example, the octagonal form of the royal church at Aix-la-Chapelle references the Dome of the Rock, the memorial mosque constructed on the site of the Jerusalem Temple. Later church lampstands were far less tied to the biblical menorah, in most cases being designed as a seven-branched "tree of life" associated with the genealogical "tree of Jesse" that culminates in Jesus Christ.

There is one exception to the general Jewish and Christian pattern of menorah illustration during the Middle Ages that is significant to our study. A group of manuscript illustrations of the menorah in books authored by Rabbi Moses ben Maimon (1135–1204 CE), known in Latin as Maimonides and in Hebrew by the acronym Rambam, show menorahs with straight branches rather than the universally accepted arced branches. The best-

Lampstand of the Convent of the Holy Trinity, Essen, Germany, ca. 1000, photograph by Steven Fine

known exemplar is an illustration to Maimonides's commentary on the Mishnah (ca. 1166–1168), thought to be written by the Rambam himself.[41] The menorah in this manuscript, now preserved in the Bodleian Libraries in Oxford, shows a highly schematic and poorly drawn lampstand, and Maimonides himself wrote that its purpose is to provide a schematic drawing of the placement of cups, bulbs, and flowers on the branches and stalk of the menorah. He even writes that while the bulbs were egg-shaped, he is drawing them schematically "so as to make it easier to draw." His difficulty as a draftsmen is obvious. The parallel branches are not always parallel. A half-moon-shaped object labeled "flower" on the far right branch, for example, is turned to the right in order to squeeze it in between branches that are not parallel, but converging. The very labeling of the menorah elements reflects Maimonides's own insecurity that they may not otherwise be recognizable. Beyond all of this, the branches were clearly too small to include all of the intended bulbs, cups, flowers, and lamps, and he was forced to write over the text of his commentary itself. Had he planned better, there was plenty of room in the bottom margin to move the entire composition downward. It would thus be easy to ignore the straight branches of this drawing for our purposes as the work of a graphically challenged hand. Fascinatingly, Maimonides's son, Abraham (d. 1237)—himself a scholar of great repute—wrote quite explicitly: "The six branches extend from the central shaft of the menorah to its height in a straight line, as depicted by my father of blessed memory, and not rounded as depicted by others."[42] Later manuscript copyists corrected some of the deficiencies of Maimonides's drawing. It is not at all clear to me that straight branches were Maimonides's intention—curved branches would have been well beyond his skill level. Nonetheless, the interpretation by his son is of great interest and is itself a careful reading of the difficulties that, as we have seen, are inherent in the Torah's description of the menorah.

The interpretation offered by Abraham Maimuni of his father's drawing is intended to undercut images of the menorah that are preserved in the Cairo Geniza from roughly Maimonides's time. Virtually all images that preceded Maimonides have rounded branches, and the Maimonidean menorah was only preserved in a small group of manuscripts that are specifically associated with Maimonides. The Maimonidean position does not reflect the realities of previous illustrations, nor the ways that later commentators—Jewish and, for that matter, Christian, imagine the lampstand. Samaritans may provide the exception. While little of their visual culture from the medieval period is extant, two Samaritan images of the menorah—one on a curtain made in Damascus in 1509/1510 and a second on a bronze Torah case—have straight branches. It is not clear to me whether this is owing to poor technical skills, or perhaps, like the Maimonidean position, reflects a form of biblical literalism (or something in

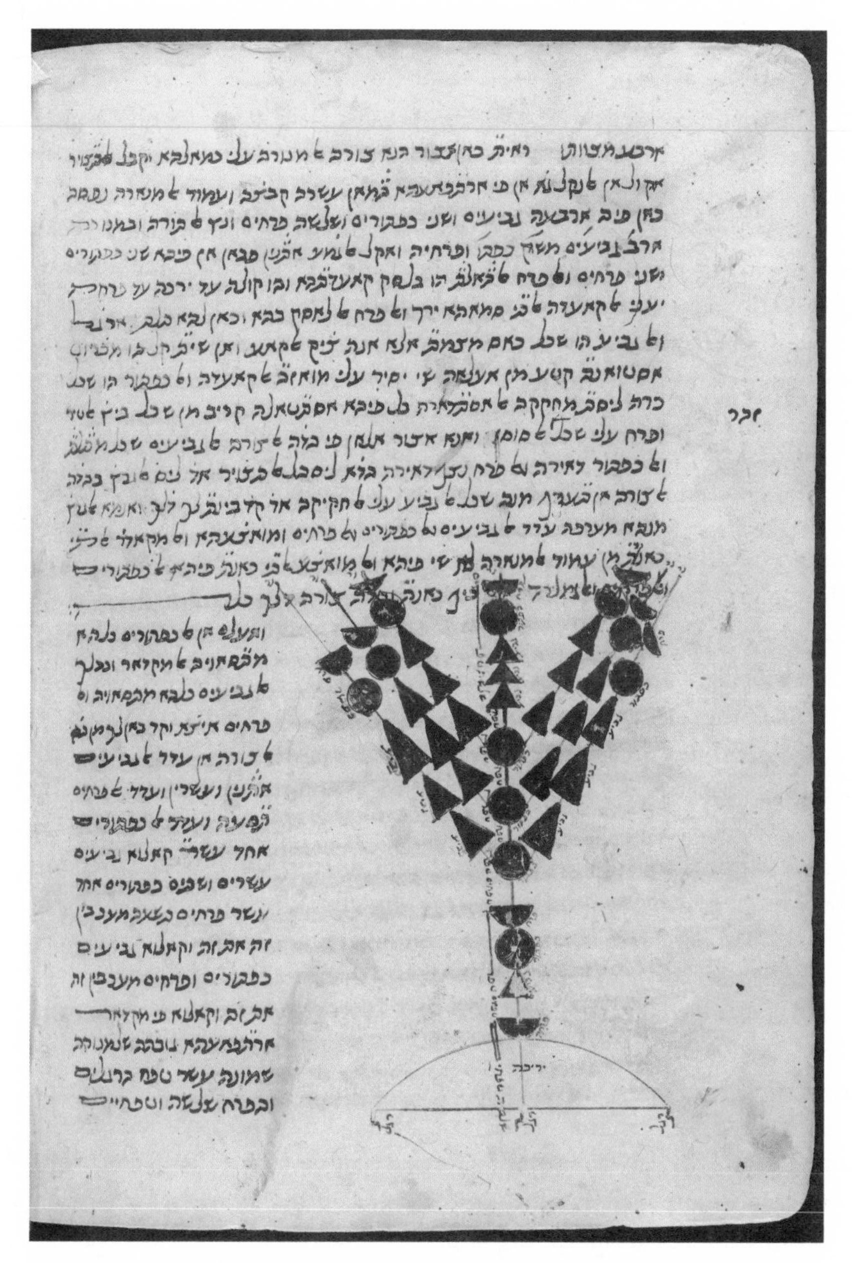

Moses Maimonides, Commentary on the Mishnah to Menaḥot 3:7, MS. Poc. 295, fol. 35b, courtesy of the Bodleian Libraries, University of Oxford

between). No Samaritan literary source clarifies this problem. Still, the parallel is worth keeping in mind.

Images of the straight-branched menorah appear in a range of Maimonidean manuscripts. These include a Cairo Genizah fragment from the thirteenth century or so (now at Westminster College, Cambridge); a Yemenite manuscript of a biblical commentary that makes use of the *Mishneh Torah,* dated to the fourteenth century (now in the Nahum collection in Holon); and a very fine manuscript of the *Mishneh Torah* that dates to Spain, circa 1460 (now at the National Library of Israel). This vision of the menorah was brought into the modern period in Yemenite manuscripts of Maimonides's writings. This significant tradition was first discussed and illustrated with a detail of the Oxford manuscript by Israeli Yemenite scholar Rabbi Yosef Qafiḥ (today generally pronounced Qapaḥ) in his supercommentary on Maimonides's Mishnah commentary (1965).[43] Qafiḥ writes that he knew then of six manuscripts that reproduce Maimonides's drawing, so this is not an insignificant tradition in Maimonides manuscript illustration. The Maimonides/Abraham Maimuni interpretation has touched on a fascinating issue in the interpretation of the menorah. While other elements of the lampstand were discussed in great detail by the Rabbis, the arc of the branches was a "given" of this image from the latter Second Temple period through Maimonides's time and into the present. Philo and Josephus explained it, giving the curved branches an astral dimension. This element was never discussed in rabbinic literature nor problematized by anyone before Maimonides/Abraham Maimuni. The arc was so basic and undisputed as to require no discussion in antiquity. Had it been disputed, I could imagine the ancient rabbis might have treated the rounded branches something akin to a *halakhah me-Moshe me-Sinai,* a tradition that is so ancient and so well established that it goes back to Moses. This is how the rabbis handled the black paint, square shape, and contents of tefillin, prayer boxes donned by traditional Jews during morning prayer. The form of tefillin precedes rabbinic discussion—as is evidenced in first-century tefillin discovered at the Dead Sea. Their form is intrinsic to the object. The same was true of the arc of the menorah branches. The Maimonides/Abraham Maimuni commentary recognizes this interpretive lapse and elides it by asserting a far more simple possibility, one certainly warranted by the biblical description of the menorah—that the branches, the *qanim,* were arranged as a series of parallel straight lines. This rather stark—and fascinating—option was virtually unknown before Qafiḥ's study, as it never influenced Jewish imagery beyond illustration of Maimonides-related manuscripts.

Early Modern Menorahs

With the advent of printing, images of the menorah became all the more standardized in European art—Jewish and Christian. Not surprisingly, a large number of menorah images occur in Rome, the earliest Christian exemplar being Raphael's *The Expulsion of Heliodorus from the Temple* (1511/1512), though there were others. It has reasonably been suggested that Raphael drew directly upon the first printed edition of Nicholas of Lyra's commentary in 1498 for inspiration. In general, church lampstands referenced the menorah through the use of a tall lampstand with seven lamps, without rendering the biblical menorah. A beautifully designed fifteenth-century lampstand in the Church of Santa Maria in Vulturella (today called the Santuario della Mentorella, in the township of Capranica Prenestina) east of Rome, is the exception. Perhaps the survival of this lampstand in a relatively obscure church on the top of an isolated mountain hints that lampstands that reference the arch menorah may have been more common. This lampstand, 1.6 meters tall, historically stood in the central nave of the church. The base, reminiscent of the arch menorah, is nonetheless quite colorful, having been made of white marble with inlaid purple porphyry and green serpentine stone. The central stalk and branches are formed to recall the bulb and calyxes of the biblical menorah. Writing in 1905, Attilio Rossi was anxious to trace the Christian pedigree of this lampstand in order to distance it from any semblance of Judaizing, as the arch menorah was so popular among Jews at this time. He carefully traces the history of Christian menorahs during the Middle Ages up to the Vulturella lampstand—going so far as to identify remains from the Jewish catacombs as Christian.

By the early modern period, Christians, and certainly Jews, were quite aware of the Arch of Titus, the arch serving as the entryway to the compound of the Frangipani family, and it was known throughout the Middle Ages as the *Arch of the Seven Branched Lamp.* The arch itself has a prominent place in Christian pageantry of the early modern period. It was central to the triumphal entrance of the Holy Roman Emperor, Charles V, on April 5, 1536, and sometimes was a station in processions celebrating the election of a new pope, which carried him from the papal compound at

St. John of the Lateran to the west of the Forum, to the Vatican, across to the Tiber to the northeast. There is ample evidence that Jews were among the celebrants, standing along the parade route with placards greeting the new pope. Amnon Linder has shown that the choice of verses on some of the extant placards reflects a kind of Jewish counternarrative to the general celebration. While verses chosen praise the pope in Latin and even in the original Hebrew, some of the verses are decidedly more critical when read through the lenses of rabbinic interpretation. In *The Religious Ceremonies and Customs of All the Peoples of the World* (1723–1743), Jean Frederic Bernard describes and Bernard Picart illustrated a practice of standing under an arch near the Colosseum, presumably the Arch of Titus, and presenting the pope with a Torah scroll—a practice that was discontinued in the sixteenth century. The last documented evidence of a Jew offering the pope a scroll dates to Pope Leo X in 1513. When responding to the Jewish gift, Leo ritually threw the scroll to the ground and proclaimed, *confirmamus sed non consentimus,* roughly, "I confirm this, but not your interpretation."[44]

Christian archaeologists, beginning with Antonio Bosio in 1602, had begun to discover Jewish tombs replete with images of the menorah—creating ever-greater cognizance of this Jewish symbol (which some—like Rossi—still continued to interpret as Christian into the twentieth century). Images of menorahs became more common in wall decoration of prominent churches in Rome during the seventeenth and eighteenth centuries, as in a painting of the Wilderness Tabernacle at Santa Maria Maggiore and plaster decoration in a side chapel of Santa Maria in Travesere. There the menorah is set in each corner of the rectangular hall, among other Tabernacle appurtenances. It was used on a medallion of Urban VII (1590) and the arch menorah sits atop the showbread table on a medallion of Benedict XIII (1724). In this way, the iconographic program claimed continuity with biblical Israel, likely cognizant of the use of this imagery by the superseded Israel of the flesh. Like the lampstand of Essen and other Christian exemplars since antiquity, the Vulturella lampstand served a distinctly Christian function. Nonetheless, Rossi relates that near his own time the lampstand had been moved to a side chapel. I wonder if this decision was a response to the very Jewish associations that he was trying to dispel. There it remains to this day.

The earliest Jewish menorah image in Rome of this period appears in the tympanum of a classicizing Torah shrine from the Sephardic synagogue, the Scola Catalana (1522/1523), and it appears often on Jewish ritual objects from this point on. Often the flames are fully ablaze—especially, most appropriately, on menorahs that decorated the back plates of Hanukkah lamps. The image of a menorah on the Torah shrine of the Scola Catalana has a tripod base, and others in Rome often have solid bases (reminiscent vaguely of the arch), not long after Raphael completed *Heliodorus.* In most cases the branches are more or less the same ratio as the image on the arch, though Jews seem to have generally avoided reproducing the base of the arch. Those few representations that reference the arch menorah base, moreover, present it most schematically and certainly with none of the animal figures—as on a monumental marble stele of unclear usage, 60 centimeters tall and dated 1574, now at St. John of the Lateran. The image seems to be influenced by catacomb menorahs and presents a stylized two-tiered base that certainly references the arch lampstand. The avoidance of the arch menorah base continued—and intensified—among Italian Jews well into the twentieth century, and presages explicit rabbinic objections to the arch menorah base that appear in writing later. In numerous examples, communal symbols referenced the branches of the arch menorah, while hiding the base behind another object. Gregorovius wrote somewhat romantically in 1853 of the connection between Jewishness and the lampstand in the lives of Roman Jews, which continued from the early modern period to his own:

> If we descend from the Arch of Titus toward the Tiber and wander through the ghetto, we notice the seven-branched candelabrum engraved here and there on the walls of the inhabited houses. It is the same design which we just now saw on the Arch, but here it is alive as the functioning symbol of the Jewish religion and to this day there dwell in these houses descendants of the Jews whom Titus once led in triumph. If we visit the synagogue of the Hebrews we see the same sculptures of the Ark of the Covenant, the golden table, the jubilee trumpet, decorating its walls. Beneath the figures of the Temple vessels which Titus once brought to Rome, the Jewish people, still persisting, still undestroyed, offers up its prayers to the ancient Jehovah of Jerusalem. Jehovah has proved more powerful than the Capitoline Jupiter.[45]

Jewish communities refrained from creating three-dimensional seven-branched menorahs from the close of antiquity until the modern period.

While such lamps are now well known from Palestine and the Roman diaspora during late antiquity, this form of synagogue lighting was not continued. This likely relates to the growing dominance of the Babylonian Talmud in Jewish jurisprudence, which by the eleventh century dominated Jewish law in Italy and northern Europe, as it had earlier established itself in the lands of Islam. This situation was occasioned by the rise of Babylonian religious leadership, the *Geonim* together with the Caliphate in Baghdad, and the decline of Palestinian rabbinic authority with the waning of the Byzantine empire. Three times the Babylonian Talmud Menaḥot 28b (and parallels) expressly forbids production of menorahs of seven branches, an assertion of the unique holiness of the lost Jerusalem Temple and its appurtenances:

> Our Rabbis taught: No one may make a building in the form of the Shrine,
> an exedra in place of the entrance hall,
> a courtyard in place of the court,
> a table in place of the [showbread] table,
> a menorah in place of the menorah,
> but one may make [menorah] with five, six or eight [branches].
> Nor [may it be made] of other metals.

Beginning in the early modern period, Jews once again began to furnish their synagogues with large menorahs, unknowingly restoring a late antique Palestinian practice. In deference to this Talmudic tradition, however, these menorahs were constructed as Hanukkah lamps, with eight branches and a ninth servitor lamp that was usually set off from the others—thus distinguishing the synagogue lamp further. They were often set to the left of the Torah ark, reminiscent of the placement of the Tabernacle menorah in relation to the Ark of the Covenant. These synagogue menorahs not only reference the menorah of the Hasmoneans, whose oil lasted eight days, but are a further fascinating step in the ideological formation of the synagogue as a holy place, a "small temple," "second (only) to My Temple."[46] It follows, however, on the very practical decision, recorded first in the twelfth century, to light Hanukkah lamps and thus to publicly proclaim the miracle of Hanukkah in synagogues. An illustration in the *Rothschild Miscellany,* an Ashkenazi manuscript from northern Italy

(Ferrara), ca. 1470, now at the Israel Museum, is the first visual representation of this practice. This manuscript shows a large golden synagogue lampstand with a broad base topped with a broad Corinthian capital. Eight candles are lit atop the menorah. This Hanukkah lamp is quite tall, being a head taller than the man who lights it using a candle set atop a pole. A fifteenth- or sixteenth-century branched Hanukkah lamp, now in the Padua synagogue, has a treelike form that is reminiscent of some of the church menorahs in Italy. By the eighteenth century, Jews in both Western and Eastern Europe were setting large brass menorahs reminiscent of the Temple menorah—complete with knobs and calyxes—next to synagogue Torah shrines. Such lamps, often portrayed with seven branches, appear in Jewish illustrated custom books as early as 1593 in the Venice *Book of Customs* (*Sefer Minhagim*).[47] These images are likely responding to print models used by the artists, as later versions are clearly corrected to represent eight branches.

Exquisitely crafted silver Hanukkah lamps were produced for the developing Jewish aristocracy beginning apparently in Frankfurt near the close of the seventeenth century. The base of the arch menorah is never reproduced, nor does it appear on images of the menorah in Jewish ceremonial contexts. Design is highly fluid based upon the standards of the age, even as most images of the branches are of the standard rounded form. Of the many forms of lamps, my favorite are the bronze synagogue lamps from Eastern Europe. These lampstands are often supported by lions—animals sanctioned by rabbis beginning during the early modern period for inclusion in synagogue decor. Some of these lampstands, whimsical in their openwork, are crowned with an eagle, symbol of Poland, or a two-headed eagle—symbol of czarist Russia and of the Habsburg Empire. In either case, Jews often interpreted the eagle as a symbol of divine protection. It may be associated with the "light of Torah" (of Proverbs 6:23 and elsewhere), "For the commandment is a lamp and Torah light." Lampstands with both double-headed and single-headed eagles survive, and could be purchased according to the needs of each community. Some are even threaded, for easy installation and removal.

We have only slight written evidence of how Jews viewed the arch menorah during this period. From what does exist, however, it is clear that some Jews looked at it with interest, and some with suspicion. Italian Jewish chronicler Gedaliah Ibn Yaḥya (d. 1587), a native of Imola, near Bologna,

Hanukkah menorah, Poland, eighteenth century, North Carolina Museum of Art, photograph by Steven Fine

seems to reflect both, turning the defeat inscribed in the arch on its head. In *Sefer Shalshelet ha-Kabbalah*, "The Chain of Tradition," Ibn Yaḥya described the arch and its reliefs with a certain pride, as he subverted notions of Christian dominance with a counterhistory of his own. "They made for him there [in Rome] a marvelous triumph[al parade to honor] these mighty acts, for it [the victory] was great in their eyes, for they know absolutely that Israel is a strong nation. They built in Rome a large monument of carved stone, called an arch, as an eternal commemoration of His might. They illustrated on this monument the image of the Temple vessels and the captive men. I saw it."[48] The Arch of Titus is transformed by Ibn Yaḥya as a monument to the strength of the Jewish people. Ibn Yaḥya was certainly influenced by a well-developed tradition of Jewish valor during the Jewish War, best known from a widely distributed tenth century Hebrew history named for Josephus, known as the *Chronicle of Josippon.* He also knew of the messianic pretender David Reuveni (d. 1535?) and his claims to command Jewish armies beyond the borders of Christendom in Arabia. Since Titus had to fight so strenuously to defeat the Jews (a war that did, in fact, take the empire eight years to win), Ibn Yaḥya reasons, he merited this triumphal arch. Thus, the "strong" Jewish captives are depicted in its bas reliefs, and the shame that Jews experienced in relation to the arch inverted. While this inversion might partly explain and be explained by the widespread use of menorahs in Jewish ceremonial art in Italy, especially Rome, it also highlights the complexities of this symbol as viewed by early modern Jews.

A very different view was voiced by the first "modern" author to discuss the arch and particularly its menorah, Moses Mendelssohn (d. 1786). Mendelssohn wrote at a moment when the Grand Tour to classical Rome was most fashionable among European elites and near-elites, and the procurement of souvenir reproductions of Roman relics was all the rage. The arch menorah was addressed within his commentary on Exodus 25. This uniquely modern commentary, the *Biur,* is included in *Sefer Netivot ha-Shalom.*[49] This volume also includes a modern German translation written in Hebrew script—all published in a format that could easily be mistaken for a traditional biblical commentary. It is not. This is a deeply transitional document, published for a community entering a painful process of transition to modernity. Mendelssohn saw himself—and many saw him—as a bridge in this process. It is no wonder that Mendelssohn would take special note of the arch menorah—his access and knowledge of Western culture was broad and deep, and the iconography of this artifact—part of a larger fascination with things classical—was pervasive.

Mendelssohn's discussion comes as the conclusion to a long and detailed commentary on every aspect of the menorah. Typical of this opus, he cites by name a wide range of rabbinic sources from late antiquity through the early modern period—displaying a deep and impressive command of this literature. Mendelssohn concludes his essay on the menorah with a very competent grammatical exegesis of Exodus 25:26, "Look and make as *I have shown you* on the mountain." Here he emphasizes the visual revelation inherent in this passage, his dissertation being nothing less than a defense of rabbinic literature—intended to buttress the commitment of Westernizing Jews to Judaism. Mendelssohn writes:

> And know that in the city of Rome, among the ruins that remain from palaces and castles there still remains to this day remains of a magnificent building of marble that they erected in honor of Titus and Vespasian called the *Arco di Tito* [*Triumph bogen dem Titus*]. Recognizable there are the bas reliefs [*temunot boltot*] of the Temple vessels that the enemy brought with him from the capture of Jerusalem—when he returned from having destroyed the house of our God—and among them the image of the menorah is easily recognizable to this very day. However, it appears from the books in which they copied there those images, they cannot be trusted at all [*ain lismokh alayhen klal*]. It is possible that the stone carver had no intention to copy them exactly—especially as the building was apparently not constructed until after the death of Titus. It is possible that he did not place the vessels themselves before his eyes when he carved them, and was not careful to make them appropriately. It is true that they took the vessels of the house of our God to Rome, and hid them there in their treasury—as our Sages, of blessed memory, remember in [Babylonian Talmud tractate] Meilah [17b], and there Rabbi Eliezer son of Rabbi Yose, who lived a few years after the destruction [of the Temple], the [priestly] frontispiece [*tsits*] and the curtain [*parokhet*] (Meilah, ad loc, Shabbat 63b, Yoma 47a, Sukkah 5b) and the end of the last chapter of the *Fathers According to Rabbi Nathan* [version A, ch. 41] says that "the grinding tool of the house of Avtimas and the table and the menorah and the curtain and the frontispiece are still stored [*munaḥim*] in Rome."[50]

It is hard to know what images Mendelssohn saw, since the standard book on the subject, Reelant's *De Spolis templi Hierosolymitani in arcu Titiano conspicuis* (Utrecht, 1716) contains excellent drawings, made on site by a competent artist. Still, images and even models of the arch, the menorah panel, and the destruction of Jerusalem were very common in his day, the most famous being Nicolas Poussin's *The Destruction and Sack of the Temple of Jerusalem* (1626). The Arch of Titus was a routine stop on the Grand Tour of Rome, and was regularly portrayed on a wide variety of tourist mementos of this trek—from table mosaics to painted fans, wall paintings, and even large-scale reproductions of the panels and cork models of the arch itself. This widespread knowledge of the arch seems to have been the source of Mendelsohn's discomfort. Writing in the *Biur,* a book that he imagined to be a classic in the making among Germanizing Jews, Mendelssohn was honest enough to admit that he himself had not seen the arch—and carrying on the biblical priority on "seeing," asserts that the artisan who carved the bas reliefs hadn't really "seen" the temple vessels. This is the source of the discrepancy, he argues, between Jewish traditional memory of the menorah and the arch portrayal. In other words—the Arch of Titus menorah was at best an intentional diversion from the original model and at worst a mistake, an act of gentile carelessness. He, by contrast, representing Judaism, presents himself as studious in his use of sources. Jewish memory of the arch, Mendelssohn claims to his Jewish readers, is superior to even that of the most exalted of all Roman sculptures. Mendelssohn's underlying concern was to maintain the dignity of Judaism—and Jewish communal memory—at a point where his acculturating readers might feel doubt.

Beyond the specific Jewish context, my sense is that the animals of the arch menorah base violate the very aniconism that, in Mendelssohn's vision as presented in his philosophical treatise *Jerusalem,* Judaism shared with Protestantism. Mendelssohn's approach to the arch menorah reflects his larger response to what we might call the colonial gaze on Judaism, and his larger attempt to provide his Hebrew audience with a counternarrative to the one normative among his German correspondents. It is the inverse of a discussion of the Ark of the Covenant that appears in *Jerusalem,* a book directed to a largely non-Jewish audience. There he argues for deep cultural knowledge as a prerequisite for cultural judgment: "In judging the religious ideas of a nation that is otherwise unknown," Mendelssohn writes, "one must . . . take care not to regard everything from one's own *parochial* point of view, lest one should call idolatry what, in reality, is perhaps only *script*."[51] Among Mendelssohn's examples of colonizing interpretation are the cherubim of the Ark of the Covenant. These biblical artifacts have a long tradition of interpretation among both Jews and Christians, since they so go against an anti-iconic strain in biblical interpretation that goes back as far as Josephus and was particularly prevalent in Protestant thought: "In plundering the Temple, the conquerors of Jerusalem found the cherubim on the Ark of the Covenant, and took them to be the idols of the Jews. They saw everything with the eyes of barbarians, and from their point of view. In accordance with their own customs, they took the image of the divine providence and prevailing grace for an image of the Deity, the Deity itself, and delighted in their discovery."[52]

Mendelssohn's comment on the ark might well have been said against the Roman sculptor of the arch menorah, which he believed to have been remade by Rome in its own (idolatrous) image, and which he clearly saw as a challenge to Judaism. Maintaining Jewish aniconism against the arch menorah base with its "illicit" images almost certainly stands behind his *Biur* tradition, especially when set against his general attitudes toward idolatry as exemplified in his strident interpretation in the *Biur* and in *Jerusalem*. The arch menorah thus stood as a bridge between Western culture and Jewish culture, a fulcrum at which to balance an increasingly complex Jewish-German identity. Its menorah was known to all as a "Jewish" artifact at the heart of Rome, a point where "Rome and Jerusalem," "Judaism and Hellenism," converge—or perhaps diverge. In a sense, it was an impediment to Mendelssohn's sense of a Jewish conservative process of integration into Prussian society—so he set out to undermine it. The "fact" that the vessels were taken to Rome is known, he argues, not merely from Roman sources, but from an abundance of rabbinic testimonials. As we will see later, the notion of Roman error become popular among traditionalist yet modernizing rabbis—particularly after the choice of the arch menorah as symbol of the State of Israel, as they struggled to maintain rabbinic hegemony over Jewish memory of the menorah. Perhaps just as significantly, Mendelssohn infers from these sources that the Temple vessels, including the menorah, were still in Rome during his day. We will return to this presence later.

Relationships to the Talmudic prohibition against seven-branched menorahs became strained during the nineteenth century. Reforming congregations explicitly referred to their synagogues as "Temples," and in Italy *templio* was used to refer to traditional synagogues as well. During the late nineteenth century, large seven-branched menorahs were a common sight in the cathedral-synagogues built by both liberal and "neo-Orthodox" communities, as brick-and-mortar expressions of emancipation. Free-standing menorahs flanking the synagogue ark became increasingly common, though there was much variety. In the Great Synagogue of Rome, completed in 1904, a short walk from the arch, the wall behind the Torah shrine was decorated with rows of lighted bronze menorahs, their branches reminiscent of the arch but, pointedly, not their bases. At the top at the roofline was a painting of a similar menorah. While the most ardently liberalizing synagogues sought to distance themselves from the traditional belief that the Temple would be rebuilt, on a liturgical level, Jerusalem temple imagery was intensified within the "temple," and large seven-branched menorahs were often prominent. This synagogue furnishing was so common that even "Orthodox" synagogues included free-standing branched menorahs—though they often procured menorahs with six branches and a decorative bronze finial in the center, eight lamps for Hanukkah, or the branches at a slight incline—all of this to both participate in the general trend of menorah usage within increasingly "templized" synagogues, and simultaneously to conform to rabbinic strictures against menorahs "like the menorah" of the Temple.

The connection between Jewish iconography and the arch menorah per se was so minimal before the fin de siècle, the end of the nineteenth century and the early twentieth century, concluding around World War I, that traditionalist Catholics in search of historical legitimization of their faith used this symbol for distinctly Catholic purposes. This new Catholic interest must be related to the renewal of the arch itself, begun in 1817 and completed under Pope Pius VII in 1821, as part of a process of reclaiming the imperial bearing of the Church. It was a battle against liberalization that Catholic rhetoric continued to frame as a victory over the Jews—who in Rome lost the rights gained during Napoleon's rule as the subjugation of ghetto life was re-imposed in 1815. Three particularly significant examples come to mind. The first is the mausoleum of the Montanaro family in the spectacular Staglieno Cemetery in Genoa, created by the well-known artist Giovanni Battista Villa in 1888 and reproduced in the tomb of Dorrego Ortiz Basualdo in the Recoleta Cemetery in Buenos Aires (1920). In

Giovanni Battista Villa, "Montanaro Family Monument," Staglieno Cemetery, Genoa, 1888, after *Camposanto di Genova* (Genoa: Fratelli Lichino, 1910)

both versions we see the arch menorah without animals on the base and lit by a virgin, loosely illustrating the parable of the ten virgins of Matthew 25:1–13, a text often ascribed with eschatological meaning. Above is a large cross with the pointed inscription "Salvation is only through the cross." In our own ecumenical age, the Genoa monument, carefully cropped to exclude the inscribed cross in photographs, is described as a sign of respect for Judaism.[53] Originally, however, this was anything but the case—it was a sign of Catholic retrenchment.

In a similar vein, the church's claim for spiritual control of the biblical lampstand is made in the Church of the Immaculate Heart of Mary, popularly known as the Brompton Oratory, in South Kensington, London (1884). This neo-Renaissance church, with clear Baroque elements, intentionally asserts the primacy of Rome through its architecture, and includes numerous facsimiles of Christian devotional art in the Eternal City. Among these are two large arch bronze menorahs, modeled rather precisely on the Arch of Titus, that flank the main altar. Designed by well-known British artist William Burges, these lampstands were presented to the church in 1879 by John Patrick Crichton-Stuart, the third Marquess of Bute—an Anglican convert to Catholicism. The two menorahs rest upon tall tapered marble bases, decorated in distinctly classicizing patterns. An early guide to the Oratory, published in 1897, opens a long discourse on church lighting with the arch lamps, explaining that "the use of lamps and lights in Divine service dates from earliest times, and is another instance of the Mosaic ritual finding its complete significance in the Christian church."[54]

Significantly, Charles Willis Wilshere (d. 1906), a major British landowner and an Anglican enthusiast of the "Oxford Movement"—a Catholic revival within the Church of England—purchased a group of Christian gold glasses from the Roman catacombs at about this time, and also one Jewish fragment with a menorah. These were displayed at the nearby South Kensington Museum, now the Victoria and Albert, for an extended period, at the same time that the Marquess of Bute's menorahs were installed. Perhaps coincidentally—though likely not—Arthur Conan Doyle's mystery "The Jew's Breastplate," first published in the *Strand Magazine* in February 1899, describes a fictitious national museum in London that not only owns the breastplate of the High Priest of the Temple, but a facsimile of the Arch of Titus menorah—so the menorah was very much present in London culture at the time. This interest in the Christian archaeology of Rome in England was very much a part of the project of the Oxford Movement. Renewed interest in the arch menorah was developed within a church in search of its own classical bearings—at just the moment when Jews were about to claim it forcefully as the symbol of their own modern identities.

From the construction of the Arch of Titus to the close of the nineteenth century, the menorah had a prominent place in Jewish iconography and thought, as it did for Samaritans, Christians, and, on occasion, Muslims. This potent symbol took numerous forms, yet was astonishingly consistent in form, even as the ways that it was fabricated and interpreted changed and served each of the many communities and places that sought out its light. As the twentieth century approached, however, this lampstand of biblical antiquity was ascribed with renewed significance among Jews. It became both a symbol for Jewish emancipation (literally "en*light*enment"), liberalizing Judaism, and Jewish nationalism—usually (but not always) Zionism—and sometimes all of these at the same time. It allowed Jews to be rooted in—and even embrace—a biblical symbol well known to Christians, and to assert continuity from antiquity to the present, as well as the ability to overcome persecution and that modern scourge, anti-Semitism. As we will see, the arch panel—and particularly the menorah—came to represent a Jewish countermemory, an alternative way of viewing and, even when taken as just a poetic expression, a powerful one. On a larger scale, the Arch of Titus, and particularly its menorah, became significant for Jews eager to ford the perceived gulf between themselves and the larger culture into which they desperately hoped to merge. It came to epitomize the bridge between the Western dichotomy between "Jew and Greek," between Hebraism and Hellenism, between Judaism and Classicism—and even between Judaism and Christianity. It gave Jews—especially those trained in the European school systems, with their strong emphasis on Greek and Latin—a stake in one of the most significant of all classical monuments—the Arch of Titus. It allowed them to see themselves and their transition as an authentic continuation over millennia. It was an ancient symbol put to a very modern use, bridging modern dichotomies that have little in common, in fact, with either ancient Judaism nor ancient Greek and Roman cultures.

3

Modernity, Zionism, and the Menorah

In 1929 Rabbi Edgar Magnin, the rabbi of Congregation B'nai B'rith, newly dubbed the "Wilshire Boulevard Temple," inaugurated a magnificent domed synagogue that was to serve as his podium as *the* rabbi of Los Angeles for the next fifty years. Magnin chafed under the religious experience to be had at Reform synagogues of his day, whose ritual he thought was staid and emotionless. He wanted to involve all of the senses in "his" temple, to provoke piety, Jewish pride, and respect for Judaism within the larger community. With this in mind, Magnin, "the rabbi to the stars," harnessed the intense visuality and theatricality of Hollywood in the creation of his "set" for Judaism—and for himself. To the left and right of the huge Torah ark he placed identical large bronze menorahs, their branches (though not their bases) modeled on the Arch of Titus menorah. This was a pretty standard feature of the large "cathedral" synagogues built during the decades preceding the Great Depression—and even of smaller Orthodox "shuls" through wall murals. It has become a standard of large synagogues ever since. As in antique synagogues, these lamps served as frames enclosing the Torah shrine podium of the synagogue. The Wilshire Boulevard Temple menorahs were lit with gas flames, and one of them was set before a mural showing the earth rising up and giving its bounty to the United States, representing the crescendo of Jewish history. The temple itself had been built in the center of the oil field that had brought wealth to Los Angeles. It must have been a deeply moving sight, a messianic statement of Israel renewed that was fitting of the Jewish Los Angeles of the era. Magnin commissioned a New York–trained muralist turned studio artist, Hugo Ballin, to paint a pageant of Jewish history ranging from Creation to Columbus in brilliant color on the walls of this octagonal shrine. Ballin created the most monumental Jewish paintings of his time.

In the "Warner Murals," donated by the studio magnates in memory of their parents, Magnin and Ballin began their story with Creation and concluded with the discovery of America. That said, Magnin, a Reform rabbi and graduate of Cincinnati's Hebrew Union College, was in fact well versed in modern Hebrew and the literature of the modern Hebrew renaissance. Early in his career he even lectured on modern Hebrew literature to popular audiences. Maxwell Dubin, the assistant rabbi, had interrupted his rabbinic studies at Hebrew Union College in Cincinnati to serve in the Jewish Legion during World War I. Dubin was with General Edmund Allenby when he took Jerusalem (1917) and must have been well aware of the art of Bezalel. Steeped in the film culture of Los Angeles, the Warner Murals are deeply imbued with the international Jewish culture of the age.

In one small corner of the paintings, Magnin and Ballin imagined the destruction of Jerusalem. Here they portrayed Josephus's emotional turmoil as he hid out at the fall of Jotapata, the battle for Jerusalem, and finally the carrying of the golden menorah out of the city. The menorah in the mural greatly resembles those lit in the Wilshire Boulevard Temple—clearly no accident. Its base is decorated with garlands and not the creatures that appear on the original in Rome. It looks like the bronze menorahs that were used by secularizing Jewish groups at the time: B'nai B'rith, a fraternal group much like the freemasons; Jewish (and nondenominational) Masonic groups, and the various Zionist groups. Jews across the Jewish community lit such menorahs. This fact would not have been lost on participants in temple religious ceremonies, many of whom were—like Magnin—Masons. In the mural the golden menorah is borne aloft as in the Arch of Titus, with a Roman soldier on horseback moving the beleaguered bearers forward. In the background is pictured the single tower, Phasaelis, that Josephus describes Titus leaving standing as a memorial to a great city destroyed. Five men bear the menorah, none with wreaths on their heads. The menorah-bearers are not the triumphal Romans of the Arch of Titus, but Jews, compelled to move forward—ultimately toward redemption in the New World.

This identification of the bearers as Jews is no accident. In fact, Magnin was insistent that in "his" temple, the Jews were the active agents in their

Above: Hugo Ballin, *The Destruction of Jerusalem,* Wilshire Boulevard Temple, Los Angeles, 1929, photograph by Steven Fine

Below: Seven-branched brass menorah, early twentieth century, collection of Leah and Steven Fine

destiny. This is a leitmotif of the entire sequence and reflects an instinct shared across the spectrum of Jewish modernizers, including Zionists. While the "ghetto Jews" of recent history were to be honored, the strong Jews of ancient history—the muscular Jews of the Bible through the destruction of Jerusalem—were to be celebrated. Ballin conformed to Magnin's instructions, which are preserved explicitly in preparatory notes for the artist: "SIEGE OF JERUSALEM UNDER TITUS_ HEBREWS CARRIED CAPTIVE_ THE MENORAH.[1] Arch of Titus, Jews but no Romans." Magnin's description of the panel soon after its dedication was clear: "The Jews march captive out of Jerusalem bearing a golden menorah or candlestick of the Temple." To achieve this identification, yet to maintain an iconographic link with the Arch of Titus, Ballin cleverly portrayed Jews carrying the menorah out of Jerusalem—and not into Rome. At Wilshire Boulevard Temple it was the Jews themselves, not the Romans, who shaped, and will shape, the Jewish future.

I begin this chapter with Wilshire Boulevard Temple, its rabbis, and artist, because they show how greatly Jewish attitudes toward the menorah had changed from just fifty or so years earlier and found expression even in then-remote Jewish Los Angeles. In fact, modern Jewish interest in the Arch of Titus, and especially the menorah, took off around 1880 or so, when a photographic reproduction of the menorah panel appeared in the Hebrew newspaper *HaZefira* on November 27, 1882.[2] Here, the editor, Haim Zelig Slonimsky, sought to restore the arch menorah to the Jewish communal agenda and, with considerable expertise, sought to set aside Mendelssohn's disdain for it. The author relates the history of the Temple vessels from the destruction of Jerusalem through Procopius before noting that, sadly, none have been discovered in the libraries and museums of Europe. He takes heart, however, in the existence of the arch panel and excitedly details to his audience the technological and scholarly innovations that were making this image widely available:

> Behold, in our days, when the art of photography has spread across the globe, and scholars of history have found in it an easy tool whereby to reproduce images of ancient architectural remains as a naturalistic image, trustworthy and exact—they have copied also the Arch of Titus in its form and likeness [*ke-demuto u-tselmo*] together with all of its interior images—and it is available to every scholar and person interested in these subjects. . . . And this image should be greatly

> valued by our people, for in it we see, as if in a vision, the horrible history of our destruction [*shever bat ameinu*] one thousand eight hundred years ago, when we lost the land of our fathers and were dispersed among the nations. Therefore, we decided to present [this image of the Arch relief] to our readership [*lifnei ha-qorim*] as it appears today in the hall of the arch in Rome—though as fits its great age, many of the more delicate parts have been lost.

Slonimsky then proceeds to argue against the specifics of Mendelssohn's objections to the form of the arch menorah based upon observation of the arch and alternate rabbinic—and even Karaite—sources. Slonimsky responds directly to Mendelssohn's objections by providing his readers with photographs. While the earliest photographs of the arch appeared as early as the 1860s—near the very origins of photography—the broad impact of this new art upon Jewish perceptions in Eastern Europe was still in its infancy. Beginning with Slonimsky's article, a veritable floodgate opened, as secularizing Jews adopted the arch menorah as their own, in a wide variety of visual and literary contexts.

The process of adopting the arch menorah proceeded at breakneck speed, as dramatic "Jewish" understandings of the menorah panel gained currency. While Jews who were exposed to classical art and literature were well aware that the menorah was borne by Romans, when less westernized Jews looked on the arch, they often "saw" their ancestors forced to carry their holiest and most beloved symbols into exile. It is astonishing how broadly Jewish authors in Eastern Europe—but beyond as well—identified the menorah bearers as Jews—even as Jewish heroes of the Jewish Revolt like the Zealots Simon, son of Giora, and John of Gischala. This identification was not one that needed to be argued, it was just considered to be so. Scholars who stepped out of the Jewish "republic of letters" and read the works of European classicists and archaeologists often found out that this identification was not the case (though even some Christians—particularly Anglophone theologians, were sure that it was). These intellectuals seem to have been something of an exception, especially among readers who could only read Jewish languages, or who never ventured beyond Jewish books.

Perhaps the most expansive presentation of this notion in any language was authored by Moses Gaster—the most significant scholar of Jewish and Samaritan folk literature of his age—in a magazine oriented toward westernizing Jewish families in Britain. A major early Zionist leader, particularly of the Cultural Zionist wing, as well as rabbi of London's prestigious Bevis-Marks Synagogue, Gaster wrote this story in preparation for the festival of Hanukkah. The piece describes Gaster's pilgrimage to Rome, a respite from an academic conference on Oriental Languages that he was attending in the month of October. Such visits to the arch are well documented from the late nineteenth century onward, and it seems that it was a standard stop on the Jewish pilgrimage route, together with Michelangelo's *Moses* at San Pietro in Vincoli. Jews ranging from Boris Schatz, founder of the Bezalel Academy of Art in Jerusalem, to noted rabbis, politicians, and simple Jews—Zionists, culturalists, Hassidim, and reformers—often made (and make) their way to the arch in a kind of ritual, reciting to themselves, in one way or another, "Titus you are gone, but we are still here, the people of Israel lives." During this period, I think, when the restored arch became more of a monument than a thoroughfare, the now well-known Jewish "tradition" of not walking under the arch took hold—a kind ritualized negation of the arch "so as not to give honor to Titus." I cite quite a lot of Gaster's amazing tale, told by a master of myth, because it says so much about the world of associations that connect to this tradition:

> Tradition will have it that the figures which are represented as carrying the sacred vessels in the triumphal procession of Titus, are not the conventional types due to the skill and inventive power of the artist who cut them in the stone, but that they are taken from life. They are the very leaders of the Captivity, who were chosen to carry the spoils for the delectation of the Roman rabble. And how life-like are these figures. Nothing of the abject fear of the man who knows the terrible fate that is awaiting him on the morrow. Cold disdain speaks from every feature—a proud hearing as it behoves the man who made Rome tremble with all her legions and all her power. At the same time the humble pride in his face for having been chosen to carry the precious vessels of the desolate Sanctuary, and the awe in his uplifted eye, the deep reverence which he feels for that very sacred burden. Picked men they were, whom Titus selected out of the seventeen thousand captives to bring with him to Rome and to follow in his triumph. Was it perhaps Simon ben Gioras himself whom this central figure represented, or one of those heroic Zealots and Has-

sidim who paid in their thousands with their life for their unbounded patriotism?

Whilst musing on this spectacle I suddenly saw that the figures on the Arch had lost their stony appearance; they were walking and carrying their burdens. The stillness which had reigned hitherto had given way to tremendous shouting. The ruins on the Palatine had disappeared. The palaces of the Caesars were standing there in all their glory. The street of which I had been the solitary occupant was thronged with a multitude that grew every minute. The road was lined with Roman soldiers, and a long procession was winding its way from the Palatine and from the Via Olympia to the very place where I had been standing. An eager crowd surged in the streets, whilst an immense multitude occupied every place where they might stand, for the triumphal procession was about to pass and a show to be exhibited, the like of which the people at that time had not seen. All the spoils of the East gathered by Vespasianus and Titus were to be carried along. Images of gods, of costly material, wonderful for size and workmanship, hangings of the rarest purples with Babylonian embroideries, pageants of three and four stories high covered with cloth of gold, the various episodes of war represented on them. On the top of every one of these pageants the commander of the city that had been taken, just as he was captured, many ships, and a vast multitude of other spoil. Vespasian and the stunted Titus, crowned with laurels and clothed with purple robes, came along, loudly acclaimed by the spectators.

A sudden hush fell upon this gathering when the last portion of this triumphal procession appeared. Clothed in garments, in order to cover the hardships which they had endured, there appeared the Jewish captives, among them Simon ben Gioras and Johanan of Giskala [*sic*], the former with a rope round his neck, and with them other Jewish captives carrying aloft the spoils from the Temple—the golden Candlestick, the golden Table, and the Law. These made the greatest figure of all. The shout died out on the lips of the Romans, an awe unspeakable seemed to have seized them when they beheld these remarkable spoils from Judea, so unlike those of any other city or nation. The tall, gaunt figures of the bearers heightened the impression, and in the stillness which suddenly ensued I heard a voice speaking to me, as from afar, a faint voice reaching my ear and saying, "Follow

> us." At the same time I felt lifted off my feet and pushed into the midst of the road. The crowd which surrounded me did not seem to notice me, and I followed in the triumphal procession, unheeded and unmolested. The way was not long. We had soon reached the temple of Jupiter Capitolinus, where they expected to hear the news of the human sacrifice which the Romans, according to ancient custom, were wont to bring on such occasions. The sacrifice selected on this occasion was this very Simon ben Gioras, the General of the Jews, spared by Titus for this purpose. The multitude shouted for joy when the tidings reached them, and the Emperors withdrew to the Palace, where the spoils were deposited
>
> I meanwhile followed the Jewish captives, and found myself suddenly in a small underground room, the only entrance to which consisted of an iron grating that served as door, for light and air.[3]

For Gaster, the living Jews of the arch literally step out of the stone and speak with him, the scholar who stood before their images and watched as the sun set. Gaster's imagination ran quite wild—imagining the deep carving of the bas-relief coming to life before his eyes. The experience that he had of the arch panels was not just a literary device—a Jewish Pygmalion coming to life and then returning to stone. This device, and this effect, was well known in his world—Europeans sometimes visiting museums late at night and exploring the "moving" images of great sculpture—the *Laocoön* being a well-trod example—by the light of torches. Under these lighting effects, Roman art did indeed seem to take on a life of its own. This fascination with shadow—one that we, used to the light of consistent incandescent (or even fluorescent) light, sometimes miss—was part and parcel of Gaster's world. The "lifelike" Arch of Titus, however, was of a different order. The arch is set along the Via Sacra in Rome in a rough east-west orientation, at something like a thirty-degree angle to the compass coordinates. What this means is that the light of the sun strobes the menorah panel with very intense light that in fact does seem to change—and make the reliefs seem to move—over the course of the day. This effect would be even stronger in October—the setting of Gaster's story—when the sun is somewhat further south—and less direct—than in the summer. In other words, Gaster's Pygmalion-like Jewish prisoners are part of the effect—intended or not—of light hitting the reliefs. The effect of the once-colored figures must have been all the more striking.

The triumphal parade concluded, Gaster's menorah-bearer, John of Gischala, offers a rather melodramatic soliloquy, where he reflects on his situation:

> Into captivity? Never. True, we are their captives, but only our bodies belong to them, not our Light, not our Law. Whilst walking in that procession it was borne upon me that we are the conquerors, and they the captives. I felt the ground shake under my feet, though I scarcely felt the weight of the Menorah; it seemed to have been supported by hands of angels. I saw the palaces sway to and fro, the temples shook and trembled, and their columns seemed as if a terrible storm was raging, and shaking them as the trees in the forest. The gods were falling from their pedestals, and the statues were hurled to the ground, at the sight of our Menorah. I felt that the fire which they had sought to extinguish was now being kindled in the heart of the whole Jewish nation, that the light once lit by my forefather, Judah, the Hashmonean [*sic*] in this very Menorah which I had upon my shoulders, had spread throughout the wide world, had kindled a great fire, which consumed all the greatness of this heathen and cruel Rome. The victor brought in his infatuation, to make a show of it in his triumph, the very instrument of his destruction and that of his empire, little dreaming that our triumph will outlast his and all his coadjutors. This Coliseum, where we will pay with our life for our faith in Him who is the God of our fathers and the God of our descendants for untold generations, who is a God of justice and mercy—this Coliseum will crumble to pieces, the proud palaces and temples will be leveled to the ground, a mere ruin will mark the ancient site; but the light of this, our Menorah, will never be extinguished.

This statement well represents Jewish responses to the arch menorah during this period. A similar sentiment is reflected in a poem that appeared in the *Menorah Journal,* which was published in Boston beginning in 1914. Publications called "The Menorah" were quite popular during the twentieth century, though the *Menorah Journal* was the preeminent one in English, continuing publication until 1962. The journal was the instrument of the "Intercollegiate Menorah Society," a group of mostly second-generation Americans who had "made it," despite quotas, to the best American universities and were looking to blend their Jewish identities with their American ones seamlessly. The menorah was their sign of "enlightenment" and participation, of wholeness and membership. It was their claim to be full members in the American "melting pot" without having to "melt" away. Representing a broad range of ideas and affiliated deeply with the cultural Zionism of Ahad Ha'am (Asher Ginsberg, d. 1927), with its notion of Palestine as a cultural and spiritual center, the "Menorah Men" (as they were called) set out to construct an American-Jewish, sometimes Zionist, sometimes religious, identity of their own. At the beginning of the movement, the "Menorah Men" came together for a banquet each year in Boston, which was widely reported in their beautifully produced journal. The program of the first Menorah banquet, in 1909, included the recitation of a Hebrew poem by the Harvard campus *maskil,* Hebrew intellectual, Harry Wolfsohn—later Harry Austryn Wolfson (d. 1974)—the great Harvard scholar of Jewish philosophy. At this point, Wolfsohn was an avid student from Ostrin (Astryna) near Vilna (in Lithuanian, Vilnius) in Lithuania and a recently ordained rabbi from the Orthodox Rabbi Yitzchak Elchanan Yeshiva in New York and a Jewish studies teacher. His original Hebrew text appears to be lost, though an English translation by his classmate, friend, and future educational innovator, Hugo M. Kallen, was widely distributed:

The Arch of Titus

Crumbling, age-worn, in Rome the eternal
Stands the arch of Titus' triumph,
With its carven Jewish captives
Stooped before the holy Menorah.

And each nightfall, when the turmoil
Of the Petrine clangor ceaseth,
Seven flames the arch illumine,
Mystic burnings, glowing strangely.

Then cast off their graven shackles
Judah's sons of beaten marble;
Living step they from the ruin
Living stride they to the Jordan.

They are healed in its waters,
Till the freshness of each dawning;

Then resume their ancient sorrow,
Perfect marble, whole and holy.

Dust of dust the wheeling seasons,
Grind that mighty archèd splendor,
Raze the Gaul and raze the Roman,
Grind away their fame and glory,

The shackled Jews alone withstand them,
Stooped before the holy Menorah.[4]

Wolfson, with Gaster, imagines "shackled" Jewish captives bearing the menorah into Rome. To the left of his poem, which opens the first issue of the *Menorah Journal,* is a reproduction of the arch bas-relief. The dark shadows and poor photographic reproduction of most images of the arch in Jewish publications of the time undoubtedly allowed Jewish readers to imagine that the Jews are "shackled." Where Gaster presents his living Judeans as the result of careful observation, for Wolfson this is clearly a literary trope. In fact, Wolfson—and likely Gaster as well—responds in this poem to nineteenth-century Anglophone poetry that imagines Jewish captives and almost always bemoans the fact that the Jews had not turned to Christianity. Wolfson responds directly to this notion, imagining Jews, Pygmalion-like, reviving themselves. He uses his poem, written in the recently "revived" Hebrew language, by a revivifying American Judaism, as proof. What would Wolfson have said had he known that "his" Judeans, "perfect marble, whole and holy," were originally fully polychromatic, even more "ready" to step out toward a new destiny, "stooped before the holy Menorah," than he could then imagine? Even before the discovery of polychromy at the Arch of Titus, Magnin and Ballin imagined just that—Jewish menorah-bearers in bright hues carrying the golden lampstand. Magnin was well aware of larger currents in Jewish thought of his time; his copies of many early Hebrew and English journals are preserved in collection of the Hebrew Union College in Los Angeles.

Wolfson's interest in the ancient Jewish fighters of the Arch of Titus was not just poetic. In 1911 he attended the Zionist Congress in Basel, before enlisting in the U.S. Army during World War I. Documents preserved in Wolfson's archive at Harvard suggest that when he received word of the foundation of the Zion Mule Corps and then the Jewish Legion, he—like many Eastern European diaspora Jews (including Maxwell Dubin)—

hoped to join the first wholly Jewish and Zionist fighting force since the Bar Kokhba War of 132–136. Wolfson went so far as to try and change his induction orders. The Jewish Legion was founded by the early Zionist leader and future founder of the Zionist Revisionist movement (the precursor of current prime minister Benjamin Netanyahu's Likud political party), Vladimir Jabotinsky, and the first Jewish officer of the czarist army, Josef Trumpeldor. Jabotinsky and Trumpeldor explicitly saw themselves as the new Maccabees and as the incarnation of Bar Kokhba's warriors. Trumpeldor wrote as much to Jabotinsky, describing the formation of the Zion Mule Corps, the precursor to the Legion, in March 1915—invoking the kinds of "shadows" that had inspired Gaster at the Arch of Titus fifteen years earlier: "How strong is the attachment of the Jewish nation to Zion. Fiery speeches were pronounced, eyes brightened with courage, and the shadows of the Maccabee and of Bar-Kochba seemed to arise from the darkness of ages."[5] The British commander of the Zion Mule Corps, John Henry Patterson, wrote in similar terms in his memoirs. He was rather fuzzy in his historical knowledge, fusing the Maccabees with later Jewish fighters:

> Now, such a thing as a Jewish unit had been unknown in the annals of the world for some two thousand years—since the days of the Maccabees, those heroic Sons of Israel who fought so valiantly, and for a time so successfully, to wrest Jerusalem from the grasp of the Roman legions.
>
> It was no light task to get uniforms, equipment, arms, ammunition, etc., for such a body of men at short notice, but in a very few days I had my men all under canvas, my horses and hundreds of mules pegged out in lines, and the men marching up and down, drilling to Hebrew words of command. Never since the days of Judas Maccabæus had such sights and sounds been seen and heard in a military camp; indeed, had that redoubtable General paid us a surprise visit, he might have imagined himself with his own legions, because here he would have found a great camp with the tents of the Children of Israel pitched round about; he would have heard the Hebrew tongue spoken on all sides, and seen a little host of the Sons of Judah drilling to the same words of command that he himself used to those gallant soldiers who so nobly fought against Rome under his banner; he would even have heard the plaintive soul-stirring music of the Maccabæan hymn chanted by the men as they marched through the camp.[6]

Or, as Patterson wrote of the legion itself, describing his own participation as commander after Allenby's capture of Jerusalem: "I have got a very great deal out of my service with this Jewish Battalion. I have had the satisfaction of proving that, in spite of all obstacles placed in its path, this new unit showed that it was worthy of the best traditions of the Maccabæans, those doughty Jewish soldiers who, on many a well-fought field, defeated the legions of Antiochus and freed Judæa from a foreign yoke."[7]

This willingness to apply this historical metaphor is directly related to the larger context of the British Army, particularly the rhetoric surrounding the British Egyptian Expeditionary Force that took Palestine under General Allenby, of which the Jewish Legion was a part. Crusader rhetoric and images of medieval knights were especially enlisted by this force, lending context for the Jewish use of historicized rhetoric. The Jewish Legion went to war bearing medals made in Jerusalem at the Bezalel School of Arts and modeled on the Judaea Capta coins. The imagery and inscriptions, however, revealed that a different process was occurring: *Yehuda Mistraḥreret* ("Judaea frees herself") is inscribed on each, the female Judaea in pursuit of the Roman soldier even as her shackles are still in place. The medal was given to each Palestinian recruit as they set out to war by the president of the Zionist Movement, Chaim Weizmann, himself.

Early Zionists well understood the significance of visual culture for the future of their still virtual nation. At the First Zionist Congress, in Basel in 1897, the movement chose the Jewish prayer shawl, superimposed with a six-pointed "star of David," as its official flag. The first institution founded, and first piece of urban property procured, by the Zionist movement was the Bezalel School of Arts in Jerusalem. Bezalel, named for the biblical artisan of the Tabernacle, was directed by the renowned artist Boris Schatz, who set about creating a rich Jewish visual vocabulary based upon historical Jewish imagery on Jewish coins, Judaica objects, manuscripts, and discoveries in archaeological excavations, as well as the flora and fauna of the Land of Israel. A museum founded to provide inspiration to artists became an integral part of Bezalel, a model drawn from such "national" institutions as the Victoria and Albert Museum in London and the Boston Museum of Fine Arts (today the Bezalel National Museum has grown and become the Israel Museum). The menorah of the arch was central to the Bezalel vocabulary, with rich imagery of the arch menorah relit by the Zionist movement emblazoned upon Hanukkah menorahs and on all manner of ephemera. An Arch of Titus menorah was set in the gable of

Ze'ev Raban, frontispiece to Boris Schatz, *Jerusalem Rebuilt* (Jerusalem: Bney Bezalel, 1924)

the "Bezalel Exhibition," the school's sales outlet near the Jaffa Gate in Jerusalem. A large wooden arch menorah was set on the turrets of the Bezalel building. Schatz imagined, writing in his novel *Jerusalem Rebuilt* (1924), that he received a vision in this spot from the biblical Bezalel—who took him on an aerial tour of Jewish Palestine one century hence, an "event" given form in a frontispiece designed by noted Bezalel artist Ze'ev Raban. Schatz's utopian fervor is palpable, causing him and his community of artists to associate deeply with the artisan of the biblical menorah, and with his artistic process—which is expressed in a series of images showing the biblical Bezalel, using the tools of a modern artisan, to fashion the biblical lampstand. Schatz was even wont to wander Jerusalem dressed in pseudo-biblicizing robes. Both he and the director of the Bezalel National Museum, Mordechai Narkiss, named their sons Bezalel—these children became noted artist Bezalel Schatz and the Hebrew University historian of Jewish art Bezalel Narkiss.

The complexity of Schatz's fervor should not be underestimated. Bezalel was a modernizing institution and, from a traditionalist Jewish standpoint, known to be antinomian. In *Jerusalem Rebuilt,* for example, Schatz imagined that his future Palestine would support pleasure gardens where the young could act on their carnal instincts (a reference to libertine trends in early kibbutzim?). Playing on Bezalel's often libertine reputation, novelist Shmuel Yosef Agnon later wrote in his novel *Tmol Shilshom* (*Only Yesterday,* 1945) of a Hanukkah ball, building upon this theme. Basing his presentation on newspaper accounts and likely oral history, Agnon's sense of the tension between traditional Jewish culture and secularizing Jewish nationalism describes precisely my point regarding the use of menorahs and other Jewish symbols within this very complex cultural environment:

> When Professor Boris Schatz made his Bezalel art school, Hanukkah came upon him, that holy holiday they started calling the holiday of the Maccabees. They went and made him a joyous party. They put up a statue of the high Priest Mattithiah, holding a sword in his hand to pierce the tyrant who was sacrificing a pig on the altar they had made in honor of Antiochus the Wicked. They spent all night in riot and gluttony. The next day, [Eliezer] Ben-Yehuda wrote affectionately about the party in his newspaper, just that he wasn't comfortable with that statue they had put up in the hall, for this Mattithiah was a zealot for his religion, for his religion and not for his land, for as long as the Greeks were spreading over our land and robbing and oppressing and murdering and killing and destroying cities and villages, Mattithiah and his sons sat in Modi'in, their city, and didn't lift a finger, but when the Greeks started offending the religion, as the prayer says, to force Thy people Israel to forget Thy Torah and transgress the commands

> of Thy will, he leaped like a lion, he and his sons the heroes, and so on and so forth, and they decided to honor the event with an eight day holiday. And now, says Ben-Yehuda in his article, and now I wonder, when they gathered last night to honor him, if they had breathed life into the statute, or if he himself were alive, if he wouldn't have stabbed every single one of us with the sword in his hand, and sacrificed all of us on the altar.[8]

This Pygmalion-Mattathias plays on a theme that we have seen associated with the living menorah-bearers of Gaster and Wolfson, and more significantly in this context, Schatz's Bezalel. Bezalel's focus on the menorah was a very modern decision—drawing on Roman iconography that seemed ancient, but outside of Rome and before photography, had been unknown to most Jews for millennia. It was the menorah as a sign of the Enlightenment, a kind of modernizing double entendre—quite consistent with the use of historical/archaeological imagery common in the civil iconography of Western countries. Just as the French had taken the Arch of Titus to Paris in the form of the Arc de Triomphe, Pius VII had rebuilt the arch to express the renewal of papal control of Rome in 1821, and the Americans had conveyed it to Brooklyn to celebrate the victory of the Union over the Confederacy (1889–1892), the Jews were now taking control of this central "Jewish" monument.

The modernity of Schatz and his Bezalel colleagues was underpinned by another set of commitments that are seldom recognized—the fact that many of these cultural Zionists were also active Freemasons. Masons shared with Jews a profound interest in the Temple of Jerusalem; it is Masonic lore that Freemasons were the builders of Solomon's Temple. During this period, Jews were initiated into the Freemasons and their Jewish counterpart, the Fraternal Order of B'nai B'rith, in large numbers across Europe, the British Empire, and the United States. Masonry was a powerful force within all of the nineteenth- and early twentieth-century Jewish secularizing communities, bringing together clergy and laity, Jews and Christians within its mysteries. Occasionally Jewish art objects mixed Jewish and Masonic imagery. We see this, for example, on an American Jewish devotional plaque, inscribed *Mizraḥ* (literally, "East"). This object was intended to be hung on the eastern, Jerusalem-aligned wall of the house. This plaque, created by one Moses H. Henry in Cincinnati in 1850, is replete with explicit Jewish, American, and Masonic imagery intertwined in its ornate program. It is now in the collection of the Skirball Museum in Los

Angeles. Similarly, the art of Ze'ev Raban makes wide use of Masonic imagery. Masonic lodges were a meeting place for secularizing Christians, Moslems, and Jews in Ottoman and early Mandatory Jerusalem. British Masonry was an impetus—and a funder—for Charles Warren's explorations under the Temple Mount in 1867. The local chapter that he helped to establish met in an ancient quarry dubbed "Hezekiah's Quarry" near Damascus Gate. When the rather grand Jerusalem YMCA was built in 1933, a small room beneath the building, reached by a narrow curling staircase, became the Masonic lodge. The altar of this lodge was built of twelve stones from the supposed site of Beit El (literally, "House of God"), one of the resting places of the Tabernacle before, according to biblical tradition, it was brought to Jerusalem. Many Zionist leaders were members. Linguist and educator David Yellin was a founder and leader of the Jerusalem Hebrew-speaking lodge (where he wrote the bylaws) and of the local B'nai B'rith Chapter, and he was one of the founders of Bezalel. So too the "first Jewish archaeologist," Nahum Slouschz, was both a Mason and a member of B'nai B'rith.

Images of Raban's Arch of Titus menorahs found their way into Judaica items, children's books, posters, and even the boxes that contain Hanukkah candles. Among the most famous is an illustration in a 1922 children's alphabet book, which, with Zweig more than a decade later, assumed that everyone thought of the menorah in terms of the small brass Arch of Titus lamps then widely available (which in fact, came in at least four sizes), and used it to illustrate the letter *mem,* for "menorah." It accompanies a poem by sometime artist turned children's author Levin Kipnis:

> My menorah gives light,
> My menorah is pure gold.
> Where was it lit?
> In our Temple
> Who lit it?
> Aaron, our priest.
>
> My menorah, O' menorah,
> Please give us again light.
> And who will light it?
> Our righteous messiah.
> When will he come?
> Quickly, in our days.[9]

Ze'ev Raban, illustration for the letter *mem,* in Ze'ev Raban and Levin Kipnis, *Alphabet* (Berlin: Verlag HaSefer, S. D. Saltzmann, 1923), Bezalel Collection of Yeshiva University Museum, gift of the Jesselson Family

As in most iconic menorahs depicted by Bezalel artists, the lamps of this artifact were lit, though Kipnis's rather traditionalist poem pushes that eventuality into messianic times. Most secular Zionists, however, were less than sanguine about this kind of delayed—and religiously determined—process, even as they employed religious imagery and metaphors to express their very modern ideology of "redemption."

The most important single artifact bearing the image of an arch menorah is the cap medallion worn by members of the Jewish Legion beginning in 1919, toward the end of the First World War. While the designer is unknown, this menorah resonates with those made popular by Raban. As with all Jewish Arch of Titus menorahs of the time, the base is maintained, though the decorative animals of the Roman original removed. Most importantly, the menorah is lit—like many of the early modern examples that we have seen in Rome. Here, however, the flame quietly yet explicitly asserts that the Zionist soldiers—the modern Maccabees, Zealots of the First Jewish Revolt, and fighters of Bar Kokhba rolled into one—were relighting the arch menorah. A British precursor to this choice was a medal of the Jewish Lads Brigade in England—a paramilitary group parallel to the Christian Lads Brigade. The founder of this association was Colonel Albert Edward Williamson Goldsmid (d. 1904), who was an avid early Zionist. A medal bearing both a bust of Goldsmid—according to its legend the "Maccabeans Memorial to Colonel Goldsmid MVO"—and on the other side a rather generic menorah was distributed to members "For long service in the Jewish Lads Brigade." Many veterans of the brigade joined the Jewish Legion.

Below the menorah pictured on the Jewish Legion hat pin is a Hebrew inscription written in a modernizing script, *kadimah,* but only for those who could read Hebrew. Latin is the only other "foreign" language used on British World War I badges, the status of Hebrew as a classical language was likely the reason that its use was allowed. *Kadimah* may be translated simply in the military sense of "forward," but in Zionist terms it takes on the added nuance "to the East"—meaning Palestine. It had been a popular term in Zionist circles from the earliest days of the movement, when, in 1882, Nathan Birnbaum founded the first Zionist students organization in Vienna and called it *Kadimah* (Freud was among the most prominent members). *Kadimah* was the title of Jabotinsky's 1903 call to Zionist action in the wake of the Kishinev pogrom, and soon of his Zionist publishing house. Its usage thus reflects both a general Zionist trope and Jabotinsky's personal branding. Another mason, though not a particularly active one, Jabotinsky had clamored and harangued British officials throughout the war to allow the official designation of the arch menorah as symbol of the Jewish Legion. A letter to a former British officer reflecting the urgency that Jabotinsky attached to this recognition is preserved in his archive, dated June 17, 1919. After recounting the service of the Jewish Legion in the war, Jabotinsky complains that

> You will perhaps remember my name if I recall that I was the initiator of the Jewish Regiment. You might also remember that in October 1917, as War Secretary, you promised that if the Jewish units distinguished themselves in the field they would be granted a special Jewish name and badge.

> Now we have three battalions in Palestine—the 38th, 39th and 40th Royal Fusiliers, over 4,000 men, of whom 3,000 are volunteers. Two of these battalions took part in the offensive of September last, were mentioned in dispatches, and the official report on the advice of the E[gyptian] E[xpeditionary] F[orce] speaks of their "good fighting qualities." We received 4 Military Crosses and 8 Military Medals. But we have not received yet either the name or the badge. The name agreed upon is "The Judaeans", the badge is the "Menorah" (the candlestick with 7 branches). I hear that in England some of our soldiers wear this badge; but here in Palestine we are still denied the honour, the hope of which was held out to us by your Lordship in an officially published statement.[10]

The British military was clearly reluctant to do what Jabotinsky urged; they were likely concerned at providing this level of official symbolic sanction for the Jewish national movement. The distribution of cap badges bearing the image of the arch menorah as official military regalia occurred only near the end of the war in 1919. The transformation of the arch menorah, so common in Zionist iconography, into a government-approved symbol of Jewish military force was of great significance worldwide as Jewish soldiers returned home—including people significant to our story—Jabotinsky, the budding "Jewish archaeologist" Eleazar L. Sukenik, David Ben-Gurion, and the future assistant rabbi of Wilshire Boulevard Temple, Maxwell Dubin. The rabbi of the legion, Leib Isaac Falk (later to serve as a rabbi in Australia, where he joined the Masons), removed his British insignia from his uniform and had himself photographed with the new Jewish symbols. In later years, images of Jabotinsky appeared that made a similar replacement, this new iconography having become increasingly significant within Revisionist circles. This insignia was worn by remnants of the Jewish Legion until 1921, when Jabotinsky's relationship with the British soured—resulting in the disbandment of the Jewish Legion. Out of such defeat, Jabotinsky grasped for future victory, the cap badge of the legion eventually becoming symbol for what would became the Revisionist youth movement, Betar. The name Betar is a double entendre. It is named for the capitol and place where messianic pretender Simon Bar Kokhba was defeated and an acronym for *Berit Yosef Trumpeldor,* the "Covenant of Joseph Trumpeldor." A particularly evocative image of Jabotinsky in his legion uniform—now with the menorah cap badge—appeared in the French magazine *Fantasio* on

November 1, 1929. Here Jabotinsky stands before the Western Wall à la E. M. Lilien's classic Zionist portrayals, arrayed satirically as something between the fin de siècle image of a medieval knight, Joan of Arc, and Marianne of Delacroix's *Liberty Leading the People.* Jabotinsky, however, holds a brass menorah in place of the knight's cross, and the menorah badge of the Jewish Legion adorns his cap. The rather sardonic legend below refers to Jabotinsky as "The Crusader of Israel." This satirical caricature clearly references both the legion and the lead taken by Jabotinsky and his followers in demanding expansion of Jewish rights at the Western Wall in August 1929—a symbolic focal point of the Arab-Jewish-British violence that erupted that summer.

Menorahs were an essential part of early Zionist iconography far beyond the obvious projection of symbols in public spaces. In 1921, for example, planner Josef Tishler formed the new Tel Aviv neighborhood of Neve Sha'anan in the form of a menorah. He created a series of semicircular streets according to then-advanced planning methods, with a central bisecting street, Levinsky Street, serving to connect the others. Each of the seven "branches" curved toward Jerusalem Street (today Sderot Har Tsion [Mt. Zion Boulevard]), where each ends at the top of the "menorah." In addition, each branch is named for a fin de siècle Zionist leader or institution, including the Jewish Legion. Only partially completed, the intended result was a planned community built loosely in the shape of a menorah. The biblical lampstand was thus implanted quietly on the urban landscape, a blending of Jewish tradition and modern city planning.

Another Jewish Legion veteran was Ephraim Hareuveni, a cultural Zionist and Jewish lover of plants in British Mandatory Palestine, who was, even by the standards of his peers, no professional botanist. Hareuveni is best known today for the relationship that he drew between the Tabernacle menorah and a rather diminutive sage plant, the *Salvia palaestina,* that grows in Israel. Not satisfied with the notion that Scripture employs botanical metaphor in a rather general way, Hareuveni yearned to identify the lampstand with a specific plant. He dubbed the *Salvia palaestina* the menorah plant, which he identified as such because of its parallel paired branches and also because it develops bulbs with calyxes on its branches in the springtime. Hareuveni planned a "garden of the menorah" on the Hebrew University's new campus on Mount Scopus in Jerusalem, overlooking the Temple Mount—thereby growing the Zionist menorah within sight of the lost Temple. He clearly hoped that there his menorah plant would grow, with the menorah, into a national symbol. The romantic

Hat insignia of the Jewish Legion, 1919, collection of Leah and Steven Fine; Rabbi Leib Isaac Falk, chaplain of the Jewish Legion, with his hat insignia, in J. H. Patterson, *With the Judæans in the Palestine Campaign* (London: Hutchinson and Co. Paternoster Row, 1922)

Adrien Barrère, "Wladimir Jabotinski: Le Croisé d' Israël" (The Crusader of Israel), *Fantasio* 25, November 1, 1929, 174, courtesy of the Jabotinsky Institute in Israel

idea that the menorah "grows" in the land has in fact become quite popular in Israel and is featured in school curricula, museum exhibitions, and even on public sculpture. It gave voice to a yearning for early Zionist science to reveal the deep rootedness of the Jewish people in the land of Israel—which is of course the case—even without this overgrown botanical folk metaphor. Scholarship since has not followed Hareuveni's lead, though his menorah plant has struck deep roots in Israeli culture through the work of Neot Kedumim: The Gardens of Israel, a botanical garden founded by his son on the road between Tel Aviv and Jerusalem, which features a "Hill of the Menorah."

Archaeology was central to the Zionist modern/national project, and the menorah quickly became a symbol for this old-new sense of historical rooting. The remains of synagogues and Jewish tombs began to be discovered in Palestine during the 1860s by British, German, and French explorers, and artifacts with Jewish symbols—known from Rome since the early modern period—began to be discovered in the Mediterranean lands by the end of the century. By the early twentieth century, modern Jewish scholars in Europe, America, and increasingly in Palestine become cognizant of this material, and particularly of the many menorahs that were being discovered—almost on a yearly basis. In Philadelphia, for example, the synagogue of the Jewish Hospital (1901) was loosely modeled on late antique synagogue ruins in the Galilee, with a menorah from the synagogue at Nabratein reproduced above its entrance. Two large menorahs typical for the period, with branches reminiscent of the arch menorah, flanked the Torah ark there. On a visit to Rome in 1922, the president of the Zionist movement, Chaim Weizmann, wrote that the local Jews were so excited by his presence that they wanted to march him under the arch from the back to the front, from west to east, in effect proclaiming liberation. Weizmann claimed that he had to dissuade them from this premature act, though they did present him with a miniature brass Arch of Titus menorah as a gift. The menorah was significant enough to Weizmann that it is preserved, together with a letter of dedication in Italian, in his archives in Rehovot. The dedication gives a real sense of how this group of Jews—and many others—viewed the arch and the potential for Zionist success: "From the Arch of Titus, symbol of the light of faith, the Associazione Popolari Ebraica presents this to Chaim Weizmann, Leader of the Zionist Organization, promoter-cultivator-guide of the millennial hope of Israel."[11] Like so many of his generation, Weizmann was enamored with the arch. His

Nahum Slouschz (center) and his team with the Hammath Tiberias menorah, 1921, in *Menorah Journal* 8, no. 6 (1922)

mansion in Rehovot, designed by architect Erich Mendelsohn (1936), is decorated with no less than three early modern prints of the Arch of Titus, including an etching by Giovanni Battista Piranesi, *Veduta del Arco di Tito* (View of the Arch of Titus), ca. 1760. Jewish interest in the Arch of Titus was, of course, part of this general cultural concern with classical roots derived from classical art, a part of this neoclassicizing visual culture.

"Jewish archaeology," as it was called, became an obsession of cultural Zionists. Happily, the first Zionist archaeologist to set out on an expedition, Nahum Slouschz, was extremely fortunate when he joined a Zionist labor group building a road south of Tiberias on the Sea of Galilee. Workers had found the post of a marble synagogue screen literally sticking out of the soil, inscribed with a menorah. Slouschz himself discovered a large limestone menorah buried under the podium, the *bema,* with which he posed most proudly for photographs and which was featured in an early Zionist documentary. This menorah quickly became a new Zionist icon, appearing on the covers of books and in a wide range of contexts—including decorating Hanukkah lamps. Similarly, Sukenik, the Jewish Legionnaire, set out to create the field of Jewish archaeology—the menorah serving as symbol par excellence for the entire discipline. Whether through literary reflections, military insignia, botany, city planning, or the new science of archaeology, the menorah was literally everywhere in the Jewish culture of the first third of the twentieth century, and particularly within Zionist contexts. The community that created this iconography was relatively small, often revolving around the Bezalel School and the Jewish Legion. Still, its members, from Schatz to Raban, Kipnis to Jabotinsky (to refer only to some who are mentioned in this chapter), formed the cultural soil within which Zionist, and later Israeli, culture grew.

The Arch of Titus Menorah in America

As the menorah had became a popular symbol in Palestine, it became so also in Jewish communities of the Western diaspora. Brass seven-branched menorahs modeled on the arch became so common in Jewish homes that novelist Stefan Zweig, writing in Vienna, imagined that such lamps had been staples of Jewish life even in antiquity: "wherever you find a Jew who continues to cherish his faith in the Holy One of Israel, no matter under which of the winds of heaven his house stands, you will find in that house a model of the Menorah lifting its seven branches in prayer."[12] This was simply not the case, except in secularizing Jewish homes of the sort with which Zweig might have been familiar. Freestanding menorahs—both seven-branched ones and eight-branched Hanukkah lamps—came to function in secularizing Jewish homes much as large crosses did for Christian families. It is not clear to me when and whether seven-branched lamps were lit in home ceremonies. The lighting of such lamps was common to B'nai B'rith ceremonies, and Jewish Masonic lodges were sometimes decorated with Arch of Titus menorahs. The Menora Masonic Temple in Boro Park Brooklyn, dedicated on June 15, 1927, is an excellent example of this phe-

Menora Masonic Temple, Brooklyn, New York, 1927, photograph by Steven Fine

nomenon. The ashlars that make up the facade of this building are modeled upon the masonry of the retaining walls of Herod's Temple in Jerusalem, most prominently the Western Wall. Reliefs of the arch menorah appear against a classicizing blue background within a medallion, enclosed by a wreath, above each of the major portals of this masonic temple. The large menorahs set to either side of the ark in modernizing synagogues, themselves classicizing and often drawing on the arch menorah, became ubiquitous at this time—the gas lamps of Wilshire Boulevard Temple being one of the more interesting and dramatic examples. The complex set of loyalties within the Western Jewish community—to modernity, to emancipation, to nationalism, and, of course, to many, to Jewish nationalism (if not to traditional piety) was the ground in which the menorah as a symbol of Zionism flourished. It spread among Jews of all sorts, in Palestine and beyond, including the non-Zionist Rabbi Magnin (himself a leader in the Scottish Rite of Freemasonry).

Two New York examples are particularly prescient. In 1930 Adolph Ochs, publisher of the *New York Times*, a prominent leader of New York's

German-Jewish elite, and the son-in-law of the founder of American Reform Judaism, Isaac Mayer Wise, made what was seen at the time as a momentous donation to the new Episcopal Cathedral of New York, Saint John the Divine. Ochs gave the church two large brass menorahs for the high altar, each of them modeled on the arch menorah. He was very particular in demanding that the lampstands express recognizably Jewish content. He even sent craftsmen to Rome to measure and draw the actual arch menorah in preparation for this project. There was much fanfare attached to the gift. Being a major voice of classical Reform Judaism, Ochs and his fellow Jewish travelers saw the gift as evidence of Jewish acceptance into New York high culture. The Episcopalian leadership was somewhat more ambiguous in their enthusiasm, some preferring that Ochs had given a less Jewish-looking lampstand. For our purposes, the fact that this sort of lamp was so unambiguously identified as "Jewish" and a "Jewish gift" is fascinating. This imagery had spread so widely over the preceding decades as to be associated distinctly with Jews and Judaism.

Another Arch of Titus menorah soon appeared just a few blocks away. In 1934 celebrated Philadelphia ironsmith Samuel Yellin, a Polish Jew who created the most significant iron gates for America's premier universities and other public institutions, created a large gate for the new Jewish Theological Seminary building at 3080 Broadway. The gate was "A gift of Mrs. Frieda and Mr. Felix M. Warburg in memory of her parents, Jacob H. and Therese Schiff," major German-Jewish benefactors of JTS, and its imagery included a Torah crown at its apex, fruits of the Holy Land, and a large Arch of Titus menorah flanked by rampant lions at its center. Visitors to "the Seminary" literally walked under the arch menorah, the opposite of the then generally accepted Jewish predilection not to walk under the Arch of Titus itself. Cyrus Adler, then president of the seminary, wrote: "And then there is the seven branched candlestick, the menorah, the candlestick of the Temple, the candlestick which was once carried into captivity by Rome and is emblazoned on the Arch of Titus at Rome, but which in spite of this has survived and gives forth its light in many places of worship and in hundreds of thousands of households each year as we recall the courage of the Maccabees."[13] Perhaps most important in Adler's comment is his indication of the growing ubiquity of the arch menorah and its symbolic association with Jewish life—as if what was in fact a recent phenomenon was timeless.

Menorah donated by Adolph Ochs to the Cathedral of Saint John the Divine, New York, 1930, photograph by Steven Fine

Toward Independence

The presence of the menorah grew in the coming decades, appearing at the peaks of water towers in Jewish towns and villages across Mandatory Palestine and early Israel. In general, though, interest in the arch menorah was most intense among Jews whose sense of Zionism formed during the first decades of the twentieth century. These Jews looked to historical themes developing in their public visual culture, forming their present in apparent dialogue with historical/religious themes. This virtual community tended toward the historically informed nationalism current in Eastern Europe and Italy, where historical motifs were given contemporary resonance among both the religiously neotraditional and the politically rightist (again, often the same people). It is no surprise, then, that Jabotinsky and his followers—for whom the arch menorah was an essential icon, were in contact with rightist movements across Europe; or that the Roman fasces was an important symbol for the similarly inclined Italian leader Benito Mussolini. Zionist socialists, like their European parallels, looked to more internationalist and future-looking imagery for inspiration, and did not tend toward the menorah. This dichotomy is not to be overstated, as there was considerable iconographic and cultural unanimity between Revisionist and Socialist Zionists.

An excellent example of this shared identity is a poster created by Tel Aviv artist Nahum Gutman in 1938 for a Zionist Hanukkah fund-raising drive that shows Jewish menorah-bearers for the first time in Palestine. Gutman, son of prominent Hebrew author S. Ben Zion, was a graduate of Bezalel with close connections to both Bezalel artists and Chaim Nahman Bialik, and was a leader of the second wave of Zionist art, this time rooted in Tel Aviv and in European modernism. Connecting further to our theme, while an art student in Rome, Gutman accompanied cultural Zionist and later Revisionist ideologue and intellectual Joseph Klausner when he toured the Eternal City in 1928. Klausner wrote on two occasions about the Jewish menorah-bearers—one of them in his memoirs recalling his visit to Rome. Gutman, a scion of fin de siècle cultural Zionism, was certainly aware of this cultural theme, which before this poster seems not to have been given visual expression. The poster, issued by the *Keren ha-Yesod* (literally, "The Foundation Fund," and in the United States, the Jewish National Fund) shows a cross-section of young Palestinian Jews carrying a lighted menorah, each of the flames labeled to represent a Zionist virtue. This poster builds on themes that were found already at the Wilshire Boulevard Temple, but which had not appeared yet in Jewish iconography in Palestine and Europe. In Los Angeles, however, the bearers are sad Jews, illustrating *Judaea Capta,* while in Gutman's poster the Jews exemplify what was later referred to as *Israel Liberata,* a Jewish people freeing itself from the stone—and bondage—of the arch. The menorah-bearer at the center wears a *kippah,* a cap, on his head and carries a large book under his arm—clearly a "religious" student; the bearer who stands before him carries a trowel—a farmer; and to the rear of the procession is a young Jewish man with a rifle. The imagery emerges from the background, as a bas-relief from stone, subtlety referencing the Arch of Titus panel. The group carries the menorah from right to left, the opposite of the arch panel, quietly carrying the menorah "home." The iconography of this poster is of one piece with the use of youths in government-sponsored social realist art that was then current in Italy, the Soviet Union, and Germany—countries that many in Jewish Palestine had so recently left. Here, strong Communist and Fascist youth bearing national symbols—the hammer, the sickle, the fasces, and the swastika—not to mention the British Crusader so prevalent in World War I memorials in Palestine—are replaced with a burden drawn from Jewish historical memory and carried by strong "Hebrew" youth of every ideological bent. I am reminded of the image of the arch menorah borne by the "precursors" of Mussolini's soldiers, helmeted like modern Italian military and not wreathed, that are portrayed in Publico Morbiducci's bas-relief *History of Rome through Its Public Works* (1939) in the new Fascist showplace at EUR (Esposizione Universale Roma), a new section of Rome built to the west of the historic center.

The accompanying Hebrew text of Gutman's poster intentionally references the Hanukkah liturgy and Mishnah Shabbat, chapter 3, which asks what types of oil and lamps and wicks may be used for Sabbath eve lighting. This text is recited in Ashkenazi synagogues each Sabbath eve, and was thus broadly known both to the religiously observant and to the secularizing majority, many of whom had been raised with synagogue observance. The upper text reads "These lamps we light," citing a Hanukkah liturgy still recited across the culture. Below the menorah image is a rhetorical question and its answer: "With what shall we light it?," citing Mishnah Shabbat 3:1. The answer, however, is a very contemporary one: "Through our donations to the *Keren ha-Yesod,* the national tax for the building of the Land."

Nahum Gutman, Hanukkah poster, 1936, Collection of Yeshiva University Museum, gift of the Jesselson Family

Donation and participation in the Zionist project is thus garbed in religious texts, and the notion of metaphorically reclaiming the arch menorah is given national sinews and Jewish historical depth through text and artifact.

During and after World War II, Jewish interest in the arch increased greatly—a kind of inverse of the broad attention given to such monuments by Mussolini, who saw himself as a new Augustus, and by Hitler, who dreamt of rebuilding Berlin—renamed Germania—on a scale even greater than Rome. On May 6, 1944, just weeks before the Allies took Rome, the daily Hebrew newspaper of the Jewish Battalion of the British army, *la-Ḥayyal,* explained this ideology to the invading Jewish troops, while seeking to displace notions of continuity so assiduously purveyed by the Fascists:

> Historians find that there is no ethnic connection between ancient Rome and modern Italy, between Nero and Mussolini. Yet many Jews continue to see contemporary Rome as the symbol of the same kingdom that killed our freedom and destroyed our Temple. The Arch of Titus stands there still today. If for the whole world its value is only art historical, for Fascist Italy it served as a source of inspiration for imperialistic and aggressive education. This modern Rome that sought to renew the war of ancient Rome against Jerusalem, to continue the thread that was first spun in the days of Pompeii and Titus, now is nothing before the Allies, and in these armies are many, many Jews. History gets its revenge.[14]

This sophisticated text calls on the authority of modern historians to discount the pervasive myth of continuity, which at this point in the war could complicate relations with the defeated Italians. Soldiers with considerable historical training were members of the Jewish Battalion, first among them the chaplain, Rabbi Ephraim E. Urbach, later a major scholar of Talmud and related literatures at the Hebrew University of Jerusalem. Many members of the Jewish Brigade of Palestinian Jews within the British Army eventually visited Rome, sang songs and wrote poetry that claimed victory over Titus/Mussolini/Hitler and his arch—collapsing the distance between recent experience and the ancient oppressor in ways that expressed both traditional Jewish attitudes toward Titus and their very modern response to Fascist ideology and display. Yiddish literature of the Hasidic community, particularly hard hit by the Nazi genocide, was especially livid in its equation of Hitler with Titus, though this was a widespread conception among Jews of every stripe.

During the immediate postwar period the arch became a place for Jewish public protests, a real turnabout from the use of the expansive Via dell'Impero ("Way of the Empire," discretely changed to Via dei Fori Imperiali, "Way of the Imperial Forums," after the war) and other sites for mass demonstrations and parades during the previous decades. On July 2, 1946, 2,000 Jews are reported to have demonstrated at the arch in response to the British crackdown in Palestine following the King David Hotel bombing by the Revisionist Irgun militia a day earlier. The Irgun bombed the British embassy in Rome on October 31, 1946, and some rightists fantasized about exploding the arch as well.[15] This comports amazingly well with the otherwise fanciful Nazi understanding of the value that Jews placed upon the arch, as reported by the *Chicago Sentinel* of July 28, 1943, a local Jewish newspaper citing the Jewish Telegraphic Service: "The Nazi-controlled radio in Italy charges that the American Government gave special training to Jewish airmen, who were particularly eager to participate in the bombing of Rome because 'the Jews want to destroy the Arch of Titus, thereby obliterating the symbol of Rome's victory over Judea and the destruction of the Jewish State.' "[16] On December 2, 1947, shortly after the United Nations decision on the partition of Palestine on November 29, the Jews of Rome and Jewish refugees of every sort awaiting transport to Palestine gathered at the arch and there they made the usual speeches and sang Zionist songs. Chief Rabbi David Prato, an avid Zionist called back from Palestine after the war to help in the rebuilding of the community, wore a miter that read in Hebrew, "I await your redemption, O' Lord" (Psalm 130:5). He, accompanied by Zionist leaders, led the crowd of survivors from across Europe carrying Zionist flags on a march through the Arch of Titus:

> A banner [*zer*] was placed on one of the stones that extend out from the arch. On this blue and white banner are recorded two dates: The date of the destruction of the Land by the Romans, and opposite it, the date of the United Nations [partition] decision. The singing of *Hatikvah* [the Zionist anthem by Naftali Herz Imber] was electrifying, and I have never heard anything like it all of my life. It burst forth from our mouths, from our hearts. Happy are we that we have merited this: *Hatikvah* beside the Arch of Titus! After *Hatikvah,*

> everyone sang *Teḥezakna* [a poem by H. N. Bialik and alternative anthem at the time] and the demonstration concluded with a procession of children and adults carrying their flags, which passed under the Arch of Titus in the opposite direction from that which the fathers of our fathers passed as slaves from Judaea.[17]

As imagined in Gutman's poster, Rabbi Prato and his throng of survivors marched through the arch from west to east, from Rome back to Jerusalem—the procession led by the Zionist flag. With some difficulty, they put aside their various political allegiances for this show of unity, which was filmed for newsreels and reported widely by Italian, international, and Jewish press outlets.

When the State of Israel was proclaimed in May 1948, the menorah, particularly the Arch of Titus menorah, was a broadly held symbol within the Jewish body politic in Palestine and internationally. Jewish religious (and even antireligious) moderns—especially Zionists (and even American reformers like Magnin), saw the arch menorah as a central Jewish symbol. It was a lamp to be lit not just at Hanukkah, but in Reform temples and even modernizing Orthodox synagogues from Eastern Europe to Los Angeles. It was kindled in Zionist ceremony, used in the ceremonies of other Jewish fraternal societies, displayed on the water towers of Jewish Palestine, and adorned the caps of the Jewish Legion. The depth of this symbolic vocabulary is the fruit of the fin de siècle. While this symbol "spoke" to European and American nationalists who sought out historical roots—whether in Palestine or in Rome, or both together, a merger of "Hellenism" and "Judaism"—those oddly bifurcated imagined categories—inspired Jewish and Christian and then Fascist thinking on the Jewish place (or, nonplace) in the West for much of the modern period. For a wide swath of the Jewish people, the menorah—and especially the arch menorah—was a significant statement of this hybridization.

4

Creating a National Symbol

Two national emblems were chosen at almost the same moment by two former British territories, separated by thousands of miles. Both were based upon stone sculptures of great antiquity, both images preserved over millennia against the odds. Both were well known and reflected a kind of cultural consensus, and both were intended to represent a new-old land in the making. I refer to the national emblems of the Republic of India and of the State of Israel. The focal element of the Indian symbol, chosen in 1950, is the Lion Capital of King Ashoka, a sculpture of four Indian lions standing back to back, on a base that includes other animals and the Ashoka Chakra, the "eternal wheel of law," which is pictured on the Indian national flag (chosen in 1947, itself a last-minute replacement for Gandhi's spinning wheel). The lions and base sit on a pedestal of a large lotus blossom sculpture. Below the image in the emblem is written, in historical Devanagari script, *Satyameva jayate* (Truth Alone Triumphs), a mantra from the *Mundaka Upanishad,* an early genre of Hindu scriptures. This assertion of historical continuity is anything but simple. The symbol contains no image of a deity—which would have offended not only India's large Muslim minority, but competing Hindu factions as well. It shows a group of lions from a long-destroyed Buddhist temple dating to 250 BCE, associated with a legendary wise king whom Gandhi and his circle found particularly compelling. It is significant that Buddhism had not flourished in India for a millennium, though it was rather fashionable among the secular national elite. The capital itself was a new-old artifact, discovered only in 1904/1905. Thus, the national emblem, while "looking" traditional to all, belonged to

Gabriel Shamir and Maxim Shamir, "Symbol" of the State of Israel, 1949, pen and ink rendering, courtesy of the Israel State Archives, photograph by Steven Fine; State Emblem of India, 1950, Supreme Court of India, Wikimedia Commons

none. On top of that, the use of lions fit well with European heraldry, and would be readily seen as such. The Upanishad text below the image is axiomatic, but likely was not comprehensible to many. The text itself is both a religious statement and a secularly palatable one, acceptable to the various sects, secularists, and Muslims. In short, the Indian national symbol is a well-thought-out attempt to represent a nation in formation, to express the things that bind, and to walk around those that don't. It is an exercise in nation construction of the first order.

The Israeli symbol is a similar exercise in nation construction. At the center of the seal of the State of Israel is the Arch of Titus menorah, an archaeological artifact that reflects a similar national consensus among Jews of most stripes. Like the lions of the Indian seal, the menorah was well known both to Jews and non-Jews, an important branding feature, and it is flanked by two olive branches—an ostensive bow to the religious factions, referencing to those in the know the olive trees of Zechariah chapter 4. This too is rather standard to European heraldry, where flanking elements, particularly laurel twigs, are common. The name of the country,

Israel, appears in Hebrew below the menorah. The script, like the styling of the composition as a whole, is rather brutally modernist, reminiscent of the kind of socialist realism current at the time—and was seen as such by the large socialist constituency within the Jewish polity. It is to some degree retro for the late 1940s, which gives this imagery a sense of being older than it is—a plus in an old-new land.

On a social level, this image, by the Tel Aviv design team of Maxim and Gabriel Shamir, was accepted unanimously by the Knesset in a vote on February 10, 1949. The general public received the national symbol quite positively. A few on the cultural edges of the new Israeli society nonetheless found it to be offensive. Salman Schocken, a pillar of liberal secular cultural Zionism and publisher of *Haaretz* newspaper, was among most disparaging of the new symbol. Immediately upon its introduction, Schocken wrote a blistering editorial in *Haaretz*. It was titled "State Symbol or Badge of Impoverishment [*teudat aniut*]?":

> This proposal, which owing to the hurried decision of the state council has become the symbol of the State of Israel, is an aesthetic horror. If this symbol is raised in the coming days above the assembly, and soon above the missions of the State of Israel everywhere in the world, it will be a demonstration of international proportions of the lack of taste and the lack of aesthetic culture of the State of Israel and of its lawmakers. It is unnecessary to discuss the motifs that might provide material to symbolize the state (the menorah, the olive branches and the word Israel). The execution is vulgar and dilettantish to such a degree that no company that respects itself would choose it as a mercantile symbol. The menorah is a poor copy of the menorah of the Arch of Titus, and there are ancient images and reliefs of the menorah that are far more pleasing. . . . The olive branches should serve as a kind of a frame, but they are so large and heavy that they overshadow the menorah—which should have been the determining image on the symbol. The Menorah is, in comparison, small and squeezed by two oversized olive branches—which are more like swords than like the branches of a tree that is the symbol of peace. The empty area above the menorah is especially ugly, and reflects the lack of skill of the designer of the symbol. The word "Israel" is written in script that shows the designer's complete ignorance of Hebrew typography. All of

this is set within a kind of plaque that is akin to those that serve as prizes at sporting events.[1]

Indeed, Schocken was repulsed by this symbol, likely because in its heaviness it so closely resembled the kind of socialist realism that had taken over Europe during the previous decades. More simply, he considered it classless. Schocken's complaint was not with the choice of the menorah, though he would have preferred a model other than the arch menorah. His essential complaint was with what seemed to him the unaesthetic work of the designers, the Shamir brothers. The image was subsequently corrected somewhat to reflect the arch menorah more closely and to decrease the size of the branches. Significantly for a man with such concern for visual imagery, the symbol of the state never graced Schocken's premiere publication, *Luaḥ Haaretz* (the *Haaretz Almanac*), which often included drawings of menorahs from archaeological sites, but never the symbol of the state.

At the other end of the Zionist cultural spectrum, a group of rabbis were also unhappy with the choice of the arch menorah as state symbol. Foremost among these was the Zionist chief rabbi, Isaac Halevy Herzog, a holder of a doctorate on the history of *tekhelet* (the Israelite royal blue) from the University of London (1913) and therefore not opposed to archaeology prima facie, as many of his peers were. He was, however, adamantly opposed to the Arch of Titus menorah as symbol of the state of Israel, a point that he made in a series of articles.[2] A sophisticated viewer, Herzog was well aware not only of rabbinic sources, but also attuned to the modernist secularizing impulses that resulted in the menorah's choice. Herzog deemed the arch menorah unacceptable both because of the shape of the base (it not being three legged) and because of the "idolatrous" animals that appear on it. We have seen that this complaint against the arch menorah goes back at least to Moses Mendelssohn and his attack on the arch menorah as inauthentic, he having of necessity been quite aware of its presence in European art of the time. Herzog sides with a position first stated by Adriaan Reelant and reiterated by a nineteenth-century British Protestant scholar, William Knight, of whose work he must certainly have been aware. Both claimed, with no historical justification or even parallel—other than a Protestant aversion to the images that appear on the arch menorah and assumptions about Jewish aniconism—that the base as we see it on the arch was made by Roman artisans. Herzog pointedly chose not to attribute the arch base to Herod the Great, arguing that "with all of his evil and proclivities toward assimilation he [Herod] would not have dared such a strange thing." He attributes this reticence to a belief in rabbinic sources, that a rabbi, Baba ben Buta, oversaw construction of the Temple.[3] Herzog proposes, following Knight, that the original base was broken en route to Rome, and that the base represented in the bas-relief was made as a replacement by Roman artisans. Herzog rejected the notion, suggested by archaeologist Maximilian Kon, that rabbis in antiquity might have tolerated the use of dragon imagery on the base of the authentic Temple menorah, in the strongest terms: "Heaven forbid that on the menorah of the Temple, the Lamp of God, there would be in the base or its stand (a sort of chest) any image of a dragon." He argues:

> In conclusion, our government is not doing well today—when we have merited again the light of Zion, which is symbolized by the menorah, by copying specifically the image of the menorah that is on the Arch of Titus—which was apparently made by foreigners and is not wholly made in the purity of holiness, as is supported by the teachings of our teacher Moses [Maimonides], the genius of geniuses [*gaon ha-geonim*] and from other sources derived by the Torah sages. Not only that, but an expert in the past (archaeologist) has testified before me that the menorahs represented on caves and in the catacombs in Rome all have three feet (tripods) as do all of the menorahs illustrated on mosaics of synagogue remains in the Land of Israel. My opinion on this is clear and determined.[4]

Herzog, ever the cultural synthesizer, dislikes the arch menorah for the same reasons that Mendelsohn did—because it does not represent rabbinic tradition. Nonetheless, he is pleased to call up an archaeologist for expert testimony when it supports his position. Herzog does not identify this "expert in the Jewish past" (*be-yedi'at qadmoniot*) with whom he conferred in constructing his argument against the arch menorah, though I would not be surprised if he was referring to an article published in *Hatzofeh*, a religious Zionist newspaper, on May 12, 1955, identifying him as archaeologist Yigael Yadin, the son of Eleazar L. Sukenik. Sukenik had been a member of the government committee that chose the symbol. In fact, Herzog illustrated his article with the Jericho synagogue mosaic, Sukenik's candidate for national emblem. This image, which met with Herzog's approval,

Beno Elkin, the Knesset menorah, 1956, photograph by Steven Fine

had previously been rejected by the Knesset, as we will soon see. This support, however, was secondary. Were all of the archaeologically derived menorahs fashioned like the arch menorah, Herzog would still have determined in favor of the Talmudic Rabbis channeled through Maimonides—who describes a three-legged lampstand—and in favor of rabbinic tradition over archaeology.

Behind this interpretation was a larger program to assert the religious significance of the new state, which Herzog himself called, in a prayer recited in Modern Orthodox (and most liberal) synagogues to this day, "the first sprouting of our redemption." Herzog must have well understood that the Arch of Titus menorah was a relatively new and distinctly secular Jewish symbol within the Israeli culture of his day. By contrast, in 1952, Herzog hesitantly endorsed Beno Elkin's Knesset menorah, a pending gift from the British Parliament to the Knesset. He endorsed the acceptance of this menorah despite the proliferation of three-dimensional human figures decorating its surface—recognizing "the seriousness of the matter in the event of a negative decision."[5] Herzog stipulated that the Elkin menorah be displayed inside the Knesset building, and not in a public garden. This did not happen. In fact, the lampstand was set in a garden beside the Knesset building. A negative decision by Herzog might certainly have been set aside by the government, thus eroding the already limited authority of the Orthodox establishment of the new state. Like his historical argument regarding the state symbol, Herzog's involvement with the Elkin menorah was a cipher for larger issues regarding the Jewish character of the Jewish state, of which he was chief rabbi.

In fact, the Shamirs had anticipated Rabbi Herzog's complaint about the animals of the menorah base, smearing the forms of the animals to the point that they are not recognizable. This was a standard Jewish technique in adopting the arch menorah, following upon the work of Christian artists of the nineteenth century. There are no animals on the bases of any Bezalel menorah, nor on the menorah pins of the Jewish Legion, and not even on the menorah created by Samuel Yellin at the Jewish Theological Seminary. However, this was not enough for Rabbi Herzog, who, in any event, was overruled even within his own Zionist Orthodox community.

The Committee on the State Symbol and the Flag

Both Schocken and Herzog would have been far more satisfied by the first choice of the *Va'adat Semel ha-Medinah shel Moetzet ha-Medinah* (the Committee on the State Symbol and the Flag). Even the term used to describe the state emblem bespoke the seriousness and complexities of the committee's charge. The biblical Hebrew term *semel* refers to a religiously illicit image. In modern Hebrew it took on the full modern range of the meaning of "symbol," with all of the complexities associated with it under the influence of Freud, Jung, and others. In choosing a *semel,* a national symbol, all well understood the gravity of the task.

Soon after the establishment of the state, the committee was formed and announced a design competition for the symbol of the new state. Its guidelines required that the symbol conform to a few general principles: "blue and white and an additional color, based upon the tastes of the designer. In the body of the symbol: a menorah with seven branches and seven stars (each with six points)." Hundreds of designs were submitted by artists throughout Israel. Among the members of the selection committee were representatives across the political spectrum and dignitaries with professional expertise, including the artist Reuven Reuven and archaeologist Sukenik, who were added at an early phase. Even these very formal documents are fascinating, as they allow us to observe the thought processes of the committee and the process of negotiation that led to the choice of a state symbol. After long deliberation, on September 21, 1948, the committee chose a symbol designed by Ismar (Itamar) David and Yerachmiel Schechter, comprising a modernized image of a roundel discovered in an ancient synagogue in Jericho in 1936, whose preservation Sukenik had secured in 1947. At the center of the seal is a large menorah, which draws loosely from the Jericho mosaic, but with heavier stems, not unlike a well-known synagogue screen relief from Ashkelon. Beneath the menorah is a quote from Psalm 125:5, "Peace Unto Israel." Above are the seven stars required by the committee, representing the days of the week. The script is historicized, and the turquoise color of the design light and contemporary. The seal itself is shaped as an oblong, drawing inspiration from ancient Israelite seals found in the Land of Israel, particularly a large bronze exemplar from Megiddo, which inspired the broad rim of the David/Schechter design. This is quite an unheraldic national symbol, unlike any European national seal both in form and in its forward-looking historicism. The choice by the committee of a recent discovery that reflected a kind of national consensus was significant. It was not unlike the Indian choice—an old-new artifact that all could agree on for a new-old nation. Similarly, the quote, written in a modernized yet historicized script, paralleled the Indian "Truth Alone Triumphs," drawn from the Upanishads, and was inoffensive to all sectors of society.

Flanking the menorah on the left in David's design are a *lulav* and *etrog*, symbols of the festival of Sukkot (Tabernacles). On the right is the shofar of Rosh ha-Shanah. Both appear as well in the mosaic, and both have deep religious resonances. When the religious content of these secondary symbols was objected to by leftist members of the committee, Sukenik assured them that "the menorah has served as the symbol of the Jewish people more than 1,500 years, the world over. In almost every case it appeared with additional symbols [*ha-simbolim*]: the shofar and palm fronds [*kappot temarim*]. These do not symbolize religiousness [*datiut*] but rather hope for the age of the messiah [*ha-tikvah le-yemot ha-Meshiaḥ*]."[6] This was a tactic he often used to secure the support and enthusiasm of secularists for "Jewish

Ismar (Itamar) David and Yerachmiel Schechter, proposed emblem of the State of Israel, 1948, courtesy of the Israel State Archives, photograph by Steven Fine

archaeology." On the same basis they might have protested the biblical menorah and the use of a biblical verse, but no one did. Within the Jewish civil religion of the late British Mandate and early Israel, a "messianic" vocabulary was fully absorbed into the Zionist ethos. The menorah was part of this consensus. Traditional Jewish terminology and concepts were often resignified nearly beyond recognition in socialist and nationalist terms. Religiously laden terms like *geulah,* "redemption," and *aliyah,* "ascent," were common parlance, *geulah* referring to land purchase and the national movement toward statehood, *aliyah* to immigration to Jewish Palestine. Ritual objects identified more narrowly with synagogue ritual, however, were apparently quite another matter for the socialist element of the Committee on the State Symbol. While this distinction may be hard for us to imagine today, it had real meaning during the early years of Israeli independence, when "Jewish" content was often esteemed, even when "religious" content was dismissed or sublimated. This parallels another potent symbol at that moment, the raising and sale of pig meat in the State of Israel. Swine were widely considered unacceptable for Jewish reasons across the Jewish polity, and not as a sign of religion per se. This distinction has widely diminished today, as distinctly Jewish content has become increasingly sectorialized, as have most areas of culture in contemporary Israel. David and Schechter's design was panned in the Israeli press as the result of a political process—a metaphor for disunity within the Israeli body politic even then. It was resoundingly—and surprisingly, to the committee members—rejected by the Knesset on September 28, 1949. It was replaced with the successful—if to some unpleasing—design by the Shamir brothers.

Much of this process of symbol formation is amply documented in the Israel State Archives, and the sequence of events narrated in a path-breaking study by Alec Mishory. What is missing from the archive, though, are details of the process whereby the David/Schechter symbol was rejected and the Shamir symbol chosen. In retrospect, this rejection is not terribly surprising. The David/Schechter design simply does not look like a state seal. The design by David and Schechter had fulfilled the parameters set out in the committee's charge as well as the culturalist instincts of some of the committee's expert members. The committee had acted upon the suggestions of Sukenik—who was clearly a driving force in this decision. It is worth noting that Sukenik's tombstone, in the Sanhedria Cemetery in Jerusalem (1953), is designed in a similarly historicized/archaeological idiom. Also, the initial Shamir proposal that served as the basis for the eventual seal was far more brutalist and steeped in socialist realist vocabulary than the rather clunky and historicized final design. The rejection of both the David/Schechter design and the first Shamir design in favor of something in-between is significant. The former is a kind of historicized, less-nationalistic, culturally literate design that would fit the liberal mores of Weimar Period Jewish culturalists—people like Schocken—while the latter evokes a far more militaristic and historicized socialist realism of the kind used most notably in Germany and Italy in the just previous era, and in the contemporary Soviet Union and the United States as well. The second design by the Shamir brothers, a more conservative choice, maintains the historicist tone of the David/Schechter proposal, and some of the brutalism still intrinsic to socialist realism of the first Shamir proposal. It was a symbol for the vast middle—an attempt to bring together the widely stretched Zionist ideological constituencies, Left and Right. In fact, the choice of the Arch of Titus menorah for the state "seal" is ascribed to David Remez, a prominent Labor Zionist leader and minister of transportation at the time.

The choice of the Arch of Titus menorah for the Shamir design fits so well with earlier Zionist iconography, that with hindsight, it is hard to imagine any other choice. My sense is that the reticence to choose this image was closely tied with the fact that the arch menorah with an inscription below had been the symbol of the Jewish Legion, which had been adopted as the symbol of the Revisionist movement, and particularly of its Betar youth organization, in the decades since. Jabotinsky and his followers, always savvy to the visual culture of their movement, had transformed the legion badge into the symbol of Revisionist Zionism. It appeared on uniform patches, posters, pamphlets, and membership cards for Revisionist groups and the Betar youth movement across Eastern Europe and Palestine to the Americas, and is today associated mostly with the rightist—and sometimes openly racist—fans of the Betar soccer teams. An editorial that appeared on February 15, 1949, in the official newspaper of the Revisionists, *Ḥerut,* associates attempts to choose an icon other than the arch menorah for the national "symbol" with an attempt to create distance from Revisionist symbolism. An unsigned editorial relates:

> The state symbol has been approved. From this point on, the menorah will symbolize the renewed independence of Israel. Long and boisterous argument preceded this decision. There were numerous attempts to influence it. The reasons offered were not always attempts to raise up a symbol other than the menorah, and were not practical or realistic. There were those who were opposed to the symbol and wanted a different symbol for the state for only one reason: this symbol has served for decades as the symbol of the movement in Israel that inscribed it on its flag from the first day of its formation as the slogan of the liberation of the motherland. The menorah—symbol of the Betar movement, the symbol that our leader, Ze'ev Jabotinsky, raised up, is not pleasing to many.

My guess is that this editorial was not far off from the truth. Throughout the war, David Ben-Gurion and the Provisional Government worked toward unification of the military branches, and even resorted to military confrontation with the Revisionist militia, the Irgun. Beyond the association with the Revisionist streams of Zionism, the menorah—and particularly the arch menorah—was a powerful symbol across Jewish and nascent Israeli society, even if leftist parties generally preferred more future-looking socialist images—the Shamir's first proposal suiting that aesthetic well. Religious or secular, for example, branched Hanukkah menorahs were generally set atop the water towers of kibbutzim, villages, and towns across Palestine/Israel—to the point that the water tower with menorah became an iconic feature of the Zionist/early Israeli landscape. By choosing the arch menorah as symbol of the state, the Provisional Government set this broadly acceptable and potent symbol in the center of the new state's civil religion, in effect depriving the Revisionists of proprietary possession of the arch menorah and seeking to integrate it, and them, into a larger body politic.

Public Acceptance of the "State Symbol"

The newly minted state symbol was particularly well received among members of the right-wing parties, both religious and "secular," as well as urban cultural Zionists of the fin de siècle, who had often been sidelined by the Socialist parties that dominated the new state. While having little political power at that time, the creative class among this group had considerable influence within Israeli society, particularly in regard to the "Jewish" content of the late Mandatory period and the new state. Cartoonists and designers, including Revisionists, had a profound influence on the formation of Israeli visual culture, even functioning at a level far more influential than the modernist high art of the period. These, together with Bezalel-trained authors and artists, most particularly Levin Kipnis and Zeev Raban, developed a visual culture in early Israel that embraced the national symbol. Writing in a 1951 children's book that was very popular within the "secular" community, author Levin Kipnis recounts a story of the first Independence Day, a Friday night, May 15, 1948. It is set at Kibbutz Degania, the first kibbutz, located on the southern shore of the Sea of Galilee. During the war it was under heavy attack. According to Kipnis's powerful first person narrative:

> It was Sabbath Eve. The radio announced the establishment our state. We, all of the people of Degania, assembled in the large dining hall. We lit the menorah of Shabbat, which has seven branches, and we

> read from the Bible. We continued to sing, and behold, the light of our beautiful menorah burned out. All of Degania was darkened. We knew that this was the beginning. The enemy hates light. The enemy loves darkness. Each of us went to his corner and prayed.[7]

In 1949, in preparation for the first Israel Independence Day festivities, the *Palestine Post* wrote in its lead story that, along with Torah processions reminiscent of "ancient times when Jewish soldiers carried the Holy Ark with them to and from battle," in "some synagogues" "replicas of the Menorah on Titus' Arch will be lit."[8] In later years, Kipnis published his own Haggadah for Israel Independence Day, 1973, which included the lighting of these menorahs—the sort of lamps that Raban had illustrated in their coproduced 1922 alphabet book. Thus, the lighting of seven-branched menorahs—known from the fin de siècle within B'nai B'rith, liberal synagogues, and Zionist ritual, was for a brief moment integrated into Israeli civil religion. Aside for a few Zionist rabbis, however, the lighting of personal menorahs on Independence Day never caught on.

A magazine for religious children (a supplement to the National Religious Party's newspaper, *Hatzofeh*), published in time for Israel Independence Day 1949, suggests the speed with which Israelis accepted the new state symbol. The cover celebrates the new national symbol and introduces it to young readers, and within its pages is printed a poem by Shlomo Sakolsky, a Revisionist poet, educator, and translator of some renown:

> Utterly silent and in decay
> On an arch in Rome you waited,
> Two thousand years, so very alone
> You dimmed, O Menorah, but were not extinguished.
>
> Ever since you were exiled, defeated
> They put you as a lesson and as an example—
> Yet in the heart of every Hebrew—you were not forgotten
> And you were like a lamp atop a lighthouse
>
> Oy, there were days of suffering and sadness
> Through blood Israel was established
> Mournfully you cried on the Arch—
> Behold you have been shown mercy by God

For behold, O Menorah, you have been redeemed
From Rome you too have been taken.
And they restored to you the light of the homeland,
and a great holiday we established.

Behold, again you are proudly displayed,
Again Jerusalem the city,
The hearts of the delegates of the people in the Knesset
Your holy flame again will glow.

Behold, again its flames shine
You were a holy symbol for the people
Show your light, my shining menorah,
The suffering that you suffered is over.

We recognize you by your seven illuminated branches,
It is you, who once shone in the Temple,
We have crowned you with wreaths of olive branches
Their oil will light a new light.

Like the dove with the news of olive twigs [having sprouted for Noah]
At the end of the flood, you rose up
And tomorrow, from the heights of the Temple Mount
You will illuminate the face of the city of David.[9]

Sakolsky's use of traditional themes and full integration of the form of the new "symbol" of the state into this poem is typical within Revisionist rhetoric. The level of association that the national religious community developed with the seal is reflected in the fact that a lighted arch menorah was the symbol of the religious Zionist Mizrachi/Religious Workers' Party list during the early years of the state, with the Hebrew caption "We will protect the flame of Judaism."[10] Similarly, British artist Rabbi David Hillman, brother-in-law of Rabbi Herzog (and trusted advisor on the Elkin menorah), created stained-glass windows for both the Central Synagogue in London and in 1958 for the then seat of the Chief Rabbinate in Jerusalem with images of the arch menorah. Mitigating—though not resolving—Rabbi Herzog's concerns, he replaced the mythological creatures of the arch with well-established animal symbols for the tribes of Israel.

Quickly the Arch of Titus menorah became an official element of Israeli culture—from government seals to Jewish New Year's cards, from passports to the plaques installed above government offices, prisons, and embassies. Prominent Israeli journalist Uriel Carlebach reveled in the fact that the Israeli seal, with the Arch of Titus menorah emblazoned upon it, hung in Rome itself, so close to the arch. He imagines "the spirit" of Theodor Herzl, the founder of political Zionism, "looking up at the Arch of Titus and searching for the menorah. It is not there. It left there and now is on its State symbol, atop a [flag] pole in Rome."[11] Images of the seal with the menorah relit, common in the art of Bezalel, especially the Jewish Legion cap pin, were illustrated by the Shamirs on the commemorative postage stamp for Israel Independence Day, 1954, and became a common theme in Israeli civil iconography.

The choice of the Arch of Titus menorah as symbol of the state created yet another urban legend. The belief is widespread that the Jewish Brigade of the British Army during World War II, made up of Zionist youth from Palestine (the vanguard of the Israel Defense Forces, and in 1948, many of its officers) had marched under the Arch of Titus in formation from west to east—in reverse—in effect carrying the menorah back to Palestine. In fact, the Jewish Brigade did reach Rome, where it was active in helping the survivors of Italian and German terror. There was considerable interest in the arch among members of the brigade, as we have seen. There was, however, no mass Zionist military parade in Allied-controlled Rome.

Iconographically, this theme was only a short step beyond Gutman's 1936 poster, which we discussed in Chapter 3. Images of Israelis, preferably soldiers, carrying the menorah "back" to Jerusalem became reasonably popular in early Israeli art. The most monumental of these is also the latest, Philadelphia-based Polish-Jewish socialist-realist artist Nathan Rapoport's massive sculpture *Scroll of Fire* (1971). Rapoport is best known for the now-iconic *Warsaw Ghetto Monument* (1948). *Scroll of Fire* was commissioned by American Jewish donors for the B'nai B'rith Forest at a rather obscure site in the Judean Hills above Beit Shemesh. In one pregnant detail of *Scroll of Fire,* we see an Israeli soldier who bears an uncanny resemblance to General Moshe Dayan, the hero of the 1967 Six-Day War, prominent among those soldiers bringing the menorah home. A related piece by Rapoport was set on the exterior wall of New York's Park Avenue

Nathan Rapoport, *Scroll of Fire,* 1971 (detail), photograph by Steven Fine

Synagogue in 1980. Reminiscent of Gutman's poster, this piece shows Israeli Jews of various sorts—a soldier, a farmer, and a student—bearing the menorah. In this image, however, angels hover above, sounding horns of redemption.

The association of Jewish Brigade/Israeli soldiers with the Arch of Titus is made forcefully, if haphazardly, in a Rosh ha-Shanah card printed in a displaced-person camp in Trani, Italy, in 1949. This rather crude montage reproduces a well-known image of Israeli soldiers marching in the first Independence Day parade. In the background is a map of Israel. To the left of the parade, Michelangelo's *Moses* looks on, and, beneath, in Hebrew, it reads "Long live our homeland, Israel." Above and to the left are an image of the arch and of the menorah. The association of the Jewish Army with the arch is clear. This iconography is refined on a pamphlet advertising a series of medallions minted by Israel Government Coins and Medals beginning in 1958, the tenth anniversary of the state. These coins commemorate "Israel Liberated," and are literally the other side of the coin from the Judaea Capta Series. They are in direct line with the "Judaea frees herself" iconography of the fin de siècle and were created by an early kibbutznik and scholar of ancient Jewish coinage, Leo Kadman (d. 1963). This design appeared in a number of variations and metals in the coming decades and was the most popular series of commemorative medals ever produced in Israel. In every version, we see free Jews in their own land—men and women and children—planting under a Judaean palm tree. The advertising pamphlet for this issue ties it back to our Jewish menorah-bearers, showing the Arch of Titus menorah relief. In the background of the pamphlet, the "Jewish captives" of the arch menorah panel transform, Pygmalion-like, into modern Israeli soldiers.

The imagery of the Jewish menorah-bearers had such deep roots in modern Jewish consciousness that on one occasion it was acted out on the streets of New York, two decades before Rapoport's Park Avenue Synagogue installation. It was adopted during the 1960s in the "Student Struggle for Soviet Jewry"—a movement with roots in New York's modern Orthodox community. Jacob Birnbaum, the grandson of Nathan Birnbaum and the founder of the Student Struggle for Soviet Jewry, had a strong flare for the historical resonances in this movement—just as his grandfather had when he dubbed the newly forming Jewish national movement "Zionism." With a well-developed sense of the theatrical, in December 1965 the younger Birnbaum "ordered a quantity of metal piping and personally supervised

Rosh ha-Shanah greeting card, Displaced Persons Camp, Trani (Bari), Italy, 1949, United States Holocaust Memorial Museum, courtesy of Schlomo Adler

Advertising pamphlet for the "Liberation Medal," Israel Government Coins and Medals, 1958, collection of Leah and Steven Fine

the all-night building of a huge candelabrum for a Freedom Lights Menorah March through Central Park." This was one of the first mass demonstrations of the Soviet Jewry movement, which called on the Soviet Union to "Let my people go"—echoing the words of Exodus—and which eventually resulted in freedom for over one million Jews from the Soviet Union. Each of the well-publicized marches was associated with a moment of Jewish redemption in the past, consciously rhyming with the rhetoric of Martin Luther King's civil rights movement. Thus the "Jericho Marches," in April and May 1965, and the "Hanukkah March" in December 1965. As the centerpiece of the "Hanukkah March," Birnbaum, himself a refugee from Nazi Europe, staged a group of Jewish youths carrying the menorah on their shoulders. These young men represented the Jews kept against their will in the Soviet Union, with strong echoes of the Jewish captives of Titus two millennia before. Birnbaum's menorah-bearers, however, marched knowing of the successes—and with a youthful surety of their own success—of both the rising civil rights movement (with its high levels of Jewish participation) and of the iconic Israeli menorah-bearers of less than twenty years before.

On a more humorous level, in a newspaper cartoon of 1949, the members of the Israeli government are shown carrying the state symbol on their shoulders up from Tel Aviv to Jerusalem, the new home of the Knesset. The bearers include figures that are still well known, including Prime Minister David Ben-Gurion, Golda Meir, and many others. Within a few years, the image of Jewish menorah-bearers was even immortalized in the design of a Hanukkah lamp, with each candle borne by an Israeli soldier into the gates of Jerusalem. Since that time, the Seal of the State of Israel designed by the Shamir brothers has become a given of Israeli culture. A 2011 exhibition at the Israeli Cartoon Museum in Holon entitled *Not Just a Symbol: The Symbol of the State in Cartoons* provides a real window into the menorah in modern Israel that goes beyond the usual citation of the Knesset menorah or noting the virtual absence of this icon in Israeli "fine arts." The cartoons range from 1949 to the present, and show the menorah used in a broad range of contexts. Among my favorites is a 1957 cartoon by the Israeli Revisionist cartoonist Kariel Gardosh, known as Dosh, which shows a startled Israeli boy standing before the Arch of Titus menorah relief. The caption below reads: "They pinched the original" (May 16, 1957). The Arch of Titus menorah was so ingrained in Israeli culture by that point that the cartoon brings a smile. Other cartoons in-

Advertising pamphlet showing the "Freedom Lights Menorah March," December 1965, Yeshiva University Archives, Student Struggle for Soviet Jewry Records, 1/14

clude one with two frames that celebrates the visit of Pope Paul VI to the Holy Land in 1964. To the right we see the soldiers of Titus bearing the menorah, with the caption: "Titus took it." To the left, the pope is handing two lampstands of three lamps each to President Zalman Shazar, with the caption: "Paul returned it."

Other cartoons are protest statements, like the 1954 image of Ben-Gurion setting the lit arch menorah and the entire country on fire as the result of a political cover-up. The menorah is subsequently used to represent the state in every possible political and social context. It was delightfully used to represent the contemporary Israel Independence Day custom of family barbecues in a 2009 cartoon, where the olive branches are replaced with kebab skewers, and the label reads, "Happy Holiday." The depth of Israeli identification with the menorah as national symbol is expressed in a 1978 cartoon by Aryeh Ben-Gurion. Here we see an Israeli in New York undergoing a chest x-ray. The doctor examining the x-ray is visibly perplexed to see that the rib cage of the Israeli is shaped like a seven-branched menorah! The message is that even an Israeli abroad is an Israeli through-and-through. This exhibition aptly represented the trends and tensions in Israeli self-awareness and civil religion portrayed through the symbol of the menorah—which the title nicely reminds us, is "not just a symbol."[12]

Competing Messianisms: Zionist Rabbis, Chabad, and the Menorah

Beginning in the 1960s, the counterinterpretation of the arch menorah that we first saw in Moses Mendelssohn's biblical commentary and then in Herzog's historicized responsum began to surface once again. I noted this first in an Israel Defense Forces magazine for soldiers called *Maḥanyim,* which was published under the auspices of the military rabbinate.[13] The Hanukkah 1959 issue is dedicated to Rabbi Herzog on his seventieth birthday and features prominently Herzog's objections to the state seal. It even reproduces a photograph of the rabbi visiting at the arch. The caption for this image asserts both Rabbi Herzog's communal and scholarly credentials to a broad Jewish studies audience: "During his visit in Italy to save Jewish children from monasteries across Europe, the chief rabbi visited historical sites, subsequently publishing legal and academic studies of these places." Rabbinic questioning of the arch menorah was thus reaching beyond the elite to a mainstream, religiously interested audience.

Among the most fascinating critiques of the state symbol by Zionist rabbis of this period was penned by Rabbi Yosef Qafiḥ (d. 2000), a Jerusalem rabbi and a leader of the Yemenite community in Israel whom we met in Chapter 2. A member of the Supreme Rabbinical Court, Qafiḥ expressed his discomfort with the Arch of Titus menorah as the symbol of a Jewish state. This view appears in a very long and unusual digression within his 1965 supercommentary on Maimonides's Mishnah commentary to Menaḥot 3:7. Qafiḥ drew attention, for the first time, to the Maimonides/Abraham Maimuni position that the Temple menorah branches were straight and not curved, which we discussed in detail in Chapter 2. In this framework, however, Qafiḥ's exposition amounted to a full-throated polemic against the Arch of Titus menorah and its contemporary prominence. He was clearly in the same camp as Rabbi Herzog on the Arch menorah:

> They [the menorah drawings in manuscripts, which Rabbi Qafiḥ illustrated] do not have any curve at all, and they are unlike the widely known image that is copied from the Arch of Titus. It has already been proven that it is fake, for it is stated in a *baraita* [an early rabbinic tradition] that [the menorah] had legs, and similarly our rabbi [Maimonides] wrote in his composition. And in the widely known image it sits on a broad base, and there are many other contradictions [*setirot*] that this is not the place to discuss.[14]

"The widely known image" is a circumlocution for the image of the menorah on the state seal, whose base Rabbi Herzog considered to be inauthentic. Where Herzog attacked the base, Qafiḥ went after the branches. In his estimation, the menorah of the arch was completely disqualified to be the symbol of a Jewish state, specifically because it goes against Jewish law. Qafiḥ's assertion served yet another purpose. By emphasizing the fealty of Yemenite manuscripts to the Maimonidean menorah tradition, he asserted the primacy of the Yemenite tradition within the larger competition between religious traditions that was brewing in modern Israel—particularly against the regnant Ashkenazi rabbinic establishment. The disqualification of the arch menorah by these Zionist rabbis had far less to do with aesthetics than with the ambivalent relationship of the rabbinic establishment to the civil religion.

Qafiḥ's position drew very little comment until the 1980s—at least in print. While broad groups of non-Zionist *Haredim* (ultra-Orthodox Jews) may have objected to the menorah on the state seal, it was not the focus of attention by most. In 1982, however, Qafiḥ's position found a powerful exponent, this time in the work of Rabbi Menachem Mendel Schneerson (d. 1994), the leader of the Chabad Lubavitch Hasidic dynasty. Schneerson's work on the menorah was as practical as it was theoretical. He had maintained an abiding scholarly interest in the menorah throughout his life, beginning with a scholarly study of the procedures for lighting the Temple menorah and the spiritual implications of this lighting that he completed in 1939 (though it was published only after his death).[15] In 1973 Schneerson began a campaign of public menorah lightings during the Hanukkah holiday. The menorahs lit in the early years were of a standard form, placed before Jewish and other public buildings—and even atop cars on busy streets. The goal in rabbinic terms was to increase the public celebration of the holiday, called in Talmudic parlance *pirsumei nisa*—literally, "spreading word of the miracle." This project was engineered to bring the menorah into the public sphere in Western countries, along with Christian symbols like the crèche and the Christmas tree. Its stated goal was to increase Jewish pride. To this end, Schneerson's followers even claimed in American court depositions that the menorah was a "secular symbol" and not a religious one. Public menorah lightings—often on town squares, intersections, and, increasingly, government buildings and national capitals—became a point of contact and recognition in cities, and even the stuff of court cases and internecine Jewish strife until the early twenty-first century. As late as 2003, in some cities, including Cincinnati, this sort of public display of Jewishness was sometimes met with anti-Semitism, and for Jews used to more private expressions of Judaism, embarrassment, anger, and even a bit of fear. The menorah lightings became a primary mode of religious "outreach" in Schneerson's project of bringing Jews and Christians closer to Judaism as part of what he conceived as a larger messianic awakening.

The success of the menorah campaign, the parameters of which have been the topics of numerous scholarly and popular presentations, led Schneerson to refine the project in 1982.[16] In that year, he unveiled a distinctly Chabad menorah. In two ritualized public lectures—*sichas*—on the subject of Hanukkah, Schneerson argued that the standard Jewish menorah, and particularly the menorah used on the Seal of Israel, is incorrectly formed. His analysis of the branches drew on Qafiḥ's commentary, which is cited explicitly in subsequent publications. Commensurate with Schneerson's general focus upon Maimonides in his teachings and legal decision-making process, Schneerson entered upon a sustained scholarly investigation of the menorah based upon the Oxford manuscript of Maimonides's Mishnah commentary that Rabbi Qafiḥ had written about. Schneerson asserted, with Qafiḥ, that Maimonides's sketch illustrating the Mishnah commentary reflected Maimonides's intention in every detail, and that it was not simply the schematic doodle that Maimonides himself describes. Thus, Schneerson argued that Maimonides's drawing of the calyxes of the menorah, described in Babylonian Talmud tractate Menaḥot 28b as

Rabbi Menachem Mendel Schneerson with the Chabad menorah, December 21, 1987, Courtesy of JEM/The Living Archive

"Alexandrian cups," are intentionally drawn upside down—citing in support the eleventh-century Spanish rabbi Baḥya ibn Paquda to explain this anomaly as an expression of Divine Light. Regarding the menorah branches, Schneerson, like Qafiḥ, drew upon Maimonides as read through the comments of his son. Going beyond Qafiḥ, Schneerson enlisted Rashi's commentary on the Torah and a range of later scholars. He argued that the Hebrew term *alkason* that Rashi used at Exodus 25:32 to describe the menorah branches refers to a strictly diagonal line. We have already seen, however, that this term is more flexible than that, and does not mitigate against a curved shape. Slightly later medieval Ashkenazi commentators, we have seen, imagined that the branches were shaped "like the branches of a tree," and manuscript illustrators routinely imagined arced branches.

Schneerson's ingenious argument, drawn through a range of rabbinic sources, was intended to disrupt standard Jewish practice and create space for a new and distinctly Chabad menorah. In her excellent description of the events that followed, Maya Balakirsky Katz tells how an artisan set out in short order to create a large, eight-branched menorah modeled upon the Maimonides drawing in Oxford, which was set beside Schneerson's seat to the right of the Torah shrine in Lubavitch World Headquarters, 770 Eastern Parkway in Brooklyn. This menorah was quickly branded as the standard Chabad menorah from that point on, used in public menorah lightings across the globe. Another factor in the popularity of the "Maimonides" menorah is its very simple angularity. It is easy to fabricate—no small matter for Chabad emissaries worldwide, who yearly construct large—sometimes gigantic—wooden or metal menorahs in public places. Finally, the angular menorah fits with modern, often minimalist experimentation in the design of branched Hanukkah menorahs. It became so successful that other fervently Orthodox (*Haredi*) groups have adopted this menorah, causing some Chabad followers in recent years to further distinguish the Chabad menorah. In Los Angeles the symbol of the "dancing rabbi"—first developed for use in relation to Chabad fund-raising telethons and widely recognized in this region—has occasionally been affixed to the face of the uniquely "Chabad menorah."

Schneerson's discussions of the menorah were not just about branding, however. They were also about unbranding. Like Mendelssohn, Herzog, and Qafiḥ before him, Schneerson had a particular distaste for the Arch of Titus menorah. Unlike them, however, he asserted that any difference between the Arch of Titus menorah and rabbinic conceptions is the result of Roman religious syncretism, maintaining his focus on the artist's intentionality that he earlier applied to the Maimonides drawing:

> On the "triumphal arch" that they built in Rome and named for Titus, may his name be blotted out, after his victory over Jerusalem, there is carved [the image of] a menorah, and there are those who say that this is the image of the menorah of the Temple. The menorah is portrayed there such that the six branches rise [from the central stem] in a half circle. . . . One can say, simply, that the menorah that is carved on the arch is not the image of the menorah of the Temple. As we see in this portrayal, a number of its details do not comport with the structure of the menorah of the Temple—to the point that the "menorah" on the Arch of Titus is decorated with a dragon. Therefore, it is logical to say that the menorah which is on the arch is certainly not the menorah of the Temple, but some other menorah that has some similarity to the Temple menorah. Since the menorah in

> the Temple was very significant even to idolaters—for the purposes of their idolatrous practice (which is the explanation for the addition of the image of the dragon, which is idolatrous)—the image on the arch was based upon one of these [idolatrous] menorahs.[17]

Schneerson posited that the arch menorah was created for gentile purposes, by gentiles (literally, "worshippers of stars and the zodiac signs"), and had nothing to do with Jews. His argument was not about Roman disinterest in verisimilitude, as argued by Mendelssohn, nor a base created after an accident, as argued by Herzog. It was closer to Herzog's rejected suggestion that the base was made to be wholly syncretistic by Herod, whom Herzog had let off the hook. To Schneerson, the arch menorah is a syncretistic pagan lampstand through and through—with a base that is pagan and branches that are wrong. Concern regarding gentile syncretism is well represented in rabbinic literature, and a sophisticated viewer like Schneerson, who spent considerable time in Berlin and Paris before settling in New York, was certainly aware of Christian interest in Jewish themes—including the menorah. Going beyond Herzog, who acknowledged the very Jewishness of the arch menorah, at least in its branches, Schneerson claimed that this lampstand had nothing to do with Jews at all. By implication, then, all other Jewish groups—including the State of Israel—were in error in using menorahs with rounded branches, and certainly in illustrating the base of the arch menorah. They were purveying gentile syncretism, he believed—as is the way of secular Zionism. Schneerson asserted here both *Haredi* disdain for Zionism as a secularizing ideology and his general concern with "assimilation" and loss of Jewish authenticity among more liberal Jewish groups. His followers quickly ceased using menorahs of other shapes in their public lighting ceremonies and started lighting only Schneerson's "authentically Jewish" lampstands. This was by far the most radical transformation of the iconography of the menorah—which had been maintained through mimetic tradition by geographically distant Jewish communities since the days of the Second Temple—a branding decision of amazing chutzpah that fit the general program of a leader who would be messiah.

This interest in the "original" forms of Jewish icons was basic to Schneerson's conception of Jewish visual culture, as he himself intended to reformulate it. He had asserted as early as 1944 when he was head of the *Merkos L'inyonei Chinuch*, the central educational arm of the Chabad-Lubavitch movement, that images of the Ten Commandments were to be shown as cubes and not arched tablets—based upon a rabbinic opinion that had seldom before been given physical form. He argued, quite astonishingly, that the arched tablets were imposed upon Jews by the Romans, based upon the Roman round arch (in fact, they were a medieval development). Forty years later Schneerson used the same tactic in order to shift the received shape of the menorah. Maimonides's menorah had never before been executed and so represented a new—Chabad—tradition in the guise of renewed traditionalism. In December 2014 the senior Chabad emissary in Milan, Rabbi Gershon Mendel Garelik, participated in an event at the Arch of Titus that was mounted to YouTube. Rabbi Garelik is seen in a small crowd of Hasidim holding up a Chabad menorah, a photograph of Schneerson resting on the arch. Garelik speaks stirringly in Yiddish (still the official lingua franca of Chabad) about the arch menorah, asserting an alternate—Chabad—vision that denies modernist Jewish transformation of the arch menorah even as it weaves it into a larger tapestry:

> Dear children, dear children [*kinderlakh, kinderlakh*]: The true menorah is like this one [he holds up a Chabad menorah]. And the menorah that hangs there [pointing to the spoils panel] is a complete lie, a complete lie [*sheqer gamur*]. It is only because that was a time of destruction, and they drove everyone crazy and they murdered millions of Jews, that they could take a falsehood [that is, a false menorah] and say that this is the [true] menorah. This [holding up the Chabad menorah] is the true menorah. The true menorah never came to Rome. It took hundreds of years and they [the "crazy" gentiles] killed millions of Jews. We [Chabad] hold this menorah, the true menorah; for it was on this kind of menorah that the Rebbe blessed the [Hanukkah] candles [*bentsht likht*]. [Today] no one persecutes [bothers] us—for now is the end of the final exile.[18]

The assembly concludes with a short communal dance. As in many postwar Jewish reflections, particularly in Yiddish, but deeply in Hebrew as well, the equation of Titus with Hitler, and perhaps Stalin, is paramount here. This event was a kind of parody of Jewish communal demonstrations that have taken place regularly at the arch since the early twentieth century, and particularly during the 1990s, when Israeli presidents and chiefs of staff were regularly filmed at the arch on patriotic pilgrimages. More to the point, groups of Jewish visitors can often be seen singing Psalm 126 or the Israel anthem "Hatikvah," "The Hope," under the arch. The Chabad gathering is closer to these ad hoc visits, except for the fact that this unpilgrimage was recorded and disseminated. "True" or not, the power of the arch and its menorah continues to attract—and provoke—even its detractors within the Jewish body politic.

Schneerson's direct model for the menorah project was the public lighting of menorahs in public spaces in the State of Israel. Even the immense sizes of Chabad menorahs hearken in part back to the large Hanukkah menorahs that are lit at the Knesset building and the Great Synagogue in Tel Aviv (as they do to American Christmas tree lighting ceremonies), as does the involvement of public officials in Chabad menorah-lighting ceremonies. While pro-Israel and arguing stridently against Israel returning any territories to Arab control, Chabad is not a "Zionist" movement. It did not make its peace with Zionist use of religious and messianic themes by the state, as religious Zionist thinkers like Herzog and Qafiḥ did. For Schneerson, then, notions of Zionism "returning the menorah" or of Israel as "the first sprouts of our redemption" were simply heresy. Nothing symbolized this for him like the lighting of the Arch of Titus–like menorahs by Jews, and the use of this lampstand as symbol of a state born in religious rebellion. The Chabad menorah, then, was—and is—a direct challenge to the notion that the existence and life of the State of Israel—meaning the government and its institutions—has religious meaning. It is countersymbolism through-and-through. The Chabad menorah gives expression in bronze and aluminum to Schneerson's assertion of exclusive rabbinic authority—and his own messianic authority—over Jewish visual culture—over the Jewish past and over its future. David Berger, professor of medieval Jewish history, rabbi, and critic of Chabad's messianic claims for Schneerson since his death, cites an anonymous rabbinic colleague's quip about the Chabad menorah—"every new religion needs a symbol."[19] What Berger's informant didn't say, and Schneerson clearly adduced and acted upon, is that the same is true of the Arch of Titus menorah as used by Zionists and other modernizing Jewish groups. The Chabad menorah expresses the real success of the state "symbol" imagined by the artisans of the Bezalel School and designed by the Shamir brothers. The emblem of the State of Israel has sparked this deeply creative countervisuality from within Jewish/Israeli civil religion.

The choice of the menorah as symbol of the State of Israel was determined in the original charge of the Committee on the State Symbol that met in 1948. The process by which the Israeli emblem (called explicitly in Hebrew by the loaded term *semel,* a "symbol") was formed is an engaging one, reflecting the broad complexities of creating a shared national culture for a new nation-state. Israel and India, two old-new nations, went through the process of creating new national identities at roughly the same time, and each made very similar choices. In the case of Israel, the arch menorah eventually did become the national "symbol"—against the wishes of some religious elements. What we have seen in almost real time is an acting out of the kinds of ideological issues described and developed in prestate times on the state of nation building. This is truly the process of imagining a polity and creating it. Uniquely, Zionism did this for a nation that initially controlled no territory and shared a religious, but not spoken, language, transforming a dispersed "virtual community" into a modern, landed nation-state. The Zionist movement, the state-in-the-making in Mandatory Palestine, and the early state of Israel made real use of images like the menorah—old-new like the state itself—in the process of forming the Jews into a political polity. This use of the menorah was complex, certainly when compared with the most widespread Zionist symbol, the Magen David. The shield or "star" of David was a new symbol developed in recent centuries. It was given a distinctly Jewish pedigree, especially in light of Nazi use of this symbol to identify Jews. The menorah, by contrast, represents Jewish tradition itself. The Zionist menorah transforms a traditional symbol into a tool of statehood, and rabbis who chose to participate in Zionism were in the unenviable position of negotiating their traditional authority within a secular polity that was often antagonistic or patronizing toward tradition. Schneerson's project to undermine Zionist iconography and harness it to his own messianic agenda represents the very strength of the Israeli state "symbol," with its rendition of the Arch of Titus menorah.

5

A Jewish Holy Grail

Television documentaries about "lost" and "discovered" artifacts have been a staple of cable television for the last couple of decades. The list of subjects includes the Ark of the Covenant, the Holy Grail, "secrets" of the Dead Sea Scrolls, Gospel fragments that undo Christianity, and, at the looniest end, space aliens who created such buildings as the pyramids as well as "runways" for extraterrestrials in the Andes. Of course, the menorah occasionally makes its appearance as well. Watching television documentaries on historical themes, it is not difficult to find a full menu of searches for "hidden" truths that were otherwise unknown but might be revealed within a fifty-minute broadcast. Some of these programs are quite legitimate, if sometimes hyped a bit more than can be sustained by the actual artifacts or the scholarship that has tried so diligently to understand them. Shots of Dead Sea Scroll fragments, for example, continue to excite—in a way that overtly religious relics scarcely do (even when the scrolls appear on the screen reversed, or even upside down). Others of these programs are simply sleight of hand, creations of well-funded filmmakers. These shows drive forward narratives that can make real experts cringe. It is often hard for the public to know if an expert is trustworthy, especially when beautiful photography and technological wizardry are punctuated with short clips of seemingly "authoritative" (and in fact, heavily edited) academic talking heads. This gets all the more confusing when these "discoveries" are associated with university-affiliated scholars and reported by legitimate news outlets, crafted as media events that cluster around Hanukkah/Christmas and Passover/Easter. When it comes to the Jewish past, few subjects are more surely draw attention than the fate of the artifacts of the Jewish temples.

It is sometimes difficult for me to fault these "discoveries," even as I shudder at their claims and am occasionally drawn in to refute them. These events often engage young students on the subjects that I find important—and bring them excitedly to my classroom and lectures. Once they are there, though, I have to inform my acolytes that the myths purveyed in these TV events—most specifically the proverbial "What if?" questions and other assumptions piled one atop the other—might be fun in historical strategy games, but are not how history is written. Quickly, they find out that "real" history is much more fun. Scratch just below the surface of most academic scholars of biblical or Second Temple history of my generation, though, and you will find a teen who fell in love with *Raiders of the Lost Ark* and longed to be Dr. Indiana Jones. For scholars just a bit younger than me, add to this the cable television programs and computer games that cause such angst. The line between scholarship and other kinds of searches—religious, antireligious, spiritualist, or even nationalist—is a very thin one, and the distinction between each needs to be patrolled vigorously. At one point, I referred to this contemporary media-driven environment as the "Da Vinci-Codification" of our culture—when the myths of our literature and the paths of seemingly objective scholarship converge.[1]

Truth is, these documentaries touch a deep chord in our culture, which for millennia has sought out holy vessels and told stories of their whereabouts. This search is rooted in Jewish literature and provides a leitmotif in Western civilization that is not discussed enough, as we tend to push it under the rug. The search for the Temple vessels goes hand in hand with the search for the ten lost tribes of Israel—a ubiquitous theme in Western civilization that was recently charted by Tudor Parfitt and Zvi Ben-Dov Benite—as well as the many supposed appearances of the Ark of the Covenant itself that Tudor Parfitt has charted—particularly in Africa. The act of searching for the Tabernacle/Temple vessels—or thinking about the search—provides deep continuity across the generations, allowing objects and people considered essential in scripture to be present, even if unseen, their "current" locations unknown. This need for continuity makes the loss of such objects simply unthinkable, firing imagination even as it fuels, ignites, or reignites anticipation of future "redemption."

Oddly, this discovery trope has particular resonance in the modern world, where we have become accustomed to regular discoveries of real significance. The premiere example of this is the "discovery" of "lost tribes" who have been brought to Israel in recent decades from Africa and Asia on the basis of medieval and modern claims and associations with Judaism. Through the instrumentality of the state, these formerly "lost" members of the ten tribes have become legally unlost. Of lesser though still fascinating significance is the recent claim that the menorah of the Second Temple and other Temple artifacts have been hidden nefariously by the Catholic Church deep in the bowels of the Vatican. This is a new myth, though one that has affected Israel-Vatican relations in recent decades, and is alive and well across the Jewish community. In this chapter I engage myths of the menorah and other Temple vessels as they have developed and been portrayed in Jewish and Christian traditions from biblical times through the nineteenth century, with a particular interest in the distinctly Roman urban myth of the menorah in the Tiber River. I then turn to the question of how menorahs and the menorah search are presented in modern literature. All of this sets the stage for Chapter 6 and my discussion of the menorah myth du jour, the menorah at the Vatican.

Myths of the Lost Temple Vessels in Judaism and Christianity from the Bible to the Nineteenth Century

The origin point for this sense of loss and memory of the Temple vessels is the destruction of the Solomonic Temple by Nebuchadnezzar in 586 BCE. The book of 2 Kings 25:1–17, the last chapter of the long saga of the Davidic dynasty, describes the loss of Solomon's treasures and the destruction of Judah. The crescendo of this loss relates to the vessels of the Temple, which the author inventories as an expression of both his pain and the latent greatness of the lost Temple:

> And the pillars of bronze that were in the house of the Lord, and the stands and the bronze sea that were in the house of the Lord, the Chaldeans broke in pieces, and carried the bronze to Babylon. And they took away the pots, and the shovels, and the snuffers, and the dishes for incense and all the vessels of bronze used in the temple service, the firepans also, and the bowls. What was of gold the captain of the

> guard took away as gold, and what was of silver, as silver. As for the two pillars, the one sea, and the stands, which Solomon had made for the house of the Lord, the bronze of all these vessels was beyond weight. The height of the one pillar was eighteen cubits, and upon it was a capital of bronze; the height of the capital was three cubits; a network and pomegranates, all of bronze, were upon the capital roundabout. And the second pillar had the like, with the network.

This dual statement of loss and greatness is made sharper yet more expansive in the biblical book called 2 Chronicles, a volume written by the returned Judean exiles during the fifth century BCE. There we read: "And all the vessels of the house of God, great and small, and the treasures of the house of the Lord, and the treasures of the king and of his princes, all these he brought to Babylon." Chronicles has it that the Temple vessels were *all* taken to Babylonia, opening the way to centuries of imaginative expression.

Continuing the narrative from Chronicles, the books of Ezra and Nehemiah, which complete the cycle, include a supposed letter from Cyrus the Great, who had subsequently conquered the Babylonian Empire and allowed many national groups to return to their ancestral territories and restore their temples. The book of Ezra opens with such a decree, which includes restitution of the Jerusalem Temple treasures:

> Cyrus king of Persia brought these out in charge of Mithredath the treasurer, who counted them out to Sheshbazzar the prince of Judah. And this was the number of them: a thousand basins of gold, a thousand basins of silver, twenty-nine censers, thirty bowls of gold, two thousand four hundred and ten bowls of silver, and a thousand other vessels; all the vessels of gold and of silver were five thousand four hundred and sixty-nine. All these did Sheshbazzar bring up, when the exiles were brought up from Babylonia to Jerusalem.[2]

Missing from this list, of course, are the most holy vessels of the Tabernacle, beginning with the Ark of the Covenant. It seems to have been destroyed in the Babylonian siege, at least according to Prophet Jeremiah, who strove to lessen the loss with messianic hope: "And when you have multiplied and increased in the land, in those days, says the Lord, they shall no more say, 'The ark of the Covenant of the Lord.' It shall not come to mind, or be remembered, or missed; it shall not be made again."[3]

The loss of Temple vessels in 586 BCE, and their restoration, provided a template for Jewish—and then Christian—thinking about loss and restoration. This is certainly how Jews have read the extended descriptions of the Tabernacle in the Book of Exodus, which are repeated twice in the traditional Jewish version of the Hebrew scriptures. Jewish tradition has certainly looked back wistfully to the Tabernacle and its vessels, and to the relatively more recent losses of the First and Second Temples. The very invocation of these Divine vessels in words, sometimes compulsively, as in Exodus, helps bring them back, and has sustained hope for their physical return throughout Jewish history.

Jewish literature of the Greco-Roman period is rich with reflections on the Temple vessels and their whereabouts. The book of 2 Maccabees 2:4–8, written by a Greek-speaking Jew named Jason of Cyrene in North Africa around 110 BCE, claims that the "holy fire" of the Solomonic Temple had even been preserved by the priests and reused to kindle the altar of the Second Temple—a real attempt at continuity from the glorious Temple of Solomon to the rather modest first iterations of the Second Temple. He goes further in this assertion of continuity from the First Temple to the Second:

> And Jeremiah came and found a cave, and he brought there the tent and the ark and the altar of incense, and he sealed up the entrance. Some of those who followed him came up to mark the way, but could not find it. When Jeremiah learned of it, he rebuked them and declared: "The place shall be unknown until God gathers his people together again and shows his mercy. And then the Lord will disclose these things, and the glory of the Lord and the cloud will appear, as they were shown in the case of Moses, and as Solomon asked that the place should be specially consecrated."

In other words, the vessels are hidden deep in the Land of Israel, awaiting Divine "mercy." Parallel to this, a Samaritan tradition mentioned by Josephus (*Antiquities* 18.85) and believed to this day, has it that the Tabernacle is hidden in a cave on Mount Gerizim. It will eventually be revealed by a messianic *Taheb,* the returning redeemer, Moses.

After the destruction of the Second Temple, speculation regarding the Temple vessels increased, as Judaeans faced yet another loss of their holy objects. A book known as 2 Baruch, completed around 100 CE, has it that when the Chaldean army was about to take the Temple, God sent an angel to save the treasures of the Temple and hide them in the earth. Baruch, Jeremiah's scribe and hero of this volume, reports:

> And another angel began to descend from heaven, and said unto them: "Hold your lamps, and do not light them till I tell you. For I am first sent to speak a word to the earth, and to place in it what the Lord the Most High has commanded me." And I saw him descend into the Holy of Holies, and take from there the veil, and the holy ark, and the mercy-seat, and the two tables, and the holy raiment of the priests, and the altar of incense, and the forty-eight precious stones, with which the priest was adorned and all the holy vessels of the tabernacle. And he spoke to the earth with a loud voice: "Earth, earth, earth, hear the word of the mighty God, And receive what I commit to you, and guard them until the last times, so that, when you are ordered, you may restore them, so that strangers may not get possession of them. For the time comes when Jerusalem also will be delivered for a time, until it is said, that it is again restored forever." And the earth opened its mouth and swallowed them up.[4]

This reflection on the loss of the Tabernacle/Temple vessels in 586 BCE, written so close to the time of the destruction of Jerusalem by Titus, clearly differentiates those earlier holy artifacts from those of Herod's Temple. Unlike the vessels of the Second Temple, which were widely known to have been taken to Rome, this tradition asserts that the far more significant vessels of the First Temple are safely stowed for future restoration.

Many variants of this story were told during the first Christian centuries, preserved both by the Church and in the writings of the Rabbis. Some Rabbis also believed that the Ark had been hidden. Mishnah Sheqalim 6:2 describes the unfortunate fate of a certain priest who came too close to discovering the Ark: "A story is told of a priest who was doing his duty, and saw that the floor was different from the other parts. He came and told his friend. He hadn't finished speaking when his soul left him, and they thus knew that there the ark was hidden." The Jerusalem Talmud makes the story all the more potent, transforming our priest from a curious observer to an active searcher: "Taught Rabbi Hoshaya: He [the priest] pounded it with a hammer and fire came out and consumed him."[5] The Ark is thus present and distant at the same time but, to the Rabbis, certainly not "lost." Belief that the Ark—and possibly other vessels—are just beneath the pavement of the Temple, or perhaps in the grottos below, is deep and wide in traditional and even modern Jewish thought, bearing the authority of the Mishnah of Rabbi Judah the Prince itself, the foundational rabbinic document.

A fascinating text of the early Islamic period, "The Tractate of the Vessels" (*Masekhet Kelim,* again, not to be confused with the Mishnaic tractate of the same name), expands in exquisite detail upon the location of the vessels, imagining that "five great righteous men wrote these recited traditions." These men formed a group that included the last Judean king, Zedekiah, and the early Second Temple prophet Zechariah, who, we have seen, prophesied regarding the menorah. Apparently written during the apocalyptic moment when Persia—then Islam—took the Holy Land, and Jews again expected apocalyptic revelation, this text claims that the five "hid the vessels of the sanctuary and the riches of the treasuries which were in Jerusalem. And they shall not be revealed until the day of the coming of the Messiah son of David—speedily, in our days, amen, and so may it be [the Divine] will." Only one manuscript of this text survived into modern times, published in 1648 in Amsterdam. A sense of the tractate's appeal, however, may be gained in a set of tiles noticed by modern scholars in Lebanon, but apparently originating in the supposed tomb of Ezekiel in Kfar al-Kafil, a village located about fifty miles south of Baghdad. These documents, dating to the nineteenth century, contain the book of Ezekiel—with its prominent vision of the Third Temple—together with long sections of *Masekhet Kelim.* I point out that the restoration of the Temple vessels is not part of Ezekiel's vision, so this addition of tractate *Kelim* might have been intended to fill a void. Alexei Sivertsev has shown that this interest in the Temple vessels parallels Byzantine Christian concern about them. This expansion of Christian interest certainly gave wings to Jewish fascination, just as Christian interest in the biblical artifacts and their whereabouts has provided rich soil—and conversation partners—for modern Jews in search of these ancient relics.

This concern for the Tabernacle and the vessels of the First Temple was applied to those of the Second soon after its destruction in 70 CE. As we have seen, rabbinic literature of late antiquity describes the presence of the

Second Temple vessels in Rome. The topic fascinated both Palestinian rabbis and those across the border in the Persian Empire. Late antique rabbis, we have seen, imagined that a selection of the Temple vessels was hidden in the palace of "Emperor Julius" (a rather generic name for an emperor) in Rome. Christians imagined their journey from Rome to Gaul to North Africa, Constantinople, and on to Jerusalem. This model was applied to the Second Temple menorah, based upon this very significant First Temple paradigm.

The path picks up again, after half a millennium of silence, during the High Middle Ages, with Benjamin of Tudela, a Jewish traveler and chronicler during second half of the twelfth century.[6] Benjamin describes the holy vessels of the Temple in Rome in his eleventh-century travelogue (and he also, incidentally, describes the lost tribes). He suggests that medieval Romans had a tradition that the Temple vessels were in Christian hands:

> In the church of St. John in the Lateran there are two copper columns that were in the Temple, the handiwork of King Solomon, peace be upon him. Upon each column is inscribed "Solomon son of David." The Jews of Rome said that each year on the Ninth of Av they found moisture running down them like water. There also is the cave where Titus the son of Vespasian hid away the Temple vessels which he brought from Jerusalem.

Benjamin was not alone in believing that the vessels were in the Basilica of St. John of the Lateran, the papal residence for much of the medieval period. Churchmen too asserted that the Ark and the menorah were eventually stored in the pope's chapel, the "Sanctum Sanctorum," the "Holy of Holies," and in other locales within the Lateran. Marie Thérèse Champagne has suggested that the development of this legend during the twelfth century was part of a larger struggle between Popes Eugenius III (1145–1153) and Alexander III (1159–1181) and the Roman Commune and Holy Roman Emperor Frederick I Barbarossa, in which they "publicly promoted the Church's inheritance of biblical Judaism in the claim that the Treasures of the Temple of Herod existed in the Lateran basilica." The legend appears already during the eleventh century in the *Descriptio Lateranensis Ecclesiae,* dated circa 1073, which locates the Temple relics under the high altar of the Lateran, asserting the connection between the Old and the New Testament relics:

> And so, in this most holy basilica of the Lateran Savior, which is consecrated by God for Jesus Christ, the head of the world, of the patriarchate and the imperium, of the pontifical seat of the apostolic cathedral, the ark of the law of the Lord is in the altar of his same principal Church, or, as they affirm, the ark is below, and according to the upper altar measurement of length, breadth, and height, the ark is concealed, between four columns of red porphyry, underneath a rich ciborium. In which in fact, the reliquary is immense, but they do not understand what it is, for they do not know its fame. Truly, it is in the altar, above which is wooden with a silver covering, and in the lower part below it, is the following relic: the seven lampstands, which were in the first Tabernacle. . . . also the clothes of purple of the same Savior and Redeemer; two ampules of blood and water from the side of the Lord. And the circumcision of the lord. . . . Today this same history is clearly understood in the triumphal arch, which is called the Arch of the Seven Lamps, which is shown to have been built next to the Church of S. Maria Nova, in memory of the predictions and the origin of all the Roman people, on which are the candelabra and the ark with its sticks, which were in the first tabernacle, and which have been in the next Temple within the altar cloth, and were understood by the evidence to have been fashioned with marvelous care.[7]

The *Mirabilia Urbis Romae,* "The Marvels of the City of Rome," a well-known guide to pilgrims written by a canon of St. Peter's Basilica named Benedict (ca. 1040), emphatically restated this point:

> During the days of Pope Silvester, Constantine Augustus built the Lateran Basilica, which he adorned beautifully. He put there the Ark of the Covenant, which Titus had carried from Jerusalem with many thousands of Jews, and the Golden Candlestick of Seven Lamps with vessels for oil. In the Ark are these things: the golden emeralds, the mice of gold, the Tablets of the Covenant, the rod of Aaron, manna, the barley loaves, the golden urn, the coat without seam, the reed and garment of Saint John the Baptist, and the tongs that Saint John the Evangelist was shorn with.[8]

A late antique box containing soil from each of the holy places of Jesus in the Holy Land was kept in the Sanctum Sanctorum until fairly recently.

Benedict clearly associated the "ark" of the Lateran with the Arch of Titus relief: "in the Circus the Arch of Titus and Vespasian . . . at Santa Maria Nova between the Greater Palace and the Temple of Romulus, the Arch of the Seven lamps of Titus and Vespasian where is found Moses' candlestick with seven branches with the Ark, at the foot of the Cartulary Tower."[9]

Similarly, a Cistercian monk described the relics of the Lateran in 1145, placing them in the Sanctum Sanctorum. Describing the Jewish War, Nicolaus Maniacutius writes that

> At that time, the ark and tablets, the candelabrum and trumpets, and other vessels of the Temple had been carried away to Rome, or at least those vessels that are read about in the Second book of Maccabees or those that had been concealed in another way by the patriarchs following the restoration of the Temple, and which obviously appear on the triumphal arch which was erected for the divine Titus, by the son of the divine Vespasian, by the Senate and People of Rome.
>
> Indeed, all that is sacred, which was carried off from Jerusalem, was contained in the sacred altar of the Lateran, where this image of the Savior was preserved for a long time, until it inspired the high priest of the Lord, so that he removed it to the Palace, and indeed placed it with honor above the most holy altar of the basilica of Blessed Lawrence, which is in the Sancta Sanctorum. At that time, the ark and tablets, the candelabrum and trumpets, and other vessels of the Temple had been carried away to Rome, or at least those vessels that are read about in the Second Book of Maccabees or those that had been concealed in another way by the patriarchs following the restoration of the Temple, and which obviously appear on the triumphal arch which was erected for the divine Titus, by the son of the divine Vespasian, by the Senate and People of Rome.[10]

The square object at the head of the procession on the Arch of Titus relief—the showbread table—was identified as the Ark of the Covenant. The arch panel was interpreted explicitly as representing the transfer of the most significant Old Testament artifacts from Jerusalem to Rome by God's agent Titus and on to papal control, setting the stage for papal ritual at the arch—particularly in the early modern period. Belief in the presence of the menorah was dispelled already in 1308, when, as the result of a fire at the Lateran, contents of the high altar were cataloged, and no lampstand was found. The Ark, however, was identified and placed in the sacristy of the Lateran until 1647, when it was placed on display in the ambulatory of the apse of the Lateran—where it remained until 1745—when it must have become obviously incorrect, and perhaps embarrassing, to identify this object as the Ark of the Covenant.[11] At that point, it was removed from display. I have not yet found out where this ark is today, or whether it was lost.

It is very easy to dismiss this kind of speculation out of hand as projection or pious fantasy. Much of it is. On occasion, however, a source appears that is hard to dismiss. Just as Renaissance and modern scholars occasionally discover artifacts mentioned in ancient texts, Jewish artifacts from antiquity did occasionally come to light. Scrolls uncovered in the Judean Desert during the eighth century were likely from the first. They were the original "Dead Sea Scrolls." Similarly, Josephus describes a Torah scroll among the booty of the Temple. He writes that the scroll was deposited in Vespasian's palace. This tidbit finds an intriguing parallel in a tradition preserved in an eleventh-century midrashic collection called *Bereshit Rabbati.*[12] According to this book, a scroll from the Temple was brought from Jerusalem and eventually deposited in a Rome synagogue: "This is one of the words which were written in the scroll that was captured in Jerusalem and was brought to Rome and was stored in the synagogue of Severos." The description of this scroll as using what later came to be called the medial *mem* and the final *mem* indiscriminately fits well with first-century Jerusalemite orthographic practice, as scholars have long noted. There is thus good reason to believe that an early Torah scroll survived antiquity in Rome, one of the rare (though not unique) manuscripts in numerous languages to survive before ultimately being lost.

Similarly complex is the case of the Copper Scroll, a Hebrew document engraved on copper sheeting that was discovered in 1952 among the Dead Sea Scrolls in "cave 3" at Khirbet Qumran. The text is essentially a list of hiding places for a vast quantity of treasure. The first interpreter of this text, John Allegro, was convinced that he had found a treasure map that would lead to the riches of the Jerusalem Temple, hidden at the time of the Roman sack of Jerusalem by Temple authorities. It makes no reference to the Temple vessels—neither the menorah nor the showbread table nor any of the other Temple objects. Allegro even enlisted King Hussein of Jordan, who in 1963 funded an excavation in search of the treasures in Jerusalem's Kidron Valley. Nothing was found. The Copper Scroll has been the subject of numerous novels that have caught the popular imagination, and in 2004 a Public Television documentary followed a search carried out by an American scholar in the Judean Desert, he too using the Copper Scroll as his guide. Responsibly, this film problematizes this (unsuccessful) search, turning the documentary format into a study in academic process. The jury is still out regarding the Copper Scroll, making speculation about it all the more alluring.

Among the most earnest articles describing Jewish participation in the search for Temple artifacts was penned by J. D. Eisenstein (1854–1956), a prominent Jewish intellectual and prolific author and publisher. Living in New York, Eisenstein was a bridge between the Eastern European Judaism of his youth, American culture, nascent Zionism, and even early Israel. He was the editor of the first Jewish encyclopedia ever, the *Otsar Yisrael,* and of numerous influential anthologies of classical Jewish sources (one of which included the "Tractate of the Vessels"). In 1901 he penned an essay in a prominent American Jewish journal, coincidentally called *The Menorah.*[13] His long forgotten piece, called "The Fate of the Temple Vessels," takes recent discoveries from his time most seriously. In the article he collects rabbinic sources that refer to the whereabouts of the Temple vessels from the beginning of the Babylonian Exile in 586 BCE through Procopius in the sixth century CE. Eisenstein opens his essay with the assertion that descriptions of these vessels "should be studied by archaeologists in order to identify them in the event that they are discovered." It turns out that Eisenstein had a specific example in mind—an incense shovel—one that we now know is typical of the Roman period. The shovel "was found with two others of nearly the same pattern in the excavations south of Mount Moriah in Jerusalem." He relates that unknown "experts have pronounced it the 'Machteh' of the Bible, and one of the Temple vessels." Eisenstein believed that he had identified an artifact from the Temple—he does not mention which Temple, though, and he tended—like so many explorers—to conflate the two.

Eisenstein was a minor player in this search. One of the most flamboyant expeditions was reported in the *New York Times* on May 1, 1911. The headline reads: "Have Englishmen Found the Ark of the Covenant? A Mysterious Expedition, Apparently Not Composed of Archaeologists, Hunts Strange Treasure under the Mosque of Omar, Sets the Moslems in Ferment, and May Cause Diplomatic Incident." The accompanying article is illustrated with a nineteenth-century model of the Ark of the Covenant and describes the exploits of a British team led by Montagu Brownlow Parker. This search also resulted in failure, but what is most interesting is the obsession behind it. Obsession with discovery of biblical antiquities continues to fuel our culture, whether we are speaking of American Christian fringe elements who continue to crawl the Judean Desert in search of the Temple treasures or modern academics who are all too susceptible to accepting fakes as real because they bespeak (or better, undermine) biblical certitudes.

Moderns were (and are) no less lured by the search for Temple vessels than their ancient and medieval counterparts. In fact, I would suggest the opposite to be the case. Where ancients imagined and projected their hopes for the restoration of the Temple vessels and thus their national aspirations, moderns set out to discover and to reconstruct and own them. This search was but a part of a larger period of exploration throughout the Mediterranean basin, the Near East, and beyond by scholars in search of treasure and biblical authenticity—a search for the roots of modern culture in classical civilization and for objects that could assert (or unseat) biblical truth through excavation. Charles Warren's explorations of the underground reservoirs of the Jerusalem Temple Mount had the patina of modern science. In truth, he was on a search for the vessels of the Solomonic Temple—which biblical and rabbinic sources claim were buried there. A passion for exploration and discovery of lost relics—particularly those with biblical significance—was thus broad and deep in the Western culture of this period. On quite a few occasions, such yearnings were well satisfied, as when British archaeologists uncovered the reliefs documenting Sennacherib's destruction of the biblical city of Lachish in 701, graphically corroborating the biblical accounts of the exile of the people of Lachish, together with the ten tribes. Searches for the Ark of the Covenant and other biblical relics continued to draw.

The Menorah in the Tiber

Another permutation of the menorah myth is particular to Rome, and is of a piece with this age of biblical discoveries. According to this myth, the menorah never left Rome. It has been sitting in the silt of the Tiber River, both present and not present. A significant context for the myth of the menorah in the Tiber was the conquest of Rome by Italian Republican forces in 1870, a moment of jubilation for the Jews of the Eternal City. Their final emancipation finally ensured, Jews soon began to spread beyond the confines of the cramped and unhealthy boundaries of the Ghetto, belatedly joining other Italian Jewries, and all Western communities, in the joys of citizenship. The tiny area of the Ghetto where they had built tenements upward only to survive, was cleared for new construction. A magnificent new synagogue, with a tall dome that—much to the consternation of the Church—could be seen across Rome (and particularly from the Vatican), was built of luxurious materials, the gables of its entranceways topped with menorahs modeled loosely on those of the arch. Israel had truly risen and taken back "its" menorah, and at the heart of Rome. Inside, the high walls were painted in brilliant neo-Arabesque designs, and rows of brightly polished bronze seven-branched menorahs—their branches (though, pointedly, not their bases) modeled on the arch menorah—illuminated the hall. Roman Jewry had made it, or at least the Jews projected themselves as the exuberant victors in the war for emancipation. Their shrine—which coincidentally stands halfway between the arch and Saint Peter's Basilica—and their menorahs reaching upward.

During this time of reconstruction, a large reddish limestone ashlar, triangular in shape, seems to have been buried in the soil of the Ghetto—someone clearly hoping that it would have been found during the construction project. This object was discovered in 1994 during renewed construction at the site and reflects a fascinating moment in the history of the menorah. The image of a large and rather typical menorah, resting on a square, classicizing base, appears on the face of the ashlar. Above and to each side of the menorah is some sort of rounded object, perhaps a helmet, though I am not sure. To the right is a hatchet, to the left a horn or a club. Below are two rampant lions. The iconography of this object is reminiscent of imagery that was common to Jewish art in Italy and across Europe in the modern period, though the objects that I have called "helmets" are very strange. More important, though, is the information preserved on reverse of this stele. At its peak are pictured two tablets of the law, with rounded tops, clearly markers of Jewish identity from the early modern period and on, but not earlier, though round topped tablets do appear in medieval Hebrew manuscripts. What is special about this stone, however, is its dual-language inscription. There we read in Latin and in Hebrew: "Here lie the three brothers of Jewish faith, Natanel, Amnon and Eliau, who found the relics of Jerusalem, the candelabrum and the ark, in the

Tiber, where they still are, three hundred seventy-five steps under the island, in correspondence with the promontory of the Palatine, they were beheaded by public axe under Emperor Honorius."[14] The names of the brothers, all biblical, do not mention their father (which is odd for a Jewish inscription—whether in late antiquity or in later periods). They are written in a rather unsure Hebrew script—a script transcribed by a stonecutter who was far less secure in Hebrew that he was in the (still none too professional) Latin. This inscription explains, it seems, the three helmets—each one representing one of the brothers. Perhaps the axe represents their method of execution. It is likely that this composition draws loosely from Jewish gold glasses found in the Roman catacombs well known from nineteenth-century publications, which include the menorah, lions, Torah scrolls that look like staffs, and other paraphernalia not so different formally from those on our stele. According to the inscription, the Jewish brothers found both the menorah and the Ark. The mention of the Ark, however, points to a Christian source, as Christians often spoke of the "Ark" in the Arch of Titus relief, and Jews had no such tradition.

Who planted this "relic" in the synagogue compound, we will never know. The notion that the menorah was dropped into the Tiber "under Honorius," the western Roman Emperor from 395 to 423, is an attempt to both place our stone at the time of the sack of Rome on August 24, 410, by the Visigoths led by Alaric and to add an element of Jewish martyrology to the story. These Jews, we are told, died for the Temple relics. Belief that the menorah was buried in the sludge of the then rather wild Tiber River was common in the nineteenth century. Some believed that it was dropped from the Milvian Bridge by Constantine in the great battle where he saw his vision of the cross—a symbol of the Christian triumph. Others, going back at least to the eighteenth century, believed that it was dropped there by the Visigoths during their sack of the city. Daniela Di Castro has speculated that a company formed in Rome in 1818, the Manifesto of Association for the Privileged Excavation in the Tiber, intended to search for the menorah. Similarly, Jessica Dello Russo reminds us that Prince Alessandro Torlonia "had considered draining the Tiber in order to retrieve ancient objects said to have been thrown into its depths during the fifth century CE invasions of Rome. Most famous among these rumored treasures is the candelabrum with seven branches taken from the Jerusalem Temple by the Roman emperor Vespasian in 70 CE. Roman Jews, for their part, very much hoped such a project would take place following the unification of Italy in 1870."[15] On April 1, 1873, three years after unification, Rabbi F. Servi wrote in an Italian journal of Jewish education in support of Jewish participation in this project:

> And who knows if some of the lost objects of the Temple of Jerusalem conquered by Titus will be found? Raids of the barbarians—wars, conflagrations, looting, and all the events experienced by that great city—are so numerous that it would not be surprising if in the bed of the Tiber some shattered statues might be found—even here some of the mementos of the Jewish War might be discovered. We mention this because we know from the stories that the vessels of the Temple were taken by Genseric King of the Vandals during the sacking of Rome, brought with him to Africa. There they remained 70 years; then Belisarius the general of the Emperor Justinian, defeated the Vandals in Africa, and after the spoiling, also took the sacred vases and brought them with him to Constantinople. But they did not remain long in Constantinople. It is a mystery where they are now. The work to be done in the Tiber may provide some evidence on this topic. We hope that the Jews of Rome will work a little more diligently on behalf of causes that are really Jewish.[16]

This notion that the menorah is in the Tiber is well represented in nineteenth-century English-language publications. A decade before Servi's essay, American Nathaniel Hawthorne wrote in his 1860 novel, the *Marble Faun,* of his party of travelers: "treading over the broad flagstones of the old Roman pavement, passed through the Arch of Titus. The moon shone brightly enough within it to show the seven-branched Jewish candlestick, cut in the marble of the interior. The original of that awful trophy lies buried, at the moment, in the yellow mud of the Tiber, and, could its gold of Ophir again be brought to light, it would be the most precious relic of past ages, in the estimation of both Jew and Gentile."[17] Objects of historical value are indeed regularly recovered from the Tiber—and other artifacts of great value are routinely discovered. Why not the Temple relics? *Israel: The Jewish Magazine* of 1900, the same issue that contained Moses Gaster's Arch of Titus story, raised the possibility quite explicitly in a short news report:

> The workmen engaged in laying the foundations of the new Ponte Cavour across the Tiber [a bridge next to Augustus's tomb, the Ara Pacis, and to the north of the Jewish ghetto, built 1896–1901] have just made a most interesting discovery, a splendidly preserved candelabrum having been extracted from the muddy bed of the river. It is of bronze, and curiously enough resembles the famous seven-branched candelabrum of the Jews, which Titus brought to Rome in triumph, after destroying the Temple of Jerusalem, and a faithful reproduction of which, in bas relief, may be seen on the Arch of Titus, near the Forum. That this candelabrum was thrown into the Tiber, after having figured in the Emperor's triumphal progress along the Via Sacra to the Capitol, is a matter of history. There have been odder coincidences than the candelabrum just discovered in one "Eternal City" should be an authentic relic of the building round which centered the other city destined also to eternity.[18]

I have not found another published mention of this "splendidly preserved candelabrum," so it is hard to know what was discovered, except that it looked something like the arch menorah in bronze. The excited response that it evoked in *Israel: The Jewish Magazine* reflects the tone of the period, when major discoveries, even some of biblical proportions, were somewhat routine. It was only a year later, in 1901, that Eisenstein declared the discovery of the Temple shovel in a very similar magazine oriented toward an American Jewish readership—and these are only minor examples when compared with the great excavations underway throughout the Near East and the Mediterranean world. The stele of the three brothers, then, is an artifact of the nineteenth or early twentieth century, an attempt to provoke a search for the menorah and the Ark in the Tiber. It was simply discovered too late to provoke real interest in the search. To this day, many elderly Roman Jews believe that the menorah is in the river to be found. The presence of the menorah in the Tiber, assumed by at least some Jews and Christians, lent greater depth to the Jewish presence in the city. The menorah, as it were, could not only be seen in the catacombs, in paintings in the Vatican, on the arch, and illuminating the synagogues of Rome even before the emancipation, but was eternally present in the Eternal City. It was in the mud of the Tiber that often flooded the Ghetto—nearby, yet unseen, awaiting redemption.

The Lost Menorah in Modern Fiction

Stories of the menorah searches, like searches for the Ark of the Covenant, the priestly breastplate, and the Holy Grail, are the stuff of modern novels—a genre described by historian of religion Mircea Eliade as the modern "sacred literature."[19] We have already noted some early cases, mentioning Arthur Conan Doyle's "The Jew's Breastplate" (1899), Stefan Zweig's *The Buried Candelabrum* (1937), and Robert Graves's *Count Belisarius* (1938), and shown through Zweig and Graves some of the ways that the art of the novel and academic scholarship have converged around the Temple artifacts. Zweig's *The Buried Candelabrum* tells the story of the menorah—and of Jewish exile—through the legends of Procopius. In a typical Zweigian turnabout, however, Justinian never returns the *real* menorah to Jerusalem, at least not to Christian Jerusalem. Zweig imagines that a Jewish goldsmith had fooled Justinian, replacing the menorah that he intended to send to Jerusalem with a reproduction. Jews spirited the "real" menorah back to the Land of Israel, where it was buried on the road from Jaffa to Jerusalem. Zweig, who had a long association with the founders of Zionism, concluded this Nazi-era Zionist novella by equating his buried lampstand with "its people, who still know no peace in their wanderings through the lands of the Gentiles"—an ample metaphor for Zweig's personal and national exile from Vienna to London, New York, and ultimately Brazil, the site of his suicide. Zweig's story concludes, as we have seen, with the well-worn hope that at some point, "someone will dig the menorah on that day when the Jews come once more into their own, and that then the Seven-Branched Lampstand will diffuse its gentle light in the Temple of Peace."[20] Zweig was well aware, of course, that the menorah had been removed from Vespasian's Temple of Peace when he somewhat ambiguously referred to the Jerusalem Temple, using the same term. I wonder if this double entendre is a piece of his own cultural ambivalence. When his work and his cosmopolitan identity were rejected by the Third Reich, he—like many Jews—reexamined his Jewish identity. Zweig's premise, that the menorah was buried and awaiting discovery—is strikingly close to that expressed (as discussed in Chapter 2) by Hans Yohanan Lewy—who, as a leading historian, might have known better. The line between story and history here is very frail indeed.

Ma'aseh ha-Menorah, "The Tale of the Menorah," by Shmuel Yosef Agnon (d. 1970) and published in 1957, shares much with Zweig's earlier novella.[21] Agnon exemplifies his almost unique ability to bring together traditional themes and sources within an almost clandestine modernist idiom. The title plays on Numbers 8:4, "And this was the making [*ma'aseh*] of the lampstand," and is indeed about both a particular lampstand and the "making" of the modern Jewish menorah. It focuses upon a large brass lampstand in the synagogue of his fabled hometown of Buczacz in Galicia—today divided by Poland and Ukraine. As the story goes, a large seven-branched menorah was given to the synagogue by the local king, a gift to a typical "court Jew" and communal leader. The gift represented what the king believed was fitting for Judaism and represents for Agnon the space between Jewish self-understanding and the ways that the dominant society understands, and influences, Jews. Agnon was well aware that seven-branched menorahs were not traditional synagogue implements, and was certainly aware that the use of seven-branched lampstands by modern Jews is anything but traditional. Accepting the gift nonetheless, the Jews removed the central branch, so as not to violate Talmudic strictures—and to maintain their own scruples and agency. This branch was lost during the well-known Chelminski massacres (1648/1649) and recovered from the local river years later. In the meantime, a large "white" eagle, the Polish national symbol, was set in place of the missing central stalk as a sign of Polish patriotism. With the Austrian conquest of Buczacz (1772), the Polish eagle was replaced—on order of Austrian army officers—with an Austrian two-headed eagle. This process repeated itself as Poland revolted, then Austrian rule restored, and then, after World War I, the Poles eventually took control again. Finally, the stalk is retrieved when a soldier, maimed in the trenches, returns to Buczacz, and digs it up from beneath the destroyed ruins of his own home, where he had buried it for safe keeping. Concerned that the Ukrainians might revolt, it is decided once again to remove the eagle! Agnon here draws his central icon from with the well-known large brass eight-branched Hanukkah menorahs from early modern Poland that were set to the side of the Torah ark. Upon the central stems of these lampstands—which often survived World War II only to be placed in museums—was the single, often removable, single-headed and double-headed eagle. The moral of the story, symbolized by the menorah and its transitory eagles, is that "One kingdom comes and another kingdom passes away. But Israel remains forever." Agnon's menorah, in all of its cultural complexity, is a metaphor for the Jewish people. Reminiscent of Zweig's *The Hidden Candelabrum,* with its romantic use of a hidden lampstand and its restoration as a symbol for Jewish hope—a story that the well-read Agnon, who corresponded with Zweig by mail, certainly knew. "The Tale of the Menorah" focuses this assertively "eternal" theme through a known early modern menorah type. While Zweig's menorah is somewhat static in its eternality, Agnon's is transforming and adapting. Agnon's menorah is set in a near-distant frame that connects antiquity with the modern Zionist/Israeli seven-branched menorah, even as it reflects real knowledge of the life—and travails—of a living religious and national community. It is not surprising, then, that in describing a brass, branched menorah topped by an eagle, the Israel Museum website immediately connects this lamp with Agnon's tale, now an important part of the Israeli literary canon.[22]

Novels that focus upon the discovery of the menorah in Rome are now a staple of modern pulp fiction. Every year or two another seems to appear, each one involving an academic searcher, criminals, and a love interest. The Vatican and the Israeli security services are involved in some, the chalice myth and the Crusaders in others. Peter Levi's *The Head of the Soup* (1979) is an early example of this genre. Levi's volume imagines the menorah for sale and concludes with its dumping (actually, the dumping of a close facsimile) into a crag at the bottom of the sea off the coast of Greece. As Levi's Israeli character explains it: "Have you thought of the pressure there would be, inside Israel, and from Jews all over the world, for us to buy it? And then what? Are we going to rebuild the Temple? There is a mosque there now. It is a distinguished ancient monument of great beauty. We have one wall to weep at. But what would the pressure be?"[23] With Zweig, the sense that a fake menorah is actually in play is raised, but in Levi's account, the protagonist argues that the authenticity of the lampstand is not the essential point: "Whatever we say, not everyone is going to believe it was faked. If someone sees it, in Israel, will he not talk about this great treasure? At this moment we are back in a position to be blackmailed. Think if someone thought it was genuine and we were breaking it up."[24] This sense that the world is better off without the menorah—even a fake one—is basic to Levi's plot. The novel ends with yet another hidden menorah: "Somewhere under the Mediterranean, a long way down underneath them, wreathed in the remnants of its sacking, was a passable imitation of the treasure of the Temple of God, scattered in a deep crag of the sea-floor."[25]

More recent examples, which appeared on the coattails of *The Da Vinci Code* (2003), include David Gibbins's *Crusader Gold* (2007), Daniel Epstein's *The Last Ember* (2009), Shifra Hochberg's *Lost Catacomb* (2014), and now Marcia Fine's *Paris Lamb* (2015). The promotional blurb for this last mentioned volume gives a sense of the contours of this professor thriller, and, as the author indicates, it is highly dependent upon Kingsley's *God's Gold*:

> The suspicious death of an esteemed professor thrusts biblical archaeologist, Michael Saunders, to the forefront of a rare antiquities auction. Coupled with an academic meeting in New York, he is beckoned from a Paris vacation to authenticate the priceless artifacts known as God's Gold. The objects, a candelabrum, silver trumpets and a sacrificial table, from Solomon's Temple in Jerusalem have traveled through the hands of barbarians and Vandals, to find their way into the Vatican for safe-keeping. Released onto the open market, world powers vie for the treasures. Impulsively, Michael returns with his Paris lamb to encounter the opposition. Michael's stance that the objects are authentic sparks confrontations with other archaeologists as well as a sinister cabal of Chinese investors. In defense of his research, his anger compounds what he feels about a revealed family secret. At the auction his life changes forever. A robust, satisfying read with a captivating love story that journeys from Paris to the Ivy League, New York, Miami and beyond.[26]

The situation is similar in video media. The best of the video documentaries about the menorah was a Canadian series produced by British-Israeli filmmaker Alan Rosenthal called *Mysteries of Jerusalem*. After a general introduction to the nature of biblical loss, the first documentary, *The Hunt for the Treasures of God* (1996), focuses upon three aspects of the "hunt": the Templars in France made popular in pulp fiction, the menorah at the Vatican, and the menorah in Jerusalem (mainly at the Nea Church, but also pursuing claims that the menorah is in a tunnel somewhere under the Temple Mount). The film describes each of these approaches, complete with the requisite academic "talking heads"—mostly archaeologists—presenting each as plausible, based upon its own internal logic. One is given the sense that each of these accounts of the whereabouts of lost treasure is potentially "true," and the overriding sense is that the narrative as a whole is trustworthy. In fact, the film covers much of the material discussed in this chapter and some in the next. The genre—carried out by filmmakers who are highly competent but are not scholars of antiquity, requires a level of sensation. Rosenthal leaves each of the storylines essentially intact, without the complex academic "teaching moment" that might have created doubt in the minds of the viewers, but that in this volume I have the leisure to pursue. Rosenthal wrote a memoir of his own process, which involved reading the novels, the pseudo-scholarship, and the myths, some of which he describes as "crazy," and others that he considers more "serious."[27] As he himself writes, "Soon after starting the research, I realized I had stumbled on a growth industry, particularly on the literary scene. History mysteries were all the rage, and if you wanted to make a million you simply dug up some incredible theory, wrote ninety thousand words, and foisted your slender hypothesis onto an avid, thirsty, naive public."[28]

The lines between scholarship and this kind of popular imagining are far narrower than most scholars would prefer. Understanding this, we can sometimes contextualize the kinds of larger popular trends that have influenced both writers of a scholarly bent and those writing and producing for broader audiences, and that are breaking down the barriers that are sometimes thought to separate them. The existence of footnotes does not a scholarly book make, and scholarly apparatus does not insulate academic life from a herd mentality. The balance is complex indeed. From the very earliest literature of the Second Temple period to the most recent novel, television special, and seasonal media event surrounding a "revolutionary discovery," then, the search for Temple vessels, and particularly the menorah, has grasped our collective imagination. Like the Holy Grail of Christ, these objects emerge changed, yet with lingering sameness from generation to generation. Over the last century or so, no single artifact has fascinated Jews more than the menorah, while Christians often focus on the Ark of the Covenant, the Holy Grail, or the Shroud of Turin. The menorah, the preeminent symbol of Judaism turned symbol of an old-new Jewish modernity, enlightenment, and, ultimately, the Jewish state, continues to inspire the imagination and the desire for physical contact with biblical reality.

6

The Menorah at the Vatican

Few Jews today will tell you that the menorah is in the Tiber. This is, more or less, a local legend—even many young Jews in Rome may not know of it. For contemporary Jews, however, belief that the menorah is hidden in some subbasement of the Vatican is widespread—across denominations and geographical location. This is astonishing, since there are few hints of this belief preserved in Jewish folklore of earlier periods. No reference to this myth appears in the broad selection of historical Jewish newspapers available via the Tel Aviv University/National Library of Israel database, even though the Arch of Titus and particularly the menorah are often discussed. Similarly, no trace of these musings has been found in the vast resources of the Israel Folklore Archive at Haifa University, until most recent times. This myth did not appear in scholarly literature of the 1950s or 1960s, where other myths of the menorah are discussed, nor in popular literature before the recent spate of writings—even when it might have enhanced the story.

Still, the notion seems to have been deeply ingrained in the modernizing twentieth-century Jewish culture of Eastern Europe, particularly among Hasidim. It has struck roots in the United States and in Israel since World War II—particularly, though not exclusively, within traditionalizing Orthodox circles. Rabbinic sources, from the Talmud to Benjamin of Tudela, that placed the Second Temple vessels in Rome, were accepted at face value, as they still are by believers in the myth. As we have seen, even the rationalist Moses Mendelssohn entertained the possibility that the vessels were still in Rome, based upon claims of sightings that appeared in classical rabbinic literature—offering real credence to this position. He did not, however, suggest that they were in a particular place. Going one step further, these rabbinic sources are taken by many today to mean that the menorah and the other Temple vessels are "hidden" at the Vatican. Since they were in Rome in antiquity, and Jewish sources provide no indication that they have been removed, then where else could they be? This myth has spread as Jews have become increasingly aware of Jewish treasures, particularly books, in the Vatican Museum and libraries, and rabbinic scholars have gone there to pursue research. I begin this chapter with a fine example of a Jewish folk tradition that was created full cloth from a well-known detective story by Arthur Conan Doyle and move from there to discuss a series of unsuccessful visits by rabbis to Rome to see the vessels. Finally, I turn to the contemporary myth of the menorah at the Vatican, a story whose development may be traced from its origins until almost the present.

Among the most flamboyant of the recent versions of the myth of hidden Temple treasures in rabbinic circles is one associated with Rabbi Yehuda Yudl Rosenberg (d. 1935), a Polish Hasidic rabbi and the author of significant studies of Jewish law, translations of the Zohar from Aramaic into Hebrew, and a large group of sources that straddle the line between traditionalist hagiographic literature, rabbinic scholarship, forgery, and belles lettres. Rosenberg's pamphlet *Ḥoshen ha-Mishpat shel ha-Kohen ha-Gadol*, "The Priestly Breastplate of the High Priest," is a case in point. Published in Piotrków, Poland, in 1913, the fact that this book appeared in both Hebrew and in Yiddish points to Rosenberg's intention to reach a broad audience. This text addresses a lost Temple implement and is attributed to Rabbi Judah Loew ben Bezalel (d. 1609), known as the Maharal. It gives the overall impression of a very serious book of traditional scholarship. The title page even produces a schematic "drawing of the words and letters on the twelve stones of the breastplate that the Maharal of Prague saw, may the righteous one be remembered for a blessing." Shnayer Z. Leiman relates the gist of the story:

> Briefly told, the Maharal related how in 1590 he learned that the twelve precious stones of the Jewish High Priest's breastplate . . .—which had survived the destruction of the Second Temple and ultimately made its way to England—had been stolen from the Belmore Street Museum in London. The Maharal immediately left for London where, by posing as a wealthy collector of antiq-

> uities, he managed to make contact with a certain Captain Wilson, who was both a charlatan and a thief. Wilson had ingratiated himself with a former curator of the Belmore Street Museum, Professor Andreas. Through Andreas, an innocent victim of Wilson's intrigues, Wilson gained entry to the museum's inner vaults and succeeded in pirating away the twelve precious stones. The actual theft took place after a new curator had been appointed: Professor Edward Mortimer. After the Maharal and Wilson had settled on a rather steep purchase price, the Maharal sought and obtained a two-week reprieve, ostensibly in order to raise the agreed-upon exorbitant sum of money. In fact, the Maharal used the two-week period to wreak havoc with Wilson's personal life by means of a series of miraculous interventions into Wilson's daily routine. By the end of the two-week period, Wilson was a broken man who repented and was only too happy to rid himself of the precious stones at no cost to the Maharal. At the advice of the Maharal, Wilson confessed the crime to Andreas, handed him the precious stones, and requested that they be restored to the Belmore Street Museum in a manner that would not incriminate him (i.e., Wilson).[1]

In the end, Wilson converts to Judaism, and is the reputed ancestor to Woodrow Wilson, which accounts, in Rosenberg's estimation, to the president's supposed pro-Jewish stance. Rosenberg credits this account to a grandson of the Maharal, and he credits a fictitious scholarly discussion of the Temple vessels that accompanies it to a Rabbi Manoah Hendel of France. This fictitious sixteenth-century Hebrew book, he suggests, was discovered in a fictitious "Imperial Library" in Metz, by a noted archaeologist and curator of the (nonexistent) "Belmore Street Museum." This museum is something akin to the British Museum or the Victoria and Albert, and in Rosenberg's hands is an anachronistic projection of the modern museum and the field of archaeology back to the sixteenth century. Rosenberg's pamphlet, which is forty pages long, concludes with a letter that he assures his readers: "was written to me by the great sage, scholar of antiquities, pious Jew in the law of Israel and its faith, Mr. Y. Werner, from the capital city London," dated April 1, 1913. In fact, the author is Rosenberg himself, and the letter is an artful conclusion to this most clever and learned volume. I translate two particularly fascinating sections:

> Three times I have searched in the government library, located near the university, and I have found nothing new regarding the BREASTPLATE that is kept in the royal treasury. Even though Professor Eduard Martimer and the great author Conan Dqoil wrote about it. When I saw that your translation, which is from Russian language books, has many lacuna, I ordered that [the story] be translated for his honor as it appears in English language books.
>
> Regarding the curtain and the headpiece of the high priest. I can respond that they are not found in Britain, and only in the royal treasury in Italy are they located—but only pieces, and some are quite small. Small pieces of them are also [located] in the museum of the papists in the city of Rome.[2]

Here Rosenberg reveals that his book is based upon Arthur Conan Doyle's mystery "The Jew's Breastplate," published in 1899, and shortly thereafter in Russian and in Hebrew. The letter even traces those language shifts, arguing that the version of Doyle's story translated at the direction of "Mr. Werner" from English to Hebrew and reproduced by Rabbi Rosenberg is superior to any other translation available in Russian or Hebrew—that is, better than the original story. The names of "Eduard Martimer" and "Conan Dqoil" appear in Latin script in this Hebrew document. The author goes so far as to camouflage Doyle's name, "misprinting" it as "Dqoil." Such errors are the bane of traditionalist Hebrew and Yiddish publishing to this day, and so a clever literary device. "Professor Eduard Martimer" is a main character of Doyle's story. It is only in this letter, at the very end of the book, that Rosenberg tips his cards and tells his most perceptive—and often clandestinely worldly—readers that the volume is a parody of traditional hagiography and rabbinic scholarship.

The correspondence with "Mr. Werner," the trustworthy Westernized Jewish professor (pointedly not a rabbi), shows Rosenberg asserting his capacity to reach beyond his community into the broader Jewish "republic of letters" to a less pious though learned Jew. Werner points out to Rosenberg the locations of small remnants of Temple vessels, though only tidbits to be sure. The placement of these particular objects in Rome is based upon well-known rabbinic sources that we have seen. That some of these are in the "Papist museum" is new and fits the institutional focus of Rosenberg's story—with its interest in museums, libraries, and modern scholars. There is, I point out, no mention of the menorah—which is not said to have been seen by ancient Rabbis in Rome in the canonical rabbinic canon. *Sifre Zuta*—the only rabbinic source to place the menorah explicitly in Rome, was not a well-known book at this time, and certainly not in Polish yeshiva circles. An edition of this book appeared only in 1910, and that was a modern critical edition. My guess is that if the myth of the menorah at the Vatican were current, Rosenberg would have included it as well. On the other hand, his scholarly bent toward textual authenticity might have led him to distance himself from blatant unsubstantiated hearsay.

Rosenberg's spoof, witty as it is, went over the heads of most readers. This is certainly aided by the fact that Rosenberg was a well-known rabbinic leader and legalist, especially after he left Poland in 1913 for Canada, eventually settling in Montreal (1919) and becoming an exponent of a modernized Orthodoxy. Once in Canada, he wrote no more folk literature. The gravitas of Rosenberg's rabbinic life, particularly after settling in Montreal, colors our view of his far more playful—that is, rebellious—life as a young Polish rabbi who seemed to be a bit closed in by his rabbinic oeuvre as he negotiated his own process of modernization. Like so many of his generation, Rosenberg scandalously learned Russian in his youth, read detective stories, and was aware of trends in "secular" Jewish scholarship. Through his stories, Rosenberg wrote a new modernizing narrative for his community that was projected onto a stellar rabbinic figure—all under the cover of pious scholarship. Pseudepigraphy—that is, pious forgery, and claims of publishing unknown manuscripts—provided Rosenberg with a level of cover—even if in his "Mr. Werner" letter he "outed" himself to his most sophisticated and worldly readers.

With few exceptions, the fervently Orthodox *Haredi* community has taken the stories far more seriously. They are regularly repeated as factual—or at least reliably traditional—"stories of our sages." Rosenberg's pamphlet was reprinted in 1984 and is reprinted periodically in magazines directed to the *Haredi*, mainly Hasidic, Yiddish-speaking audience. It has been mounted on pious databases as an exemplar of authentic rabbinic scholarship. In fact, I was recently discussing this story with a Yeshiva University undergraduate student, Mordechai Friedman, who grew up in the Satmar Hasidic community in Montreal. At one point, Mordechai excitedly told me that as a fourth-grader his teacher had rewarded his students for good behavior by reading this story aloud in daily installments from the Yiddish version. The continued life of Rosenberg's story sets the tone for a whole genre of stories about rabbis and their searches for the menorah and other vessels, stories that both present fervently Orthodox rabbinic culture heroes successfully negotiating the modern world and explain to later generations the seeming worldliness of earlier generations of sages, on the claim that they were in fact carrying on the age-old—and "unchanging"—work of redemption. Rosenberg's story, then, is both a tale of modernization and, for some, a historical "fact."

Other stories followed and continue to develop. They are related to a larger Hasidic interest in their holy leader, the Rebbe, and with objects associated with the saints and pilgrimage to their courts and tombs. The setting for many of the rabbinic travel stories is the reality that rabbis, particularly rabbinic leaders, made ample use of recently developed train and shipping lines to travel far beyond their usual environs—sometimes for medical care, for psychoanalysis, sometimes to enjoy distant hot spring baths, on pilgrimage, and occasionally for purposes of scholarly research, study, or even curiosity. This newfound mobility became the stuff of legend, even as rabbinic visits to Rome in search of the Temple vessels now were quite plausible. This is all the more true because Jewish scholars were now allowed to examine and copy Jewish manuscripts at the Vatican, occasionally making significant discoveries. Since priceless Jewish manuscripts are at the Vatican, the logic goes, why not the Temple vessels? More to the point, this genre provides a viable explanation to increasingly insular communities of the greater worldliness of earlier generations of fervently Orthodox leaders, who not only are said to have traveled great distances in search of the Temple vessels, but sometimes even engaged in modern methods of scholarship. At base these stories represent earnest attempts to rebalance in a world that they controlled less and less, to reclothe traditionalist Judaism in Western garb without losing a cultural "essence" by imagining and modeling ways to address cultural change.

The earliest story I have found of an Eastern European rabbi traveling to Rome in search of the vessels appears in the writings of Baruch Shneur Zalman Schneersohn (d. 1926). Schneersohn relates that on the Sabbath eve of February 12, 1915, Sholom Dovber Schneersohn, the fifth Rebbe of Chabad, told of his own visit to Rome in 1906 in search of the Temple vessels:

> He told of his experiences in the city of Rome. He [the rabbi] was there ostensively because he had heard that some vessels from the Temple were there. He came to Rome on the eve of the holy Sabbath

> and went on the Sabbath with his servant Abraham (Gorelik) from Bobruisk to the study house. This is because he had heard that the rabbi of the city frequented the study house, and he had been told that he [the city rabbi] could make this happen.
>
> However, since this the study house was a choir synagogue [*kor shul,* that is, a mega-synagogue with a choir and modernized liturgy] he did not want to go there. This is because it is strenuously forbidden to be in such a place, since it is built, unfortunately [*le-havdil*] like *their* houses of worship [that is Christian churches]—the prayer leader stands with long hair, unfortunately, like their priests in their houses of worship [churches]. None of the men are there to pray at all.[3]

This homily then expands on the prohibition of entering such a modernizing synagogue (which, incidentally, is often called a "cathedral synagogue" by contemporary architectural historians). Schneersohn relates that "even for the Temple vessels that he was after [*she-ratsah*] he took no action, since the rabbi was not in the study house [and the Rebbe was unwilling to enter the choir synagogue]. He had gone [to Rome] for no gain, a great distance." Even as it enlists notions of rabbinic travel as a context for this tale, this story is far less about Rome than about instructing followers how to respond to modernizing impulses within Eastern European Jewry. As the story goes, Sholom Dovber chose not to enter a modernist Orthodox synagogue—though he was willing to deal with a rabbi associated with the selfsame community. His commitment not to enter the synagogue was so great that he was willing to forfeit seeing even the Temple vessels. The Temple vessels are thus secondary to the story, which is intended to instruct the rabbi's followers not to enter a "choir synagogue." Whatever historicity lurks behind Schneersohn's story (and there was enough to make the tale believable), the real purpose of this homily was to warn against entering modern "temples." In Italy *tempio* is the term for synagogues, including modernized Orthodox edifices. Schneersohn set this boundary even at the expense of not finding the vessels of the Jerusalem Temple in Rome.

This ancillary use of the Temple vessels suggests that for the audience of this story, the presence of Temple vessels in Rome, and of rabbinic travel, was a given. One fascinating case is that of Gershon Henoch Leiner, the Rebbe of the Izhbitzer-Radziner Hasidic dynasty (originally from Poland, now in Israel). In 1887 and again in 1888 Leiner traveled to Naples to visit its then state-of-the-art saltwater aquarium. He was in search of the long-lost source of the biblical royal blue, *tekhelet,* the discovery of which would have messianic implications. Based upon his research, his followers began to wear the blue string on their ritual fringes, and still do. Alas, his "discovery" was apparently a hoax played upon Leiner, as the active agent of the dye he found was synthetic Prussian blue. While Leiner failed, his work was continued by Rabbi Isaac Halevy Herzog in his University of London dissertation (1913). The source of the dye was successfully discovered by archaeologists in modern Israel. The results have been adopted within messianic Zionist circles, whose members can often be seen wearing ritual fringes, *tsitsit,* dyed with the ink of *Hexaplex trunculus,* a type of sea snail—a modernizing restoration of a lost Jewish practice. Hasidic folklore has it that while in Italy, Leiner stopped off in Rome to examine garments of the High Priest and the priestly head plate (*tsits*) at the Vatican. More recently, the menorah has been added to this list.

Another story, this one from North Africa and Israel, began its life in a biography published in 1946 of a prominent Libyan rabbi, Yitzḥak Ḥaï Bokovza (d. 1930). According to this text, Rabbi Bokovza, then chief rabbi of Tripoli, hosted King Victor Emmanuel III in the central synagogue of the city during a royal visit to this Italian colony. Some months later, the rabbi received a telegram inviting him to the wedding of the king's son. In fact, the king did visit the synagogue in October 1929, and his son Umberto was married on January 8, 1930. The rabbi made the journey, and according to the biography, Victor Emmanuel invited him to a private meeting. The biography reports that "all of his [Rabbi Bokovza's] requests for his community were fulfilled." He returned to Tripoli ecstatic.[4] The author is clearly thrilled by this newfound attention from the king and its implications for his community. By the 1970s, the story had developed further:

> A short time after the wedding the rabbi went to say goodbye to the king, and to request his permission to return to his place [to Tripoli]. The king and his household received him with great honor. Toward the end, the king called him into a room, and asked him if perhaps he was lacking something. He [the rabbi] responded that he lacked nothing. The king offered him a raise in salary. The rabbi responded in the negative. The king asked, whether the community [needed anything] or whether his office [needed anything]? The rabbi responded that, thank God, nothing is lacking.

But the king was insistent that the rabbi request something. The rabbi responded that his only request is that he might visit the Vatican and see the vessels of the Temple. The king responded that this would be difficult for him, since he had no capacity to allow him to enter, since it was not in his jurisdiction, but rather was controlled by the pope.

The rabbi retracted [the idea]. The king was nonetheless adamant that the rabbi request something else, but the rabbi said that he had nothing to ask.

The rabbi left the king and his family, and prepared to return home, but the king would not rest and was not silenced. He contacted the Pope and told him that the rabbi, with whom he had met, wished to visit the Vatican but that he hadn't permitted this, since it was not his jurisdiction. The king explained that it hurt him greatly that he could not fulfill the rabbi's wish.

The Pope replied that he [the rabbi] may come [to the Vatican] at such and such a time, but he must come alone. The king immediately contacted the rabbi, and told him that it was all agreed with the Pope, and that he would show him the Temple vessels.

The day and time were set, and the honored rabbi went [to the Vatican], and was received graciously. He went down into the basement, to the place where the vessels are kept. When the servant was about to open the curtains [and show him the vessels] the rabbi told him that he has seen enough, and that he is not capable of seeing more. . . .

We do not know, and will not know, what the rabbi saw. He returned from there to the ship and from the ship to his house. In his house he went up to his bed, [where he stayed] for forty days after which he was summoned to the heavenly yeshiva. The secret was hidden with him. This is what I heard from Ben Zion Ḥayya, of blessed memory, the husband of his [the rabbi's] granddaughter Yehudit.[5]

This second story appears in a collection of reminiscences of the rabbi, attached to an anthology of Bokovza's well-respected legal responsa. Its authenticity rests on hearsay from the husband of Rabbi Bokovza's granddaughter. While this chain of transmission may add credence to the story within the community that reveres the rabbi's memory, for us it is useful as an outstanding example of the ways that folktales develop and integrate well-known themes. This version is far less connected to the original event reported in the biography. The teller(s) and their audience now live in Israel, far from Italian Libya, its colonial culture, and its natural attachment to Rome. This nostalgic story of a rabbi-hero is Israeli, and directed to Hebrew-speaking Israelis of Libyan Jewish decent and to a more general Sephardic rabbinic culture. The historical referents fade, as the trip to Rome and the piety/spiritual power of Rabbi Bokovza become all the more significant. If the rabbi was in Rome and had come so close to power, the logic goes, how could he not have asked to see the Temple vessels? Still, the sense of suspense with which the story concludes—with the death of the Rabbi Bokovza after presumably having seen more than he could bear—whatever that was, adds to the aura of the sage. The afterlife of this story is assured by an imprimatur to Rabbi Bokovza's collection of legal works that also appears in this volume by Rabbi Ovadiah Yosef (d. 2013), the leading Sephardic legal authority of his day.

The most recent permutations of the search for objects of the Second Temple in Rome relate specifically to the arch menorah, an artifact activated in the Jewish consciousness by Zionism and the State of Israel. These searches are deeply related to contemporaneous events and have little to do with the menorah itself. In this case, the germinating point of this menorah legend is the Second Vatican Council. I have heard other "evidence" of sightings. An American Sephardi Israeli was adamant in telling me that the great early modern rabbi and traveler Ḥayyim Joseph David Azulai (d. 1806), known as the *Ḥidah,* saw it (he did not). In 2000 an American resident in Jerusalem told me a version that bears a distinctly Anglo-Israeli flavor. According to this embellishment, the pope showed Chief Rabbi Isaac Halevi Herzog the golden menorah during a visit to the Vatican. Pius XII refused to return it. There is a kernel of historicity buried deep in this folktale. Rabbi Herzog indeed met with Pope Pius XII on March 10, 1946, at the Vatican in his effort to reclaim Jewish orphans in Europe. We have seen that he had a particular interest in the Arch of Titus menorah—particularly in the shape of its base. While in Rome, he—like so many Jewish leaders—made a pilgrimage to the arch and was photographed with the menorah. More recently, this association with Herzog has spread to popular literature.

The most significant and sustained story of menorah sighting at the Vatican surrounds Oscar Goodman of Queens, New York (d. 1997). My sense is that this oft-repeated story is the "source" for the modern myth of the menorah at the Vatican and so is of considerable significance. Happily, Goldman related the story of this visit on a number of occasions, and at least two recordings of his experience are extant. Oscar Goodman owned an electronics supply business and was active in his Modern Orthodox synagogue in Kew Garden Hills, Queens, New York. Goldman was born in Poland and spoke English with a thick Yiddish accent. Goldman relates that in 1962 he and his wife, Mitzi, were invited to the Vatican to meet Pope John XXIII, during the era of the Second Vatican Council. The invitation came as the result of a good deed toward a Catholic colleague, who arranged for the visit while the Goldmans vacationed in Rome. In fact, many Jews were welcomed to the Vatican during those years, as part of the rethinking of the relationship to the Jewish community inaugurated by the pope. Goldman was well aware that his visit related to a new openness, which he, like other members of his community found most astonishing and a bit transversive. In the recordings, Goldman ascribed the early death of the pope to an assassination by traditionalist elements in the Church. John was murdered, in Goldman's telling, for reaching out to the Jews, which included the sin of showing him the Temple relics. In reality, the pope died of stomach cancer. After meeting with the pope as part of a delegation, Goldman relates that he and his wife were escorted down a number of flights of stairs to a dark room with a heavy door. Joseph Frager, a New York physician and Orthodox activist, described Oscar's recollection in the *Jewish Press,* a New York Orthodox weekly, in 1994:

> Oscar remembers the room he was taken down to as though it happened yesterday. '"I'm sure what I saw," says Oscar. The room was poorly lit but Oscar remembers vividly seeing a number of artifacts including a gold Menorah which stood about three feet by three feet [one meter square] in a corner. There was no pedestal or tripod. He was impressed by the fact that it looked as though it could have been made out of one piece of pure gold. Its branches were curved. Its overall appearance was similar to the Menorah depicted on the Arch of Titus except for the fact that there was no base or pedestal. In addition to the Menorah, Oscar remembers seeing a wooden table about eight feet [2.4 meters] long, the "kiyor," and a number of blackened-with-age pans and pokers that could have been used in the Temple service.

> The visit only lasted a few minutes but Oscar has kept his memory burning. He was visited by a Polish Cardinal Wojeiech [*sic*, should be Wojciech] Adarniecki several years ago. The Polish Cardinal ostensibly was looking for a way the Polish people could make amends for their complicity in the Holocaust.
>
> Oscar just wants to see the artifacts he saw on that fateful day be returned to their rightful owners, the Jewish people.[6]

Goldman's recollection is somewhat different in the audio recording, where he describes the menorah resting on the table. The interview questioners are somewhat leading, excitedly asking Goldman questions that would give ever greater credence to his "testimony." Joseph Frager tells me, though, that in conversation Goldman was not completely certain that he had seen the Temple menorah, instead suggesting that it could have been a medieval one. In other words, because of his great desire to see the Jerusalem relics—to fit his unusual and at some level transverse vacation into known categories—the legend of the menorah at the Vatican took flight.

Frager relates how he brought this "evidence" to then-Knesset member (later prime minister) Ariel Sharon and to Vatican and U.S. Government officials. Perhaps the greatest popularizer of Goldman's sighting, however, was Moshe Yehuda Blau (d. 2003), a Chabad rabbi from Brooklyn. Blau was a person of broad connections in the Jewish world, and deep interests. The son of a Modern Orthodox rabbi—his father was trained in the Hildesheimer Rabbinical Seminary in Berlin—Blau was also a relative of Alexander Marx, the legendary librarian of the Jewish Theological Seminary of America in New York. Like many Modern Orthodox German Jewish youth of his generation, Blau gravitated toward the "authenticity" and seeming spirituality of Eastern European Jewry, studying at the Lithuanian Mir Yeshiva and going to "great lengths to receive the blessing of the Chofetz Chaim [Rabbi Israel Meir Kagan, d. 1933]," the leader of a fervently Orthodox Lithuanian yeshiva movement in prewar Poland. Fleeing to Shanghai during the Second World War, Blau eventually settled in Brooklyn and associated with the Chabad Hasidim. Blau is best known for his privately published editions of medieval rabbinic texts, beginning his studies with those in the charge of Marx as well as those in the collection of Yeshiva University. These relationships were clearly transverse within his Brooklyn yeshiva community—and have resulted in the shading of Blau's biography to fit more recent self-perceptions within fervently Orthodox culture. The *Chabadpedia* online biography of Blau never mentions the institution where Marx worked, but only that he, Blau's "cousin," had "procured a large library of medieval rabbinic texts [*rishonim*]."[7] It notes approvingly that, in consultation with Chabad leader Rabbi Menachem M. Schneerson, Blau declined a full-time position in the rare books collection at Yeshiva University—an institution whose Rabbi Isaac Elchanan Theological Seminary was still "Orthodox" and worthy of mention by name, but was too liberal for a full-throated association. The *Chabadpedia* explains that such a position would require his regular presence on campus—which was not acceptable to Blau's sense of Judaism.

Blau developed close relations with librarians at the Vatican, a fact that is unmentioned on *Chabadpedia.* A 2003 online biography discusses his connections there, though it is quick to note, "The family pointed out that Reb [rabbi] Moshe Yehuda never entered the Vatican library."[8] This point is verified by Blau's unpublished Hebrew memoirs, with no value judgment, but only mentions that "he had never traveled to Rome or to Italy."[9] Blau there recalls that his conduit to the Vatican was a Catholic priest/doctoral student whom he befriended in the rare book room at the Jewish Theological Seminary: "Once I was visiting in the library of the Seminary to examine manuscripts and sitting opposite me was a priest wearing a *kippah* [a skullcap], with a cross hanging around his neck. I was curious what a person of this sort was doing in the library, and I asked him what he was looking for." Blau goes on to explain how he helped this Spanish priest with his research on the medieval vocalization of Hebrew biblical manuscripts. As a result, he developed a long-distance relationship with the Vatican Library. The 2003 article, not surprisingly, erases the fact that this took place at JTS, and is far less friendly toward the priest than Blau's own writings are. Moshe Blau was clearly a man who traversed the usual boundaries for a fervently Orthodox rabbi, even a Chabad rabbi.

Blau traveled widely within North American Jewish communities to sell and gain economic support for his publication projects; speaking often in public fora—he even found his way to my own community in San Diego. A number of informants—widely dispersed across the United States—have told me that Blau described how he himself visited the Vatican and knew someone who saw the menorah, though I wonder if their memories are truncated. In his memoir, Blau describes Goodman's sighting and makes no claims about himself. He writes in a kind of legal idiom, which lends an air of sobriety to his presentation:

> Mr. Goldberg, who lives in Kew Garden Hills, gave testimony before me and before my son-in-law and before my family members that the room containing the menorah was opened before him and Rabbi Yitzchak Pinsky, of blessed memory, [that he] saw the curtain and the priestly headpiece and the table. And in truth, there are many headpieces stored in the Vatican and among them, I should note that they were like [*ke-middat*] those of the high priest, as Rashi interprets in the [Torah] portion of *Tsav* [Lev. 8:9]. Rabbi Eisenbach, who was born in the holy city [Jerusalem] and is a student of the Yeshiva of Telshe-Chicago testified before me that that when he made a sick call as a "youth" in a hospital in Chicago a Jewish electrician carried out his final confession before him close to [the man's] death. This is the story:
>
> A number of years ago the electricity in the Vatican went out, and they needed a tradesman to fix it. That Jew, [who was later in Chicago] went there, and as he walked in the basement, he came upon a childhood friend from the yeshiva of Holesov [Holleschau] in Moravia [Czechoslovakia]. He called out, "Chaim, what business do you have here?" This Chaim put his hand on his mouth, and signaled [that I should be] silent. Late in the night he brought him into a room in the depths of the basement, and revealed to him all of the hidden treasures there—volumes of the Talmud so heavy that they need two people to pick them up, [manuscripts] that had not been tampered with by the censors. When the electrician asked with wonder how Chaim had survived [the War], he admitted to him that when the edicts were announced by Hitler and his accomplice Mussolini to annihilate, kill and destroy all of the Jews [a reference to Esther 3:13], he apostatized and changed his religion. Since he had studied in yeshiva, and become expert in the Hebrew language and in Talmudic literature, he was appointed secretary of the library. Of course, before he would release him peaceably, [Chaim] warned his friend the tradesman not to tell anyone the things that he had seen with his own eyes, lest he be pursued by the "Mafia," which would kill the librarian and the tradesman. This is the story that Rabbi Eisenbach told.[10]

The folklore motifs inherent in this story are quite remarkable, if somewhat standard. Stories of Jews entering forbidden places late in the night, of hiding for protection among the gentiles during wartime, of craftsmen gaining secret knowledge, and of the threat of death for revealing the story are common fare in Jewish lore. The power of the story is enhanced by the fact that this is a deathbed confession (a very standard rabbinic literary motif) and thus cannot be verified even as it maintains an aura of veracity, all the more so because it is vouched for by a trusted rabbinic authority. In fact, many Jewish manuscripts, including Talmudic literature, are, of course, held in the Vatican, and Jewish scholars—including Blau—have had access to these since the nineteenth century. Microfilms of all of these are maintained at the National Library of Israel in Jerusalem, and many may now be viewed on the Vatican Library website.

Behind the entire episode, however, is the fact that prominent Jews did take refuge in the Vatican and other Catholic institutions during the Holocaust, some converting to Catholicism. First among these was Israel Zolli, chief rabbi of Rome, who abandoned his community and apostatized in 1945, teaching at the Sapienza University of Rome and the Pontifical Biblical Institute (Rabbi Prato, whom we discussed earlier, replaced Zolli after the War). Like Goodman's excursion to the Vatican in search of the menorah, this story of Jews crossing the *limes,* the boundary, separating Jews from Catholics on the shared territory of Hebrew books must have appealed greatly to Blau—who himself crossed boundaries in search of manuscripts, in promoting his project and in the publication of otherwise understudied volumes of rabbinic tradition from a broad range of libraries—including the Jewish Theological Seminary, Yeshiva University, and the Vatican.

In a similar way, a Satmar Hasid living in Israel, one Rabbi Yisroel Miller, reports that his father, a textile merchant from the Carpathian Mountains, had worked for the Hungarian army under the Nazi regime.[11] Rabbi Baruch Miller, we are told, had a "friend" who had held an Italian passport during the war. This man disguised himself as a gentile and went to the Vatican out of curiosity, hoping see the Temple vessels. As in the story told by Rabbi Blau, the wartime experience allowed the storyteller to posit the presence of a Jew in the Vatican—not the usual haunt for fervently Orthodox Jews. In a YouTube interview with Rabbi Yonatan Shtencel, whom we will soon see has recently engaged in his own menorah search, Rabbi Miller is quite sure that the friend, whose name he does not remember, but like his father, is dead, saw many authentic artifacts from the Second Temple—but not the menorah. The fact that a Satmar informant did not stress the menorah is not surprising. Satmar maintains a very ambivalent relationship with the national trappings of the State of Israel, and the menorah is the symbol for the State of Israel. A popular legend among Satmar

Hasidim tells of their leader, Rabbi Yoel Tannenbaum (d. 1979), visiting the Arch of Titus, but leaving quickly when he learned that the site had become central to Zionist ideology. In other words, while the Satmar community participates in the stories shared by many traditionalist Jews, their versions often reinforce distance from distinctly Zionist content.

The myth of the menorah at the Vatican is so pervasive even among liberal Jews that in 1979, it found its way into the catalog of the first major exhibition of Jewish manuscripts from the Vatican Libraries to be presented under Jewish auspices—itself a milestone. This is all the more astonishing because the exhibition was organized by the Union of American Hebrew Congregations, today called the Union for Reform Judaism. Father Leonard Boyle, former director of the Vatican Libraries, felt the need to address the myth directly. Father Boyle tells of Orthodox Jewish tourists from the United States entering the library during their touristic visits to the Vatican and, with all naiveté, telling Father Boyle that their rabbi teachers had instructed them to go find the menorah during their visits to the Vatican. In this way, the most holy pilgrimage complex in Western Christendom, and Rome's most popular museum, is turned into a Jewish pilgrimage site—or at least is made into a religiously palatable option for Jews uncomfortable with visiting Christian sites yet have no intention of missing the Vatican. On a recent visit to the late antique synagogue remains at Capernaum, a Christian pilgrimage site on the northern shore of the Sea of Galilee that is overseen by the Franciscans, I overheard an Israeli tour guide matter-of-factly explaining the image of a menorah on a synagogue frieze to Christian tourists/pilgrims: "the seven-branched menorah of the Temple is now, as everyone knows, stored in the basement of the Vatican."

All of this might amount to a kind of quaint Jewish urban myth, except that in 1996 the myth received international prominence. On January 18, 1996, Israeli minister of Religious Affairs Shimon Shetreet met with Pope John Paul II for the first time. This was a momentous event, as the Vatican was about to establish diplomatic relations with the State of Israel. Having abandoned the notion that Jews, as deniers and killers of Christ, were eternally damned, and that their exile was a divine punishment, the Church was preparing to fully embrace the principles of the Second Vatican Council as expanded by Pope John Paul II. After the meeting, Sheetret reported that: "he had asked for Vatican cooperation in locating the 60-kg. gold menorah from the Second Temple that was brought to Rome by Titus in 70 CE. Shetreet claimed that recent research at the University of Florence indicated the menorah might be among the hidden treasures in the Vatican's catacombs. 'I don't say it's there for sure,' he said, 'but I asked the Pope to help in the search as a goodwill gesture in recognition of the improved relations between Catholics and Jews.' "[12] The Israeli newspaper *Haaretz* reported on this event in May 1996. Witnesses to this conversation, reports Ronen Bergman in *Haaretz,* "tell that a tense silence hovered over the room after Shetreet's request was heard."[13] Shetreet's request was followed in short order by requests by the two chief rabbis of Israel on their first visit to the Vatican and then by that of President Moshe Katzav for the Vatican to help find the menorah. The urban legend had snowballed.

At this point, I noticed that something strange was in the air; that a belief that I had always dismissed as quaint and harmless had become an irritant. I began by following up on the "recent research at the University of Florence," writing to both Shetreet, as Minister of Religious Affairs, and my academic contacts in Florence. No one in Italy could point me to the researchers involved, and I received no more help from Israel. I became dubious that such "research" actually took place—though its mention surely added a level of authority to the entire event—especially because it is described as Italian scholarship and cited approvingly by a Hebrew University law professor. I had no luck at all. Only recently, in 2015, did my research assistant uncover a 1997 article in an Italian art journal by University of Florence art historian Fulvo Cervini. Cervini describes a bronze lampstand modeled loosely on the biblical menorah created by the famous Renaissance craftsmen Maso Bartolommeo for the Cathedral of Prato (1440). Cervini has nothing to say about the location of the Temple menorah. Still, at least someone in Florence was writing about a menorah. Urban legends always contain a germ of the possible, otherwise no one would believe them.

Increasingly curious, I started to look into the myth. I sent an e-mail asking the Israeli Ministry of Foreign Affairs for an official response. Much to my surprise, I received one back:

> The requests by Shetreet, the president, and the chief rabbis reflect the long-held belief that the Catholic Church, as the inheritor of Rome, took possession of the empire's booty—as documented by the Arch of Titus. It is thus assumed that, among other treasures looted from the Jewish people, the Temple menorah is stashed away someplace in the storerooms of the Vatican.

> This is not to say that 2,000 years or so have been enough time for the Foreign Ministry to formulate a policy on the matter. Unofficially at least, we look forward to the restoration of the treasures of the Jewish people to their rightful homeland, but do not anticipate this will occur before the coming of the Messiah.[14]

This response assumes that Catholic doctrine that asserts continuity from Peter and Paul during the first century to the current pope actually reflects historical reality, and that Jewish beliefs that the menorah is at the Vatican are ancient. Neither of these positions, of course, is historically accurate. The papacy established itself long after the destruction of Rome, and with it the Temple of Peace—and the Vatican myth is of very recent vintage. I am not the only academic to pick up on the question in the wake of this odd request. No less than five of my academic colleagues—Americans and British—have also written on the menorah in Rome since 1996, showing the ways that scholarship develops in response to larger cultural questions.

Israeli president Katzav's interest in the supposed menorah at the Vatican continued, and, at his behest, the Israel Antiquities Authority quietly sent a team to Rome in 2004 to search the Vatican storerooms for signs of the Temple vessels and to catalog archaeological artifacts of Jewish significance—just to put an end to the matter. This visit was not made public, but was revealed by an Israeli lawyer, Nissan Sherefi, in the sectorial newspaper of an Orthodox political party, the Sephardi Torah Guards, *Shas,* on December 28, 2006. According to the daily, *Yom le-Yom,* Sherefi learned of the visit in a letter received from the office of President Katzav, which attempted to convince him that no treasures were or will be found at the Vatican. The headline speaks otherwise: "The Temple Vessels Are Stored in the Vatican Vaults." The subtitle continues: "Investigators of the Antiquities Authority Examined Artifacts at the Vatican and Found Jewish Treasures. New Evidence from Rome That Has Been Transmitted to *Yom le-Yom.*" The research trip was subsequently confirmed by Chava Katz of the Israel Antiquities Authority, in the mainstream media outlet *Maariv.* Its purpose was to produce a joint catalog with the Vatican Museum of unpublished Jewish artifacts. Katz reported that nothing significant was discovered, and so a catalog unwarranted.[15] Conspiracy theorists can always argue, of course, that some deeper vault had been hidden from the researchers—even against the actual evidence.

With the ascent of Pope Francis in 2013, I fully anticipated that the Vatican menorah myth would appear once again, and it did. This time, it was brought up by Rabbi Yonatan Shtencel, a modernized Hasid from Bnei Brak, a fervently Orthodox suburb of Tel Aviv. Shtencel, himself a person who crosses boundaries within Israeli *Haredi* culture, made international press with a letter written to Pope Francis requesting the menorah. In it, the rabbi collected a group of "proofs." This is a fascinating and rambling document. I reproduce some poignant sections, which really do express a palpable sense of loss and longing:

> In the year 70 AD, year 3828 from the creation of the world according to the Hebrew calendar, Roman soldiers entered the Jewish temple on the Temple Mount in Jerusalem, which was then the Kingdom of Judea, brought about its destruction and took from the temple the holy vessels that had served the people and the priests for their worship of the only G-d of Israel in their permanent and temporary temples. In this matter, I appeal to you, as you have only recently attained high office, imbuing it with a new and creative spirit:

A. I am a member of the Jewish People. I do not represent anyone, rather only my faith and the wish of my people wherever they are, and I am acting by power of my inner desire and recognition to bring about, with your assistance, a real transformation after many years of stagnation, imperviousness and disregard of historical truths.

B. I have learned in a short time, observing your service as Head of the Christian Church and as one who occupies such a high position, to whom the eyes of millions of Christian faithful all over the world are lifted, that you have been endowed, among your other virtues, with the willingness to listen to other nations, and to people with all their weaknesses and limitations.

C. As one closely acquainted with the edicts of Christianity in general and the history of the Jewish People in particular, including your familiarity with the Jewish faith on all its levels, I believe that it is time, especially on the eve of your visit to Israel—the Holy Land, that this visit, which in itself has special and historical dimensions, be utilized by Your Holiness to return the holy vessels which, as is known to the entire world and proven strongly by historical and other proof, are located in the archives of the Vatican under your control.

D. The return of the holy vessels, particularly through your intervention, shall lend special status to your position among all nations, and shall serve as a real complement to the Jewish prayer "My house shall be called a house of prayer for all nations."

. . . For all these reasons, I ask that you devote a little of your time to real and deep inner observation of those aspects of your heart and soul that brought you to your lofty position, and that you make use of this position in a special and unique way, and direct that the vessels—the holy vessels—be prepared, gathered, packed and taken with you when you come to Israel in order to hand them over to the Jewish People to guard forever.[16]

Much, I think, to his own surprise, Shtencel—who has a real sense of media and public presentation—received a response to his letter from the papal ambassador, the Nuncio for Israel and Palestine, Archbishop Giuseppe Lazzarotto:

Dear Rabbi Shtencel:
I have received you[r] letter of November 14th and I wish to assure you that I have given a serious attention to the issue that you raise with the Holy Father.

Your affirmation that the sacred vessels of the Temple "as known to the entire world and proven strongly by historical and other proof, are located in the archives of the Vatican" cannot be underestimated. This would suggest that, for some unspecified reasons, the Vatican would maintain a negative attitude and hostile feelings towards the Jewish people. I think that you would agree with me that this is against all the evidence of at least the last fifty years of dialogue and friendly relations between the Catholic Church and the Jewish people. If the sacred vessels were kept anywhere in the Vatican, John XXIII, John Paul II, Benedict XIV and Pope Francis would have certainly made sure that they be returned to the legitimate owners.

If you can provide me with evidence that the sacred vessels are indeed kept in the archives or somewhere else in the Vatican, I will be very pleased to forward your request to the Prefect of the same archives and to Pope Francis himself.[17]

Archbishop Lazzarotto was clearly trying to deal with this issue in as polite a way as possible, particularly in advance of Francis's visit to Israel in May 2014. Reading the letter with a deep-seated sense of suspicion, Shtencel believed that he had been rebuffed and threatened to take the Church to the International Court of Justice in the Hague. He would not have been the first to use court proceedings to advance the agenda of returning the menorah. In 2009 rightist leader Baruch Marzel filed suit against Pope Benedict XVI, demanding the return of the menorah, days before the pope's arrival in Israel.[18] Emboldened by his new notoriety, which was widely published in the Orthodox press in Israel and the United States (though ignored in the mainstream Jewish and Israeli press), Shtencel moved forward with his menorah agenda. In preparation for a "prayer meeting" that included Palestinian president Mohammed Abbas and then-Israeli president Shimon Peres at the Vatican in late May, Shtencel authored yet another letter detailing his "proofs." He hoped to convince Peres to raise the question of the menorah with the pope. This letter reached me.

Coincidentally, at that moment I was teaching an undergraduate seminar on the history of the arch at Yeshiva University. It was a general education course, made up of two premeds, a history major, an architecture major, and a freshman. I set these students to studying the sources detailed by Shtencel and to respond to his claims. Some were anxious for the challenge, others were concerned that I harbored an anti-Orthodox agenda. Then they studied the material and spoke with the informants, some of whom had to be tracked down in Israel. The group came to the conclusion that the "proofs" adduced were not sufficient to be accepted in either a rabbinic court or a court of law—and certainly not by a historian. They were at best hearsay. The students composed an open letter to President Peres in which they explained the incorrect assumptions that have been used to claim that the Vatican is hiding the menorah—piece by piece. Much to my surprise, this project was noticed by the *Wall Street Journal,* which spread news of our research to every corner, in both English and in Hebrew.[19] As a result, Rabbi Shtencel and I entered into a fascinating dialogue. It is not often that a scholar of antiquity gets to correspond in real time with one of his informants. In the course of our discussions, the rabbi admonished me for making the menorah campaign more difficult (I pled guilty), even as he confided in an e-mail that "I am not sure that it is really there," admitting that there are holes in the evidence.

The urban myth of the menorah at the Vatican is amazingly potent. It is a conspiracy theory tied to deep-seated distrust of the Vatican and assumptions that the Roman Catholic Church is secretly plotting against non-Catholics. For Jews this is not so crazy. Jewish relations with the Roman Catholic Church were never amicable. In fact, from the High Middle Ages until the 1960s Jews were at best tolerated, at worst persecuted; as late as the nineteenth century their children taken from the Rome Ghetto and baptized, their holy books "acquired" by the Church. One scholar refers to the modern phenomenon as "the Popes against the Jews," and the often-tepid response of too many within the Church to the massacre of European Jewry during the twentieth century is still an open wound. Many of those who continue to believe that the Church is hiding the menorah are Eastern European Holocaust survivors, or the children of survivors. For them, the Catholic Church is a persecutor, a kidnapper, and a thief of Jewish property—from medieval manuscripts to the Temple curtain, the priestly headpiece, and the menorah itself. At a moment when others were demanding the return of Jewish manuscripts and books from the Vatican, some Jews upped the ante and demanded the menorah. Having little historical training and a long history of distrust, they assume that since the menorah decorates the arch and the Church is the inheritor of Rome, then the Church has the menorah—and they hope it does. Even the government of Israel bought into this myth, the Antiquities Authority sending a team to resolve the issue.

The menorah at the Vatican is an urban legend, often believed by people of goodwill who really want the menorah to exist. For them, the menorah is the symbol of the Jewish people—all the more so once the Arch of Titus menorah was chosen for the Symbol of Israel. This decision opened a new pathway, making the arch menorah all the more present—on government buildings, passports, official documents, and on all sorts of textbooks and posters. In 1949 placement of the state "symbol" above the door of the Israeli embassy in Rome was taken by some to be a kind of triumph. In that way, it is far more than the legend of the menorah in the Tiber. As long as the menorah exists, some tie with eternity is maintained. It is a relic seen and unseen, seen in the arch and seen in Raphael's painting and seen in the Jewish catacombs and in the museums, but unseen in its golden brilliance. It is symbol of the State of Israel, called in Israeli liturgical texts "the first flowering of our redemption," but not the hoped for messianic kingdom for which all traditionalist Jews wait.[20] When the menorah is restored, many believe, the messiah will be that much closer. The Vatican menorah myth is the newest stage in the long Jewish and Christian "search" for the Temple vessels. It is a Jewish version of the Holy Grail, the stuff of Stefan Zweig's *The Buried Candelabrum,* Dan Brown's *The Da Vinci Code,* and countless novels. It reflects the assumption for many that the Catholics cannot be trusted.

Can they? Who could imagine a religion of over a billion members, with a nineteen-hundred-year history of the most rabid anti-Semitism, working to change itself? It is as hard to believe as the repentance of the city of Nineveh must have seemed to the author of the biblical book of Jonah. It is indeed astonishing to many Jews, even fifty years after the Second Vatican Council, that Catholic children are being taught that anti-Semitism is a sin, and that for the first time, Catholics and Jews, the Vatican and the State of Israel, are building an amicable relationship. This is the very moment that the myth of the menorah at the Vatican kicked in. "They must be hiding something," "this must be a conspiracy," is the assumption of some Jews—especially traditionalists who, as a matter of habit and intention, are suspicious of change. More significant for our purposes, though, is what this case study teaches about the ways that an urban myth of recent vintage but deep progeny spreads in modern society, and how it is maintained specifically because it draws on traditional themes among a population undergoing its own radical transformation. This myth has had serious consequences—as politicians, lawyers, newspapers, clergy, and scholars have been absorbed in digesting the realities created by this myth—and they (we) have responded to that reality.

7

Illuminating the Path to Armageddon

Religious radical fringes, Christian and especially Jewish, show considerable interest in the menorah. A rather classic example of the former occurred in the former Soviet republic of Moldova on Hanukkah, 2009, when a large-branched Hanukkah menorah was ceremonially dismembered and set upside down before a statue of Stephen III of Moldavia, known simply as Stephen the Great (d. 1504, sculpture installed 1928). Created to replace a statue of the czar, this sculpture suffered a fraught history through the Soviet period. It is located opposite the main government building in the capital Chisinau, a place of considerable Moldovan national significance. The *Jerusalem Post* narrated the scene:

> The Anti-Defamation League on Monday condemned the "despicable" removal of a *Hannukiah* in Moldova, apparently led by an Orthodox priest. Video footage of the event, uploaded to YouTube, shows a group of dozens of people looking on as the menorah is pulled down with hammers and iron bars and replaced with a cross. Officials in the Moldovan capital of Chisinau said that the 1.5-meter-tall ceremonial candelabrum was retrieved, reinstalled and is now under police guard. The video shows an Orthodox priest, identified by Moldovan media as Fr. Anatoliy Chirbik, leading the Sunday demonstration at Stefan the Great Square and saying, "We are an Orthodox country. Stephan the Great defended our country from all kinds of kikes, and now they come and put their menorah here. This is anarchy."[1]

Naturally, the Moldovan government deplored this sacrilege and acted against it, though Moldovan law did not provide a vehicle for prosecution. Father Chirbik was fined the equivalent of fifty dollars, as the government pressed the Moldovan Orthodox Church to sanction the priest. More importantly, this sort of incident has not been repeated. To me, what is fascinating about this event was its ritual performance. In a video uploaded to YouTube, Father Chirbik appears in full clerical robes, leading a group that carries a large eight-branched Hanukkah menorah modeled on the Arch of Titus menorah—the sort common in modernizing Eastern European synagogues before World War II. The Orthodox Christian clergyman fumigated the menorah and sprinkled holy water as his followers broke it in two, separating the base from the branches. Then they carried it to the base of the statue of King Stephen and left it upside down there. The World Jewish Congress website added significant details and a haunting response to the event:

> The Russian Orthodox Church in the former Soviet republic of Moldova has indirectly blamed the Jewish community for the recent anti-Semitic march by Christian fundamentalists in the capital Chisinau in which a public menorah was dismantled. A church statement said: "We believe that this unpleasant incident could have been avoided if the menorah had been placed near a memorial for victims of the Holocaust."
>
> On Chanukah, some 200 fundamentalist Christian protestors, led by a priest of the Orthodox Church, marched through Chisinau and removed the 5-foot-tall menorah, using hammers and iron bars from a major downtown square. "The Jews can try to kill us, to traumatize our children, but Moldovan Orthodox believers will resist," the priest told the crowd, many of whom carried large crosses. Moldova, he said, was an Orthodox country, and Jews were trying to "dominate people." Allowing the menorah to be set up had been "a sacrilege, an indulgence of state power today."[2]

Members of the group carried a large banner that declared "Moldova is an Orthodox Country," and others carried the flag of czarist monarchists. Clearly Father Chirbik and his followers, and to some extent the official church, were offended by the seeming brashness of local Jewish leaders who placed the menorah in the most public space possible, often at the center of local, regional, or national power. To Father Chirbik's telling, the Jews (expletives deleted) had overstepped into the public—Christian—square, apparently with the approval of a government that Chirbik did not support. As in antiquity, Chirbik's actions were carried out on a local level, but this kind of protest had serious implications for the nature of contemporary Moldova. As in the past, this testing of power relationships was carried out to the detriment of the local Jewish community. To me, the fascinating—and chilling—thing about this event is how closely it holds to the kinds of scripts known from antiquity and the Middle Ages for the destruction of synagogues by Christians, led by their priests. We have already seen graphic evidence of this from Laodicea, in Asia Minor, where a cross was superimposed on a menorah—a transformation in stone that might well have been associated with the kinds of prayers, incense, and sprinkling of holy water that we have seen in Moldova. Did Father Chirbik know that he was breaking up a menorah modeled on the Arch of Titus lampstand, or at least the symbol of the State of Israel? If he did, he didn't say so. Whatever the case, this sort of rightist behavior is generally held at bay by local governments, in part as a litmus test of their status as non-anti-Semitic, that is, civilized, countries.

Far more ominous than the Moldova incident was a little-noticed procession that took place in Jerusalem on the second night of Hanukkah, December 6, 2007—preserved on YouTube by its organizers. On that day the leadership of Jerusalem's *Mekhon ha-Miqdash*, the Temple Institute, staged a procession through the streets of the Jewish Quarter of the Old City, carrying a large seven-branched menorah, bronze but plated with 42.5 kilograms of gold (at an estimated cost of $1,000,000), provided by Ukrainian-Jewish businessman Vadim Rabinovitch. The lampstand was carried from the rather nondescript place in the excavations of the Byzantine Cardo—today a shopping area in the Jewish Quarter—where it had been exhibited since 2000 to a broad landing on the main staircase leading down to the Western Wall—a site with a brilliant view directly opposite the Al-Aqsa Mosque. The site had recently been designated "Menorah Square," so there was no ambiguity as to its purpose. The large, and apparently quite heavy, menorah—which looks roughly like that of the Arch of Titus, was lifted into a protective glass case with stepped benches surrounding it—a spot that invited tour groups and other tourists to rest en route up the steps from the Western Wall—a "tourist destination" in the making. Soon it spawned a large number of tourist trinkets, all for sale at the Temple Institute, just a few meters up the hill on the next stoop in the stairway.

It was a fascinating, if rather understated procession, attended by well-wishers and American post-high-school "gap year" yeshiva students—a crowd that can always be counted on to sing and dance exuberantly, and like most students their age, with varying levels of nuance and understanding. The ceremony culminated in the blowing of two silver horns, crossed before the menorah in clear reference to the horns of the Arch of Titus relief. The menorah is almost home, the rhetoric went. Zionism brought it back to the Land of Israel, this parade proclaimed, but did not go far enough. The state has failed in its messianic mission of settling the entire land, restoring the Temple, and bringing the messiah. Beginning with the Oslo Accords (1994), which agreed to redivide the Land of Israel between Israelis and Palestinians, and continuing with the evacuation of Gaza in 2005, the State of Israel is no longer seen by this rightist polity as an instrument of redemption—for some, it is now an impediment. It is up to us, so the reasoning goes, those who truly are committed to the Land of Israel and the Temple of God, to finish the task. This procession is a microcosm of a larger process of movement from exile to redemption. It has a liminal existence that has continued after the State of Israel moved beyond its most explicitly messianic rhetoric, stuck in the "doorframe" between unfulfilled redemption and the end of time. Thus, this celebration brought the menorah—the redeemed and redeeming "Arch of Titus" menorah—within sight of the Temple Mount itself. This procession gave expression to an increasingly sectarian form of post-Zionism—not its well-known leftist expression, but its less discussed and sometimes violent rightist variant.

The Temple Institute was founded in 1987 by Rabbi Yisrael Ariel, whose influence is pervasive to this day and whose biography is widely known. Ariel, originally Stieglitz (Ariel is one of the biblical names for Jerusalem), a former student of the ultranationalist Merkaz ha-Rav Kook Yeshiva, was one of the soldiers involved in the capture of the Temple Mount/Haram al-Sharif during the Six-Day War in June 1967. He is a follower of Rabbi Shlomo Goren (d. 1994), a major thinker and actor of the religious Zionist "Land of Israel" movement and a former chief rabbi of the military and of the State of Israel. Goren was well known for his messianic stance. According to Uzi Narkiss, the commander of the Jerusalem District in 1967,

Temple Institute Menorah, Menorah Square, Jerusalem, 2013, photograph by Olivier Lévy, Wikimedia Commons

Goren urged that the Israel Defense Forces "blow up the mosques" and begin rebuilding the Temple (a claim refuted by others, but consonant with Goren's general approach). Since then, Ariel has held leadership roles on the fringe of the Israeli body politic. An extreme voice who called on soldiers to refuse orders to evacuate the Sinai settlement of Yamit in 1982, Ariel went on to serve as number two on the Knesset list of the Kach Party of the radical American immigrant Rabbi Meir Kahane during the early 1980s, before the party was barred from the electoral system for violation of racism laws in 1988. Indicative of his often impassioned rhetoric is Ariel's eulogy for Baruch Goldstein, an American immigrant doctor who, in 1994, entered the Tomb of the Patriarchs in Hebron with his military-issue M-16 and gunned down twenty-nine Arab worshippers on the Jewish festival of Purim, mostly shot in the back as they prayed. Ariel is reported to have said that: " 'Baruch Goldstein is from now on our intercessor in heaven.' The rabbi added that 'this was not an individual act.' According to the rabbi, Goldstein 'heard the cry of the land which is being stolen each day by the Ishmaelites.' Rabbi Ariel concluded: 'The land will not be procured through peace agreements, but only through [the shedding of] blood.' "[3]

Ariel leads an organization dedicated to the rebuilding of the Temple in the near future, which in fact believes that it has already begun the construction with the fabrication of the Temple service vessels. Avoiding the kinds of illegal activities carried out by others on the radical Right (including a 1984 attempt to bomb the Dome of the Rock, Goldstein's attack in 1994, and the assassination of Yitzhak Rabin in 1995), Ariel and the Temple Institute began an educational campaign to insinuate their naturalistic messianic vision—it has been correctly called an "alternate memory"—into the religious Zionist, fervently Orthodox, and "secular" mainstreams. Sarina Chen, who has written extensively about the religious program of the Temple Institute, has insightfully noted that even the Hebrew name for this organization, *Mekhon ha-Miqdash*, expresses the ambiguity of its messaging and project. *Mekhon ha-Miqdash* represents a kind of double entendre fitting for this organization. Derived from biblical Hebrew usage, the Modern Hebrew word *mekhon* has the secular meaning simply of a public institution. In biblical Hebrew—the underground and almost covert code where the Temple activists derive meaning—however, the verb root *k.n.n.* has given messianic overtones. We see this, Chen notes, in Exodus 15:17: "Thou bringest them in, and plantest them in the mountain of

Thine inheritance, the place [*mekhon*] of your dwelling, an act of the Lord, the sanctuary, O Lord, which Thy hands have established [*konenanu*]."[4] Eschewing the kinds of protests that characterized his youth, Ariel has chosen an incremental approach to achieving his messianic vision. As he explained in another context: "If you make things happen on the ground, people feel that you are the address, and this draws people. This in itself establishes authority" (my translation).[5]

The Temple Institute, up the stairs from the menorah, displays a model of the Temple as it was and will be once rebuilt and various Temple vessels built in accord with Jewish legal traditions that they claim may actually be used in the Temple. These are the result of studies carried out by a research institute led by Ariel dedicated to establishing exactly what Jewish law has construed as rules for the fabrication of the Temple instruments, which range from the priestly garments to all manner of shovels and pans, the showbread table, and the menorah. While these texts were essentially an academic exercise for millennia, the authors never lost faith that they would eventually have practical import. For Ariel, the moment for their practical implementation has arrived. Elements requiring Divine input or miracles that Jewish tradition considers necessary for the fabrication of the vessels are limited and overcome through reinterpretation. For example, while the stones of the priestly breastplate are to be carved by a stone-eating mythological creature known as the Shamir, the scholars of the institute have found legal ways to circumvent the Shamir, allowing human artisans to carve the stones.

The vessels built by the Temple Institute—first among them the menorah—are not just models, meant to be display items, even as they build on display techniques that were used for model Temple vessels that go back to the nineteenth century and were embraced by Zionism. In fact, they were favorite features of local exhibitions and the Palestine pavilions organized by the Zionist Organization at international fairs throughout the first half of the twentieth century. Such models have been rather common in Christian, particularly Anglophone Protestant, circles for generations, and displays of such items can be visited across the southern United States today (most expansively at the Holy Land Experience, a Christian theme park near Disney World in Orlando, Florida). Rather, the Temple Institute vessels are actual Temple vessels, built to serve in the rebuilt Temple. Thus, the priestly garments are occasionally worn by priests in practice ceremonies in preparation for their service in the Temple sacrifices. According to the rhetoric of the Temple Institute, preparation of these artifacts—and of the personnel to use them—is the first step in the replacement of the mosques with the Temple and the resumption of the Jewish sacrificial regimen.

In the spring of 2014, for example, the Temple Institute staged practice sessions for priests conducting a mock Paschal sacrifice, which was strangely reminiscent of the well-publicized Samaritan Passover sacrifice that many Jews observe on the assumption of its biblical authenticity.[6] These events, overseen by Ariel and accompanied by priests in white robes and the blowing of silver horns, were presented in a Hebrew video geared to an Israeli religious audience and in an English video intended for Jews and Christians. They were covered with curiosity by major press outlets. These are likely to become large and very public events, intentionally rivaling the Samaritan Passover. Similarly, in a YouTube video filmed on Hanukkah 2013, "Rabbi Yisrael Ariel Conducts Holy Temple Menorah Lighting Rehearsal," Ariel promises the assembled crowd that a large, purpose-built, wooden seven-branched menorah is suitable for use in the Temple "this very evening."[7] A priest, in full regalia, is shown next to the menorah and recites a blessing based upon the Hanukkah liturgy but composed by the Temple Institute: "Blessed are you, Lord [*Hashem*] our God, King of the Universe, who has commanded us, through the sanctity of Aaron, to light the menorah of the Temple." In this instance, the Temple Institute attempts to usurp contemporary public menorah-lighting practices (best known through Chabad's public lighting ceremonies), while transforming standard liturgical texts for sectarian purposes. Thus, the widely known Hanukkah blessing, "Blessed are you, Lord our God, King of the Universe, who has commanded us to kindle the Hanukkah lights" has been turned into a Temple blessing of recent vintage (though of ancient parts). This radically new ceremony—like the sacrifice of the paschal lamb—"looks" kosher and stays just within the line separating the permitted from the forbidden in traditional Orthodox practice. It even includes a costumed priest.

The Temple Institute sees itself as preparing the Israeli public for this redemptive eventuality—which Ariel carefully states will occur "as soon as the government allows." Its educational programs and publications are intended to help open Israeli society to their project. Not surprisingly, much of the support for the Temple Institute comes from American evangelical and fundamentalist Christians, who see the rebuilding of the Temple as a part of their own apocalyptic vision—as a necessary prelude to the Second Coming of Christ. In fact, many of the graphics prepared by the institute are reminiscent of nineteenth-century Protestant Bible illustration of a sort still well represented within these Christian communities, and the Temple Institute works closely with a network of Christian supporters and partners—particularly in the United States, but worldwide. Funding also comes from the rightist government of Benjamin Netanyahu. According to a 2013 study, "The State of Israel directly funds various Temple movement activities. In the years 2008–2011, the Ministry of Culture, Science and Sports and the Ministry of Education supported the Temple Institute and the Midrasha [advanced school for women] at an average rate of NIS 412,000 [approximately $137,000] per year. In 2012, the Midrasha, the educational arm of the Temple Institute, received NIS 189,000 [approximately $63,000] from the Ministry of Education."[8] In 2013, Army Radio reports, the Temple Institute received a total of NIS 416,000, approximately $139,000, in direct government funding. These sums do not include intangibles, such as staffing by women who fulfill their national service through work at the institute. Ariel's publications—a primary form of outreach—are published by Carta Press, a well-known Jerusalem publisher of academic publications and atlases, as well as tourist publications—mostly directed toward Christian evangelical pilgrims. In recent years, the Temple Institute has successfully integrated itself and its vision within the nationalist "Modern Orthodox" polity, having recently negotiated for the publications to appear with the prestigious, and previously apolitical, Koren Publishers. Its most significant publications are a series of prayer books and study editions of rabbinic texts that provide glossy images of the Temple service and a commentary that connects directly the many aspects of Jewish prayer that focus on the Temple and its sacrifices to the current activities of the Temple Institute. The unstated claim is that Ariel's reading of biblical and rabbinic sources represents both historical and eternal truth (these books contain no reference to Second Temple period literature that is external to the rabbinic canon, nor modern scholarship). The Temple Institute has vigorously sought to regularize its menorah, using it as a symbol for the movement and populating *Wikipedia* articles in Hebrew, English, and many other languages with the image of their lampstand.

The menorah in "Menorah Square" is the centerpiece of Ariel's project. The process leading to its fabrication by artisan Chaim Odem is documented in a large and beautifully produced coffee-table book and in a video presentation. Ariel's fascinating study of the menorah discusses each element of the lampstand, and this work serves as a guide and explanation for his process of building a menorah that will serve in the Temple. The design of the volume is meant to evoke modern—if not academic—credibility. It is printed on glossy paper, with numerous color illustrations interspersed. It also uses the tools of scholarship—footnotes, indices, image captions, and clear, thesis-driven chapters. This volume uses the language of the academy, and Ariel's followers seek to participate in academic conferences. The book systematically sets out Ariel's agenda that it is possible—and indeed a Divine imperative—to construct a usable menorah. Ariel argues for the use of archaeological discoveries as legal evidence—an approach generally frowned upon by contemporary rabbinic jurisprudence. The Temple Institute, a kind of eschatological post-Zionist "Orthodoxy" (it might even be "post-Orthodox"), pushes both Zionist/Israeli realpolitik and Orthodox Judaism toward messianic fulfillment. The religious Zionist notion that the State of Israel is "the first sprouts of our redemption" is thus provided with a guidebook for those advancing the actual creation of vessels suitable for service in the Temple.

Ariel begins his menorah book by setting out his sense that the biblical commandment to create and light the menorah is not specific to any particular period but is an imperative for the present. He even goes so far as to suggest that the making of a usable Temple menorah requires the recitation of a specific blessing, "Blessed are you, Lord our God, King of the Universe, who has commanded us regarding the fabrication of the holy menorah."[9] Ariel spends considerable effort arguing against Maimonides's imagined straight-angled branches on the menorah and for the rounded ones that Jews have accepted since the Second Temple Period. Further, Ariel's numerous fellow travelers within the Chabad movement and other fervently Orthodox groups have of late accepted Maimonides's proposition and as a result have branded their own recognizable menorah. Coming from the Zionist branch of Israeli Orthodoxy, Ariel, clearly was committed to the rounded "Arch of Titus" branches of the menorah and engaging archaeology as a source for religious decision making, argues directly against the Maimonides interpretation. His goal throughout is clearly a menorah that is as similar to the arch menorah as it appears on the national "symbol" as possible. Thus, Ariel reproduced the arch menorah base, though he removed the mythological creatures, replacing them with pomegranates, and added three small feet. In fact, this menorah bears a striking resemblance to the smaller brass menorahs used by Zionists, B'nai B'rith, and Masons at the turn of the twentieth century. It is the supersized version. Solving a major technical problem, Ariel argues that a menorah built without messianic supervision may be built of materials of lesser value than "pure gold." This follows on a tradition in the Babylonian Talmud Menaḥot 28b (and parallels) that we earlier encountered, with its description of a lead Maccabean menorah built upon the cleansing of the Temple in 164 BCE, and the menorah's continual upgrade from lead to silver to gold throughout the Hasmonean Period. In fact, Ariel's menorah, built of brass and gilded, has the appearance of pure gold, though by 2013 the gold was peeling from the lampstand.

On a recent public tour of the Temple Institute (July 2013), the English-speaking guide, fulfilling her national service, explained that "we believe that the menorah is hidden at the Vatican. Until it is returned, we will light this menorah when the Temple is rebuilt." Another member of the Temple Institute community, Rabbi Mordechai Persoff, made a similar claim, enthusiastically endorsing Rabbi Shtencel's efforts in trying to retrieve the menorah from the Vatican, in an article dated August 22, 2014, that appears on the Temple Institute website. More recently, on October 4, 2014, clearly in response to my public questioning of the whole notion of the menorah at the Vatican (my *Wall Street Journal* piece also appeared in Hebrew translation), a spokesman tried to distance the Temple Institute from this broadly disputed contention. The "International Director" of the Temple Institute, American-born Rabbi Chaim Richman, who has considerable media savvy, was cited in a newspaper oriented to the nationalist Orthodox community, *Makor Rishon,* to the effect that: "Even if there are vessels in the Vatican, this does not release us from the contemporary imperative to prepare the vessels of the Temple. Even if we could search and compare [the Vatican vessels to] the vessels that we are creating at the Institute for Ancient [Temple] Vessels and if it became possible to use in the Temple some of the original vessels—if and when they will return—we prefer to act according to the traditions available to us and to progress to the extent that we can" (my translation). The Vatican connection is clearly a side issue for their apocalyptic, yet gradual, project of rebuilding the Temple.[10]

As I described earlier, the Temple Institute has placed their menorah as close as they can to the Temple itself. The placement of the menorah on Menorah Square was orchestrated as a public procession, with silver horns similar to those of the arch crossed and blown before the approaching lampstand. While Zionism had succeeded in bringing the menorah "home" to Israel, the Temple Institute was intent upon taking up the metaphor, creating an actual Temple menorah and completing its transfer to within sight of the Temple Mount. In fact, through the branches of the menorah, the domes of the two mosques can readily been seen, bringing the replacement of the mosques—whether by divine, messianic, or human hands, that much closer. This positioning of the menorah, together with the vast array of literature, videos, and images created by the Temple Institute that show the rebuilt Temple in place of the golden dome, might clearly—and clearsightedly—be seen as a threat both by those looking outward through the windows of the Al-Aqsa Mosque and by mainstream Israel as well.

Messianic rhetoric, so central to Zionist and early Israeli identity, has been maintained and enlivened by Israelis and diaspora Jews who inhabit the rightist side of Jewish politics—some of them religious, many not. Secular and Left-leaning Israel has generally relegated this kind of imagery—together with rhetoric relating modern Zionism to such epic heroes as the Maccabees, the Zealots of the Jewish War, and Bar Kokhba—to elementary-school curricula. It is for them a piece of the national civil religion, the stuff of children's books, but not the motivating factor it once was. Archaeology, once a central national interest, is thus not a process of discovering a "deed" in the land as it once was, with each discovery at a Jewish site seen as strengthening a Jewish claim to the land. This claim is already self-evident to many. This distancing from nationalist symbols is part of a larger Western disconnection from nationalism, particularly in Western Europe, but with a very local twist. In Israel it is a response developed since the period of the Oslo Accords, with their promise of "two states for two peoples" and acceptance of Palestinian claims to pieces of historical Eretz Israel/Palestine. As the Israeli Left has distanced itself, however, the Right has moved in the opposite direction. For this community, Jewish settlement in the West Bank and Gaza was and is not just a security decision—though that position is well represented, but a nationalist and religious one. It is a direct continuation, they argue, of the earlier Zionist program of settling the land "from the Sea to the Jordan" and, for followers of Jabotinsky, in all of Mandatory Palestine—which includes the territory of the Hashemite Kingdom of Jordan.

If the impetus for the Temple Institute and its very public menorah was the Oslo process, further radicalization of the menorah within the Zionist religious Right was caused by the 2005 evacuation of the Jewish settlements in Gaza (organized collectively as Gush Katif) under Ariel Sharon—a general who has been described as the "architect of the settlement movement." The level of disappointment among many of the settlers about their removal from the Gaza Strip and northern Samaria in August 2005 was deep and active. Symbolic of this angst was the destruction of synagogues and the removal of Torah scrolls and other sacred items into Israel proper. This removal was seen by many as a forced exile, and imagery drawn from Jewish descriptions and depictions of exile were well reported in the Israeli media. Perhaps the most dramatic—or at least the most staged—removal ceremony took place at the village of Netzarim, the last Gaza settlement to be evacuated. There a large menorah was ceremonially removed from the roof of their synagogue and carried back to Israeli territory, eventually to the Western Wall and now to a memorial site and community center called the Gush Katif Museum in a Jerusalem apartment block.

This procession from Netzarim was filmed by Israeli television, and like the others that we have examined in this chapter, it was posted on YouTube.[11] It began with the removal of the menorah from the roof of the synagogue by a group of men. The video then shifts to a kind of ritual procession, with clearly anguished supporters lining the way. The procession begins with an elder, with a large white beard, holding a Torah scroll. Behind him is a large group carrying the Menorah, which rests on two planks in a manner that resonates with our Arch of Titus panel. The scene merges two well-known icons of Israeli civil religion—the Arch of Titus relief, with "Jews" bearing their holy objects into exile, and Samuel Hirszenberg's often-reproduced painting *Exile*, which shows a group of Jews walking into an unknown exile, led by a bearded elder carrying a Torah scroll. This painting, now lost, is nonetheless well known in Israel, owing to its frequent reproduction and artist Nathan Rapoport's rendition on the Warsaw Ghetto memorial (both in Warsaw and in its iteration at Yad Vashem, Israel's central Holocaust memorial, in Jerusalem). The marchers of Gush Katif may also have had in mind the well-known photograph of the capture of an Israeli soldier at the Suez Canal by Egyptian forces in October 1973, who was carrying a Torah scroll with him. The procession was likely seen as a rendition of both.

The procession from Gaza likely influenced the Temple Institute's Hanukkah procession two years later. The event in Gush Katif, however, was

Evacuation of Netzarim, Gaza Strip, August 19, 2005, photograph by Yossi Zeliger

far more complicated. Like the Hanukkah event, the Netzarim procession was sparked by the religious calendar, which is of central significance to religious Israel, but at times less noticed by secular Israel—particularly such dates as the fast of the Ninth of Av. The infusion of Temple/exile imagery at Netzarim was exasperated by the unfortunate—I would say Jewishly tone-deaf—decision of the Sharon government to carry out the Gaza withdrawal in July and August. It was originally to be concluded on August 1, 2005—the ninth day of the Jewish month of Av—which is known as Tisha B'Av and observed as the anniversary of the destruction of Jerusalem by the Babylonians in 586 BCE and by Titus in 70 CE. It is the day that Jews traditionally commemorate the destruction of synagogues and their communities throughout history. Recognizing the error too late, the disengagement was moved to the day after, which just was not sufficient, owing to the generally negative associations that the three weeks before the fast, and all of the month of Av, have in Jewish life. As the ancient Rabbis wrote, "When Av enters, joy decreases."[12] The Sharon government inadvertently wrapped the destruction of Gush Katif into this mix of lamentations. To this day, more than a decade later, Israeli and American Wikipedia pages still list the "exile" from Gush Katif among the tragedies that have befallen the Jewish people in the month of Av, and some Jewish settler communities recite specially written liturgical lamentations (*kinot*), modeled upon ancient prayers for the Temple, in memory of Gush Katif.

The symbolic value of this unfortunate choice was obvious to observers who viewed the events through even the most minimally traditional Jewish lenses, and it provided an opportunity for the messianic community and its broader constituency to think in larger metaphors than they might have were the withdrawal to have taken place in some religiously more neutral time of year. This circumstance was not missed by Aharon Shevo, a Holocaust survivor and well-known designer of stamps, medals, and coins for the Israeli government, as well as illustrator of his own Passover Haggadah. In the days before the evacuation of Jewish settlements in the Gaza Strip in 2005, Shevo published a protest poster showing the Arch of Titus panel. The panel is rolled like a scroll on its lower edge, and the legs of the men carrying the menorah are replaced with those of Israeli soldiers. Below is written in Hebrew the Jewish date—Tisha B'Av, 5765. According to Shevo, the poster represents the Jews carrying the menorah into exile, and Israeli soldiers (who by sectarian definition are not "Jews") forcing the "Jews" of our own day, those of Gush Katif, into "exile" from their homes. The secular state is thus seen as interfering in the messianic process of redemption, and so this theme has been used in Israeli political discourse. This interpretation is in line with the interpretation intended for the pamphlets that accompanied the Medal of Liberation that was first minted in 1958—the standard to which Shevo responds. It represents real disillusionment with the claim imbedded deep in Israeli civil religion that the founding of the state brought the menorah home and that this redemption was carried out by Palestinian Jewish soldiers out of the ashes of the Holocaust.

Perhaps the most evocative, and in an Israeli sense, threatening, use to which Shevo's image was put during the Gaza withdrawal was on a poster calling on soldiers during the Tisha B'Av fast to refuse to participate in the evacuation of Gaza. The accompanying text well expresses the spirit of Shevo's image, connecting the events of 2005 to this iconic Jewish tragedy:

> *Eikha*—Whence?
> Two thousand years ago Jews were exiled from their land,
> Settlements in the Land of Israel were destroyed.
> Then this was done by Romans.
> Jewish soldier.
> Do you want to join them?
> This is not why you enlisted.

The poster provides hotline numbers for soldiers to call for support in refusing to participate in the withdrawal—a real red line in mainstream Israeli civil religion. While I have presented the procession at Netzarim and Shevo's visual appropriation of the Arch of Titus in succession, moving from Netzarim to Shevo as far as cause and effect, the historical reality may have been quite different. Shevo claims—my guess, correctly—that his posters served as the impetus for the Netzarim event. Thus, the *tableau vivant* performed at Netzarim, the reenactment of the Arch of Titus bas-relief, was prompted by an intermediate step—Shevo's powerful poster.

The procession at Netzarim was a refutation of the validity of the State of Israel and parallels a trend within the messianic community to avoid or alter the "Prayer for the State of Israel" and its claim that the state is the "first sprouts of our redemption." These attitudes, which have always confused the line between Judaism and the civil religion, are embedded in liturgical poetry that continues to be recited among the aggrieved a decade later. One lamentation, *kinna,* composed by a resident of Shilo in the West Bank, Yehoshua Buch, recalls each of the Gush Katif and northern West Bank (Samaria) communities that were removed in turn. Regarding Netzarim he wrote:

> He [referring directly to Sharon] oppressed all of my gallant [ones] to crush youths,
> They pursued her and captured her *bein ha-metsarim* [literally, "between the straits," the three week semimourning period between the breach of the walls of Jerusalem on 17 Tammuz in 586 BCE and the Ninth of Av];
> Oppressors saw her, they mocked heroes;
> They became as foreigners, the sprouts of Netzarim.[13]

Poster calling on soldiers to resist service in Gaza, with Aharon Shevo's Arch of Titus poster, August 2005, collection of Leah and Steven Fine

In Buch's poem, Ariel Sharon and the Israeli army take the place of Roman oppressors, using the same terminology used in ancient poetry for these enemies. As the author explains, "The *kinna* [poem] blames all Jews who took part in the *churban* [destruction] and expulsion and describes them in harsh words such as 'enemies', "pursuers,' etc." Whereas in antiquity, gentiles destroyed Jerusalem and occasionally synagogues, here, as in Shevo's interpretation of his art, the oppressors—those who cause the *churban*—are Jews who act against the "redemption." This complex story is rooted deep in the polemics and mutual miscomprehension of the secular Left and the messianic and nationalist Right in contemporary Israel, especially since the Oslo Accords. For now, however, I point out the sophistication with which the Israeli religious Right has transformed the Zionist menorah. No longer a metaphor to be "returned," the arch menorah is now a cipher for the messianic community and its practical steps toward settlement of the land and the rebuilding of the Temple—steps that are supported financially by Israel's current rightist government. For the Israeli messianic Right, the menorah is a symbol that reaches from Roman and Christian exile to Zionist return, to "leftist" Israeli "betrayal," and, for the most extreme, onward toward apocalyptic fulfillment.

Conclusion

New Light

If the Romans hadn't commemorated their victory
In the Arch of Titus, we wouldn't know
The shape of the menorah from the Temple.
But the shape of the Jews we know,
Because they begat, and begat right up until me.

—Yehuda Amichai, "I Feel Good in My Pants," 1980

In 2010 the *New York Times* reported on the largest menorah in the world. This menorah, nineteen meters tall, was not built in Israel or in New York, as we might expect, but above the city of Manado in Indonesia. It was constructed with a conical central stalk and rests on a large square base with scalloped edges—giving this menorah a real Indonesian aesthetic that only broadly resembles "Jewish" menorahs. The Manado menorah, like all menorahs for millennia, both participates in the larger biblical saga and in the very local issues of its builders, in this case, tensions between the Muslim majority in Indonesia and the active Christian evangelical community in this region. In fact, the menorah was constructed with government funds. According to one informant cited by the *Times,* a goal was "to attract tourists and businessmen from Europe. . . . It is also for the Jewish people to see that there is this sacred symbol, their sacred symbol, outside their country," he said. The *Times* reported that two years before construction of the menorah, a ninety-eight-foot-tall statue of Jesus was built upon a hill by a real estate developer. The Manado menorah is just the largest example of the Christian adoption of the seven-branched menorah and other Temple imagery that has taken place in recent years, most prominently within fundamentalist and evangelical communities—though also within more mainline and even Catholic churches.

The year 2014 was a particularly good one for Christian menorahs. In December, the town of Cosenza, in southern Italy, was decorated with large illuminated images of the Arch of Titus menorah. These golden menorahs were suspended on either side of the local pedestrian mall in commemoration of yet another variation on the menorah myth. According to early medieval tradition, Alaric I, king of the Visigoths, died in Cosenza sometime after the sack of Rome in 410 CE. He was buried, together with his treasure, in the bed of the Buzenzo River, which runs through Cosenza. In 1937 this myth brought even Heinrich Himmler to Cosenza in the hope of discovering the lost treasures. In its most recent iteration, of course, this treasure includes the menorah. Lurking behind this local myth is Procopius and his claims about the removal of the menorah from Rome by the Visigoths—claims that continue to inspire claims in France, Jerusalem, and even the West Bank. The mayor of Cosenza, Mario Occhiuto, explained the presence of the menorah-lighting fixtures, saying, "Cosenza has a tradition of being an open city, a city for dialogue and encounter for different people and cultures. We want to revive this tradition and in this sense, the connection with our Jewish heritage and the present Jewish life is extremely important to us." More recently, as I was preparing this book for final submission, an article appeared in the British newspaper the *Telegraph* that tells of excavation and tourism plans in Cosenza. While the menorah is the least of the treasures emphasized in the article, the subtitle speaks to other concerns: "Italy to dig for ancient Roman treasure sought by Nazis. Haul from tomb of Alaric, king of the Visigoths who sacked Rome, thought to include gold, silver and priceless Menorah looted from Second Temple." Cosenza is thus the newest claimant for the unseen, but never lost, menorah.

On July 31, 2014, the "Neo-Pentecostal" Universal Church of the Kingdom of God in São Paulo, Brazil, christened its 10,000-seat megachurch, its facade loosely modeled on a well-known model of the Herodian Temple, now at the Israel Museum in Jerusalem. Described as a modern-day "Temple of Solomon," the interior of this eighteen-story edifice is replete with imagery drawn from the Jerusalem Temples. This use of Temple imagery goes farther than that of traditional Christian groups by not only reaching back to contemporary Jewish/Israeli imagery but pushing forward to a unified iconography with fellow travelers in the post-Zionist, post-Orthodox Israeli apocalyptic Right. Among the artifacts of this Christian temple is a model of the Ark of the Covenant and a large golden seven-branched menorah on the front stage, which bears an uncanny resemblance to the Temple Institute lampstand. The church's interior walls are illuminated with twelve menorahs, reminiscent of Solomon's Temple. At the dedication of the church, the ark was escorted to the stage to a rousing chorus of "Hatikvah," the Israeli national anthem.

Before its completion, this church, a statement of growing evangelical power in South America, served as the backdrop for a short film by Yael Bartana, *Inferno* (2013). Blending Jewish/Israeli, evangelical, and Brazilian imagery, Bartana presents a cycle of dedication, destruction, and memorialization of the Temple—now in São Paulo. This somewhat sardonic film begins with the arrival of the ark and the menorah suspended from helicopters by cables, then pivots to the destruction of the Temple by fire. This includes a kind of *tableau vivant* of the arch menorah relief panel in which desperate men dressed in white—Jews—one wreathed, one bloodied, rush the menorah from the burning Temple. For this Israeli filmmaker, the menorah-bearers are pious practitioners and not the destroyers, "Jews" and not "Romans." Finally, as the shrine crumbles, a single wall of the "Temple" remains and develops as a site of memory in the model of Jerusalem's post–Six-Day War Western Wall plaza. A variety of menorah souvenirs are for sale—of the kind sold to pilgrims to Israel and in Christian stores worldwide. I have seen them in evangelical and sometimes Catholic settings. Even coconuts emblazoned with menorahs are for sale in Bartana's rendition. Benjamin Seroussi and Eyal Danon, curators of an exhibition focusing on this film, write that "*Inferno* is simultaneously an archaeology of the future and a forecast of the past." Much like the book that you are reading, "In *Inferno,* art can also show how mythical pasts are invented."

One more menorah (it is hard to leave the lampstand behind): Atop Mount Gerizim, overlooking Nablus in the West Bank, is Kiryat Luza—today the home of the Samaritan people, an ancient nation that sees itself as the descendants of the biblical northern tribes of Israel. The Samaritans moved to the peak of their holy mountain from the old town of Nablus during the intifadas, fleeing attacks by Palestinian fighters, though they have cordial relations with the Palestinian Authority. At the center of Kiryat

Luza is a large Samaritan synagogue, the sacrificial area for the yearly Passover lamb sacrifice, and a large community center. Within the center, on one of its walls, hangs the emblem of the State of Israel. Samaritan existence is a precarious thing, perched between the local Palestinians and a "family" association with the Jews that goes back millennia. This relationship was strengthened by the Zionist Movement, which took the Samaritans under its wing from early in the twentieth century. The "symbol" of the state has appeared on Samaritan calendars and, not surprisingly, in the homes of members of the far more "Israeli" Samaritan community in Holon (a Tel Aviv suburb)—an Israeli minority group whose children serve in the military and whose priests—like Jewish rabbis—are government funded. There is something unique about the Samaritan emblem. The word "Israel" below the menorah is written in the ancient Samaritan Hebrew script that hearkens to biblical times, and not in the Aramaic "square" script used for Jewish Hebrew. The emblem of the state is thus transformed to symbolize the "Israelite Samaritans," *ha-Yisraelim ha-Shomronim,* as they now call themselves—in contradistinction to the general Jewish population, whom they call the "Israelite Jews," *ha-Yisraelim ha-Yehudim.* Ironically, the menorah of the Samaritan seal is the arch menorah. Though the menorah has been a Samaritan symbol since antiquity, appearing, as we have seen, on a wide variety of mosaics, the Samaritans were not "exiled" by Titus. The arch menorah has nothing to do with them. The olive branches of the emblem are based on Zechariah's vision, which has even less to do with Samaritans. Zechariah was not their prophet, and his book does not appear in their scriptures. Nonetheless, through association with the very Jewish emblem of the State of Israel, the Samaritans stake their unique place within the Israeli and, more importantly, the Israelite, collective.

Zionism and the State of Israel brought the seven-branched lampstand from a symbol of a forlorn people to the emblem of a modern nation-state—with all of the complexities that have come with the insertion of messianic imagery into inert, secular time. Apocalyptic post-Orthodox post-Zionism—together with its evangelical and fundamentalist fellow travelers—has run with this imagery, to the very edge of the Temple Mount and to the center of modern Israel's struggle between normality and the End of Days. Responding to Zionist iconography and messianism, the Chabad Hasidic movement, with its own millennialist ideology, has gone one step beyond Zionist thought, placing their own uniquely shaped Hanukkah menorahs—and ideology—on the steps of every significant capital. They have garnered the support of national leaders from Reagan and Obama to Putin for their push for "Moshiach NOW," for immediate redemption—for the "Messiah NOW." Unlike the most militant "post-Zionist" religious messianists, however, they have no guns, and have no inkling to remake the Temple Mount before the divinely ordained "Coming of the Messiah."

In this volume I have related aspects of the history of the menorah, the oldest religious symbol in all of Western culture, from its origins in biblical Israel through the present, using the Arch of Titus menorah—the most famous of all—as our touchstone and guide. It has enlightened our path from Bezalel, son of Uri, the artisan of the biblical menorah, through the Babylonian Exile, the Temple of Herod, late antique synagogues and churches, medieval manuscripts, and on to the present—though past usages and understandings do not always lead "naturally" to contemporary understandings. Thanks to the unique position of the arch menorah at the matrix of Jewish and Christian/European consciousness, it has been a meeting place for these communities, as it continues to be to this day. The arch menorah became a veritable "Rorschach test" for modernizing Jews from the nineteenth century to the present—and particularly after it was chosen as the national "symbol" of modern Israel. While this has been a story of a single significant symbol, it as much a story of discontinuity, of cultural twists and turns of profound significance—under the cover of continuity. It is a story of memory created and re-created, of a past forgotten and sometimes re-remembered—again and again. In this sense, the history of the menorah is a test case for thinking about symbols and ideas and institutions and relationships that appear to be "timeless," and a challenge to maintain relationship with our root symbols even as our culture reaches toward its inevitable next stages.

This has been a personal history—the history of my own search to understand the menorah, and my attempt at using the tools of my discipline to make sense of my beloved lampstand for our own complicated times. It began as early in my own life as I can remember, and reached its heights—quite literally—standing on scaffolding within the Arch of Titus, within centimeters of its grey stone. It has been a place of discovery—not just of the polychromy of the arch menorah, but also of the many paths and palimpsests that are the menorah. Having brought to bear primary sources from across the human experience, from biblical Israel to ancient Rome, medieval Europe to North Africa, America, and even Indonesia and Brazil,

I conclude this exploration with an explicit "primary source" of my own making, drawn from my own Facebook posts of a "research trip" I took with my then thirteen-year-old son (and research assistant), Koby, to Rome and Israel in May 2014. The reader will note the ways that I, the father, and not necessarily the historian, introduced my own child into the myth of the menorah and reported home the process of our pilgrimage to two eternal cities:

> May 8, 2014
> We found it!
>
> After waiting what felt like hours with thousands of our fellow travelers, speaking at least 70 languages crammed on long hallways we braved our way through the Vatican Museum and FOUND the MENORAH.
>
> It was painted on a high wall by Raffaello, illustrating the attempt of Heliodorus to rob the Temple.
>
> After that, we found it on two pieces of Jewish gold glass and two oil lamps, not to mention yet another wall painting.
>
> Alas, the remains of the Jewish catacombs were not on display, or we would have found even more.
>
> You see, the Menorah IS at the Vatican—just not the one brought to Rome by Vespasian!
>
> :-(
>
> Tomorrow, we follow another lead, this one at the Jewish Museum.
>
> Ciao.
>
> Signed, the Menorah Men.
>
> Final Installment, May 12, 2014
> The Menorah in Rome
> At the Temple of Peace we visited the Church of Sts. Cosmas and Damian, built over the ruins in the 6th century. Above the main arch is the image of seven lights, perhaps a Christian reference to the menorah. Proceeding to the Jewish Museum, we found numerous menorahs, many dating to the 16th century. Some show definite influence from the Arch menorah. The biggest surprise was a stone discovered in 2003 that describes three Jewish brothers who hid the menorah in the Tiber near the Synagogue in the 5th century.

Mark Podwal, "A Song 1948: Those who plant in tears will harvest in joy (Psalm 126:5)," 2014, courtesy of Mark Podwal, study for the Terezin Portfolio

We thought that we were close, but alas the stone is a fake, dating to around 1900. So much for that myth. In the Great Synagogue there are menorahs everywhere, the branches modeled on the Arch. On Shabbat we visited the Via Balbo synagogue (1914) which has even more. There are even two menorahs in pictures at Santa Maria Maggiore, a major church nearby.

In Rome there are menorahs everywhere!

Our next stop, on Sunday, was the Terme Museum, where Koby may have discovered color on the menorah of the Seasons Sarcophagus. He looked very closely and carefully, and perhaps found bits of yellow. . . .

Our investigation ended where it began, at the Arch of Titus. There, alone in the night, we thought about the arch, and escorted the menorah, so to speak, back to Jerusalem.

We write this from the plane to Israel! Maybe the menorah is there after all!

Shalom, the Menorah Men.

NOTES

BIBLIOGRAPHIC ESSAYS

INDEX

Notes

Introduction

Shelley's "Arch of Titus" is cited from Nora Crook, "Shelley's Jewish 'Orations,'" *Keats Shelley Journal* 59 (2010): 59.

1. Suetonius, *Lives of the Caesars, Vespasian* 23.
2. See romereborn.frischerconsulting.com/.

1. From Titus to Moses—and Back

1. Flavius Josephus, *Jewish War* 7.159–162.
2. Ibid., 7.148–152.
3. Pliny the Elder, *Natural History* 34.6.
4. Philo of Alexandria, *Questions and Answers on Exodus* 75.
5. Philo of Alexandria, *The Life of Moses* 2, 102–103.
6. Philo of Alexandria, *Preliminary Studies* 6–8.
7. Ben Sira 26:16–17.
8. Josephus, *Jewish War* 5.216–17.
9. Flavius Josephus, *Antiquities of the Jews* 3.146.
10. Caspar Levias, "Numbers and Numerals," *The Jewish Encyclopedia* (New York: Funk and Wagnalls, 1907): 9:349.
11. Exodus 37:17–24.
12. To *Antiquities* 3.146. Loeb ed., 4, 384, n.b.
13. Josephus, *Jewish War* 6.387–391.
14. Ibid., 7.44–45.
15. Babylonian Talmud, Menaḥot 28b, and parallels.
16. Mishnah Middot 2:3.
17. 1 Maccabees 13:27–29.

18. Josephus, *Antiquities* 7.336.

19. Ibid., 8.195.

20. Ibid., 3.137.

21. Josephus, *Jewish War* 1.647–655; *Antiquities* 17.149–163.

22. Babylonian Talmud, Menaḥot 98b, and parallels.

23. Zechariah 4:1–14.

24. The Ein Gedi inscription is translated and briefly discussed in Steven Fine, ed., *Sacred Realm: The Emergence of the Synagogue in the Ancient World* (New York: Oxford University Press and Yeshiva University Museum, 1996), 175.

25. *The Liturgical Poetry of Rabbi Yannai,* ed. Z. M. Rabinovitz (Jerusalem: Bialik Institute, 1987), 2:242, lines 71–72.

2. Flavian Rome to the Nineteenth Century

1. *The Liturgical Poetry of Rabbi Yannai,* ed. Z. M. Rabinovitz (Jerusalem: Bialik Institute, 1987), poem 109, 2:37–8, Hebrew.

2. Mark 13:12 and parallels.

3. *Sifre Zutta on Numbers,* ed. H. S. Horowitz (Jerusalem: Wahrmann, 1966) to Numbers 8:2.

4. Shulamith Laderman, *Images of Cosmology in Jewish and Byzantine Art God's Blueprint of Creation* (Leiden: Brill, 2013), 139–140. See also 140, n. 63.

5. Following the Kaufmann manuscript of the Mishnah.

6. Josephus, *Antiquities* 3.139–144.

7. *Avot de-Rabbi Natan,* ed. Solomon Schechter (New York: Feldheim, 1967), version A, ch. 41, 133.

8. *Otot ha-Meshiaḥ* (Mantua, 1546), 5b.

9. Procopius of Caesarea, *Gothic Wars* 8.21.11–14.

10. Procopius of Caesarea, *History of the Wars* 5.12.41–42.

11. Ibid., 4.9.1–9.

12. Procopius of Caesarea, *On Buildings* 5.6.

13. Ferdinand Gregorovius, *History of the City of Rome in the Middle Ages,* trans. Annie Hamilton (London: G. Bell & Sons, 1896), 1:215–216.

14. Ibid., 1:213.

15. See the excellent translation of Constantine VII Porphyrogennetos's *The Book of Ceremonies,* ed. and trans. Ann Moffatt, and Maxeme Tall (Canberra: Australian Association for Byzantine Studies, 2012), 1:8, n. 1.

16. Hans Yohanan Lewy, "A Note on the Fate of the Sacred Vessels of the Second Temple," *Kedem: Studies in Jewish Archaeology* 2 (1945): 125, in Hebrew.

17. Stefan Zweig, *The Buried Candelabrum,* trans. Eden Paul and Cedar Paul (New York: Viking Press, 1937), 106.

18. Lewy, "A Note on the Fate of the Sacred Vessels of the Second Temple," 125.

19. Kingsley, *God's Gold: A Quest for the Lost Temple Treasures of Jerusalem* (New York: Harper Collins, 2007), 286–287.

20. Ibid., 300.

21. Ibid., 305.

22. Robert Graves, *Count Belisarius* (New York: Literary Guild, 1938), 266.

23. Heinrich Strauss, "Menorah," *Encyclopedia Judaica* (Jerusalem: Keter, 1971), 11:1367.

24. *Liturgical Poetry of Rabbi Yannai,* poem 109, 2:35.

25. Ibid., 2:37.

26. *Midrash Tanḥuma,* ed. Solomon Buber (Warsaw: Lewin-Epstein, 1910), *be-Ha'alotkha* 11.

27. Adolph Jellinek, *Bet ha-Midrasch* (Jerusalem: Wahrmann, 1967), 2:88–91, 4:17–18; James R. Davila, "The Treatise of the Vessels (*Massekhet Kelim*): A New Translation and Introduction," in *Old Testament Pseudepigrapha: More Noncanonical Scriptures,* ed. Richard Bauckham, James R. Davila, Alexander Panayotov (Grand Rapids, MI: Eerdmans, 2013), 1:393–409, esp. 405.

28. *The Targum Sheni to the Book of Esther: A Critical Edition Based on MS. Sassoon 282 with Critical Apparatus,* ed. Bernard Grossfeld (Brooklyn: Sepher-Herman, 1994), chap. 1. My translation generally follows *The Two Targums of Esther,* ed. and trans. Bernard Grossfeld (Collegeville, MN: Liturgical Press, 1991), 107–111.

29. A. E. Cowley, *The Samaritan Liturgy, The Common Prayers* (Oxford: Clarendon Press, 1909), 65.

30. Eusebius of Caesarea, *Historia Ecclesiastica* 10.4.36–46, in L. Michael White, *The Social Origins of Christian Architecture* (Valley Forge, PA: Trinity Press International, 1997), 2:94–99.

31. John Osborne, "The Jerusalem Temple Treasure and the Church of Santi Cosma e Damiano in Rome," *Papers of the British School at Rome* 76 (2008): 173–181, esp. 179.

32. *Bede, on the Tabernacle,* trans. and ed. Arthur G. Holder (Liverpool: Liverpool University Press, 1994), 32.

33. Ibid., 35.

34. Zechariah 4:2, *Pesiqta Rabbati: A Synoptic Edition of Pesiqta Rabbati Based upon All Extant Manuscripts and the Editio Princeps,* ed. Rivka Ulmer (Atlanta, GA: Scholars Press, 1997), 1:101.

35. *Bede, on the Tabernacle,* 44.

36. John Chrysostom, *Against the Jews,* 6.1–2, is cited from the ecumenically titled *Discourses against Judaizing Christians,* trans. P. W. Harkins (Washington, DC: Catholic University Press, 1979), 164–165.

37. Peter Bloch, "Siebenarmige Leuchter in christlichen Kirchen," *Wallraf-Richartz-Jahrbuch* 23 (1961): cat. 1, 182; cat. 17, 184; Julius Schlosser, *Schriftquellen zur Geschichte der Karolingischen Kunst* (Vienna: C. Graeser, 1892), nos. 390, 574.

38. Chap. 6, *Baraita De-Melekhet Ha-Mishkan: A Critical Edition with Introduction and Translation,* ed. Robert Kirschner (Cincinnati, OH: Hebrew Union College Press, 1992), 193.

39. Joseph ben Isaac Bekhor Shor, *Perushe Rabbi Yosef Bekhor Shor al ha-Torah,* ed. Yehoshafaṭ Nevo (Jerusalem: Mossad Harav Kook, 1994) to Exodus 25:31–40.

40. Rashi's *Commentary on the Bible,* Munich, BSB Cod. hebr. 5, fol. 65, an illustration that diverges from the commentary in significant ways, shows angular branches. For arced branches in other medieval manuscripts of Rashi's Bible commentary, see Franconia, ca. 1250, Paris, BnF hébr. 155, fol. 110v; Franconian Bible, South Germany, Franconia (?), 1294/1295, Paris, BnF hébr. 5, fol. 118.

41. Moses Maimonides, *Mishnah im Perush Moshe Ben Maimon,* trans., ed., and commentator Yosef Qafiḥ (Jerusalem: Mossad Harav Kook, 1965), to Menaḥot 3:7 (3:117–120). See also Qafiḥ's commentary to Maimonides's *Mishneh Torah, Hilkhot Beit ha-Beḥirah* 3:7 (Jerusalem: Makhon Mishnat ha-Rambam, 1983), 12:54–58.

42. Abraham ben Moses ben Maimon, *Perush Rabbenu Avraham ben ha-Rambam z"l al Bereshit ve-Shemot,* trans. and ed., A. Y. Weisenberg (London: Solomon David Sassoon, 1959), 296–297.

43. Maimonides, *Mishnah im Perush Moshe Ben Maimon,* trans., ed., and commentator Yosef Qafiḥ (Jerusalem: Mossad Harav Kook, 1965).

44. Daniela Di Castro, *Et Ecce Gaudium: The Roman Jews and the Investiture of the Popes* (Rome: Museo Ebraico di Roma, 2010), 22–36.

45. Ferdinand Gregorovius, *The Ghetto and the Jews of Rome* (New York: Schocken, 1966), 20.

46. Babylonian Talmud, Shabbat 21b; *Targum Jonathan* to Ezekiel 11:16.

47. *Sefer Minhagim* (Venice, 1593), 58a. See the facsimile at http://www.kb.dk/books/judsam/2010/maj/jstryk/en/object59318/.

48. Gedaliah Ibn Yahya, *Shalshelet ha-Kabbalah* (Jerusalem: *ha-Dorot ha-Rishonim ve-Korotam,* 1962), 253.

49. Moses Mendelssohn, *Sefer Netivot ha-Shalom* (Berlin: George Friederich Starcke, 1783).

50. Ibid., to Exodus 25:40.

51. Moses Mendelssohn, *Jerusalem, or, On Religious Power and Judaism,* trans. Allan Arkush (Hanover, NH: Published for Brandeis University Press by University Press of New England, 1983), 113.

52. Ibid., 114.

53. See http://www.staglieno.comune.genova.it/en/node/112.

54. Henry Sebastian Bowden, *Guide to the Oratory, South Kensington* (London: The London Oratory, 1897), 33.

3. Modernity, Zionism, and the Menorah

1. Wilshire Boulevard Temple Archive, posted at http://wbtmurals.weebly.com/how-the-mural-was-made.html.

2. Haim Zelig Slonimsky, "Tsiur Atiq Yomin mi-Zikhronot Yemei Qedem," *HaZefira,* November 27, 1882.

3. Moses Gaster, "The Menorah," *Israel: The Jewish Magazine* 3 (1900): 167–169.

4. Harry A. Wolfson, "The Arch of Titus," trans. H. M. Kallen, *Menorah Journal* 1, no. 4 (1915): 201.

5. Letter by Josef Trumpeldor to Vladimir Jabotinsky, n.d., Tel Aviv: Jabotinsky Institute, Zev Jabotinsky Archive, file 1/6/4/110.

6. J. H. Patterson, *With the Zionists at Galipoli* (New York: George H. Doran, 1916), 46–47; 53–54.

7. J. H. Patterson, *With the Judæans in the Palestine Campaign* (London: Hutchinson and Co. Paternoster Row, 1922), 82.

8. Shmuel Yosef Agnon, *Only Yesterday,* trans. Barbara Harshav (Princeton, NJ: Princeton University Press, 2000), 406.

9. Ze'ev Raban and Levin Kipnis, *Alphabet* (Berlin: Verlag ha-Sefer, S. D. Saltzmann, 1923), *mem.*

10. Jabotinsky to Edward G. Derby, Jabotinsky Institute, Letter 3394, Reference Code A 1–2/9, http://www.infocenters.co.il/jabo/jabo_multimedia/files/%D7%90%201%20_%202_9/3394.pdf.

11. Wiley Feinstein, *The Civilization of the Holocaust in Italy: Poets, Artists, Saints, Anti-Semites* (Madison, NJ: Farleigh Dickinson University Press, 2003), 183–184, translated from the original document.

12. Stefan Zweig, *The Buried Candelabrum,* trans. Eden Paul and Cedar Paul (New York: Viking Press, 1937), 40.

13. *Dedication of the Seminary Gates, September 26, 1934* (New York: Jewish Theological Seminary, 1934), unpaginated (6).

14. "Al ha-Pereq: Al Shiḥrur Roma," *la-Ḥayyal: Alon-Yomi le- Ḥayyilim be-Yaveshet Europa* 79 (May 6, 1944): 2, my translation.

15. Central Zionist Archives KRU\16790; "Jews in Italy Hold Mass Demonstrations and Fast Protesting Palestine Raids, Arrests" Jewish Telegraphic Agency, July 3, 1946.

16. *Chicago Sentinel,* July 28, 1943, 15.

17. B. Nicht, "Be-Roma im ha-Besorah al Hakamat Medinah Yehudit; Mikhtav me-Italiata," *Davar,* Monday, December 15, 1947, 2.

4. Creating a National Symbol

1. *Haaretz,* February 11, 1949, 2.

2. Isaac Herzog, “The Shape of the Menorah in the Arch of Titus,” *Scritti in memoria di Sally Mayer* (Jerusalem: Fondazione Sally Mayer; Milan: Scuola superiore di Studi Ebraici, 1956), 95–98, in Hebrew.

3. See, for example, Babylonian Talmud, Baba Batra 3b–4a.

4. Herzog, “The Shape of the Menorah in the Arch of Titus,” 98.

5. Letter to Lord Herbert Samuel, October 24, 1952, now in the Israel State Archives, Office of the Speaker of the 4th Knesset, Public Inquiries, כ/ 12 / 592.

6. Minutes of *Va'adat ha-Semel ve-ha-Degel shel Moetzet ha-Medinah* (the Committee on the State Symbol of the State Council), September 29, 1948, 3, Israel State Archives, 19.7.48–9.2.49, 395/1-ג.

7. Levin Kipnis, *Gan Gani* (Tel Aviv: N. Twersky, 1962), 3:34, in Hebrew.

8. “Nation in Holiday Mood as Israel Rounds out Year, Shofar Will Be Sounded as Symbol, *Palestine Post* (May 3, 1949), 1.

9. Shlomo Sakolsky, “Menorat Yisrael,” *ha-Tsofeh le-Yeladim* 3, no. 20, February 2, 1949, 235.

10. Central Zionist Archives, KRA\1490, http://www.zionistarchives.org.il/Pages/ArchiveItem.aspx?oi=09001e15806faa11&ot=cza_poster.

11. Uriel Carlebach, “Ruḥo shel Herzl be-Roma,” *Maariv* (August 11, 1949): 2.

12. Daniela Gardosh, and Yoram A. Shamir, eds., *Lo Raq Semel: Semel ha-Medinah be-Karikaturah* (Holon: Israeli Cartoon Museum, 2011), in Hebrew. For those cartoons cited here, see 34, 35, 36, 42, 60.

13. Isaac Herzog, “ha-Menorah be-Keshet Titus,” *Maḥanyim: Mesekhet le-Ḥayyil le-Ḥag ha-Ḥanukkah* 37 (1959): 9–12.

14. Yosef Qafiḥ's comments appear in his supercommentary to *Mishnah: Im Perush Moshe Ben Maimon,* 119–120.

15. Menachem Mendel Schneerson, *Reshimat ha-Menorah: Seder Hadkaqat ga-Nerot be-Beit ha-Miqdash* (Brooklyn: Kehot, 1998).

16. Menachem Mendel Schneerson's most complete discussion appears in his Schneerson, *Hilkhot Beit ha-Beḥirah* (Brooklyn: Kehot, 1986), chap. 8, 50–51. See also his *Liqutei Siḥot, Tetsaveh* 7, no. 2 (Brooklyn: Kehot, 1982), 209, n. 17.

17. Schneerson, *Hilkhot Beit ha-Beḥirah,* 119–120.

18. https://www.youtube.com/watch?v=U6Ey7z7-UK8. For a clear and impassioned explication of Rabbi Schneerson's essays on the menorah, see Levi Yitzchak Garelik, http://legacy.theyeshiva.net/Video/View/372/What-Was-the-Real-Shape-of-the-Menorah.

19. David Berger, *The Rebbe, the Messiah, and the Scandal of Orthodox Indifference* (London: Littman Library of Jewish Civilization, 2001), 62.

5. A Jewish Holy Grail

1. Steven Fine, "Concerning the Jesus Family Tomb," *SBL Forum,* March 2007, http://www.sbl-site.org/publications/article.aspx?ArticleId=655.

2. Ezra 1:8–11.

3. Jeremiah 3:16.

4. 2 Baruch 2:5–10, trans. R. H. Charles, *The Apocrypha and Pseudepigrapha of the Old Testament in English: With Introductions and Critical and Explanatory Notes to the Several Books* (Oxford: Clarendon Press, 1913), 2: with modifications.

5. Jerusalem Talmud, Sheqalim 6:2, 49c.

6. Mortimer N. Adler, *The Itinerary of Benjamin of Tudela* (New York: Philip Feldheim, 1967), 7, in Hebrew, sect. 8.

7. John the Deacon, *Descriptio Lateranensis ecclesiae,* 373 336.17 to 337.5, 337.17–19, 341.25 to 342.23, in *Codice topografico della città di Roma III,* ed. Roberto Valentini and Giuseppe Zucchetti (Rome: Tipografia del Senato, 1946), 326–373, translated in Marie Thérèse Champagne, "The Relationship between the Papacy and the Jews in Twelfth-Century Rome: Papal Attitudes toward Biblical Judaism and Contemporary European Jewry" (Ph.D. dissertation, Louisiana State University, 2005), 164.

8. Benedict, *The Marvels of Rome, Mirabilia urbis Romae,* 2nd ed., ed. Francis Morgan Nichols (New York: Italica Press, 1986), 29; Champagne, "The Relationship," 47.

9. Benedict, *The Marvels of Rome,* 6; Champagne, "The Relationship," 47.

10. Nicolaus Maniacutius, *Historia imaginis Salvatoris,* in Gerhard Wolf, *Salus populi Romani: die Geschichte römischer Kultbilder im Mittelalter* (Weinheim: VCH, Acta Humaniora, 1990), 322–323; Champagne, "The Relationship," 53.

11. Champagne, "The Relationship," 173.

12. *Midrash Bereshith Rabbati,* ed. Ch. Albeck (Jerusalem: 1940), *Va-Yigash* 45:8. See Saul Lieberman, *Hellenism in Jewish Palestine* (New York: Jewish Theological Seminary, 1940), 23–24.

13. J. D. Eisenstein, "The Fate of the Temple Vessels," *The Menorah: A Monthly Magazine for the Jewish Home* 31 (1901): 169–178.

14. Daniela Di Castro, *From Jerusalem to Rome and Back: The Journey of the Menorah from Fact to Myth* (Rome: Museo Ebraico di Roma, 2008), 1–2.

15. Jessica Dello Russo, "An Archival and Historical Survey of the Jewish Catacombs of the Villa Torlonia in Rome," *Roma Subterranea Judaica* (2012): 3, n. 9.

16. F. Servi, "Cronaca Mensile Italiana," in *L'Educatore Israelita,* 11 (1873): 116–117.

17. Nathaniel Hawthorne, *The Marble Faun: Or, the Romance of Monte Beni,* (Boston: James R. Osgood, 1876), 1:200–201.

18. *Israel: The Jewish Magazine* 3 (1900): 72.

19. Douglas Allen, *Myth and Religion in Mircea Eliade* (New York: Garland, 1998), 181, 274.

20. Stefan Zweig, *The Buried Candelabrum,* trans. Eden Paul and Cedar Paul (New York: Viking Press, 1937), 148–149.

21. This story was first published in *Atidot: Rivon le-Noar,* eds. Shimshon Meltzer and Benyamin Benshalom (Winter 1957): 3–11. "The Tale of the Menorah" was translated by David Stern in *A Book That Was Lost and Other Stories,* ed. Alan L. Mintz and Anne Golomb Hoffman (New York: Schocken, 1995), 227–240.

22. http://www.imj.org.il/imagine/galleries/viewItemE.asp?case=34&itemNum=371778.

23. Peter Levi, *The Head of the Soup* (London: Constable, 1979), 168.

24. Ibid., 169.

25. Ibid., 183.

26. See http://www.amazon.com/Paris-Lamb-Marcia-Fine/dp/0982695276/ref=sr_1_1?s=books&ie=UTF8&qid=1429421976&sr=1-1&keywords=Marcia+Fine%27s+Paris+Lamb.

27. Alan Rosenthal, *Jerusalem, Take One! Memoirs of a Jewish Filmmaker* (Carbondale: Southern Illinois University Press, 2000), 191.

28. Ibid., 189.

6. The Menorah at the Vatican

1. Shnayer Z. Leiman, "The Adventure of the Maharal of Prague in London: R. Yudl Rosenberg and the Golem of Prague," *Tradition* 36, no. 1 (2002): 26–58, esp. 30.

2. Yudl Rosenberg, *Ḥoshen ha-Mishpat shel ha-Kohen ha-Gadol* (The Priestly Breastplate of the High Priest) (Piotrków: Feldmann, 1913), 40, in Hebrew and Yiddish.

3. Baruch Shneur Zalman Schneersohn, *Reshimot ha-Rabash* (Brooklyn: Kehot, 2001), 116.

4. Moshe David b. Nissim, *Sefer Maamar Ester* (Djerba, Tunisia: Hai Haddad, 1946), 32b–33b, n. 1.

5. I have cited the story according to Daor Yehuda, "Memories of Rabbi Yitzḥak Ḥai Bokovza," in Yitzḥak Ḥai Bokovza, *Sefer Beit ha-Laḥmi* (Jerusalem: ha-Maarav, 1975), 22.

6. See http://www.ottmall.com/mj_ht_arch/v23/mj_v23i60.html#CRP.

7. See http://chabadpedia.co.il/index.php/חיים_משה יהודה_בלוי

8. See http://crownheights.info/blogs/380656/our-heroes-rabbi-moshe-yehuda-hakohen-blau-1913-2003.

9. Blau's memoir is posted at http://myblau.blogspot.com/2015/07/blog-post_23.html#more, 10.

10. Ibid.

11. Yisroel Miller's conversation with Yonatan Shtencel has subsequently been removed from the Web.

12. Lisa Palmieri-Billig, "Shetreet: Pope Likely to Visit Next Year," *Jerusalem Post,* January 18, 1996, 1.

13. Ronen Bergman, "The Pope's Jewish Treasures," *Musaf Haaretz,* May 10, 1996, 18–20, 22, Hebrew.

14. E-mail from the Israeli Ministry of Foreign Affairs, 2004, first published in my "The Temple Menorah: Where Is It?" *Biblical Archaeology Review* 31, no. 4 (2005): 20.

15. Yitzhak Qaqon, "The Temple Vessels Are Stored in the Vatican Vaults," *Yom le-Yom* (December 28, 2006): 3, Hebrew; The story appeared in the general press in Gilad Shinhav's "Following the Temple Treasure," December 28, 2006, *MaarivNRG,* in Hebrew, http://www.nrg.co.il/online/1/ART1/523/773.html.

16. This letter was provided to me by Yonatan Shtencel.

17. Nesanel Gantz, "Vanished Vessels of the Beis Hamikdash: Vatican Responds to Claim that the Church Has Our Holy Kelim in Its Possession," *Ami Magazine,* November 27, 2013, 119–126.

18. Avraham Zuroff, "Pope Named as Defendant over Plunder of Temple Vessels," *Arutz Sheva,* May 8, 2009, http://www.israelnationalnews.com/News/News.aspx/131257#Vpg6TvkrKaE.

19. Sophia Hollander, "Yeshiva Students Challenge Myths of the Menorah: Theory That Golden Treasure Is in Vatican Disputed by Research," *Wall Street Journal,* August 14, 1994. The Hebrew version appeared at http://www.bhol.co.il/forums/topic.asp?cat_id=4&topic_id=3059259&forum_id=771.

20. Joel Rappel, *Zehuto shel Meḥaber ha-Tefillah le-Shalom ha-Medinah: Maḥzor Koren le-Yom ha-Atsma'ut ule-Yom Yerushalayim,* ed. Moshe Taragin, Binyamin Lau, and Joel Rappel (Jerusalem: Koren, 2015), 305–311.

7. Illuminating the Path to Armageddon

1. http://www.jpost.com/Jewish-World/Priest-leads-attack-on-Moldova-menorah.

2. The World Jewish Congress, "Moldovan Church Indirectly Blames Jews for Anti-Semitic Incident," December 23, 2009, http://www.worldjewishcongress.org/en/news/moldovan-church-indirectly-blames-jews-for-anti-semitic-incident.

3. Ilana Baum and Tzvi Singer, "Gibbur, Tsadik, Qadosh," *Yediot Aḥaronot,* February 28, 1994, 9, in Hebrew.

4. Cited by Sarina Chen, "Between Poetics and Politics—Vision and Praxis in Current Activity to Construct the Third Temple" (Ph.D. dissertation, Hebrew University of Jerusalem, 2007), in Hebrew, 92.

5. Ibid., 183.

6. Videos of the 2014 Paschal sacrifice appeared in English and in Hebrew, the English version geared for a Christian audience: https://www.youtube.com/watch?v=5kgbRusmqjs; https://www.youtube.com/watch?v=WiyEKJgBU4U. To view historical footage of the Samaritan Passover sacrifice, see https://www.youtube.com/watch?v=QpRr5ln1asM.

7. "Rabbi Yisrael Ariel Conducts Holy Temple Menorah Lighting Rehearsal" (2013), https://www.youtube.com/watch?v=xmI2yL7XKMo.

8. Keshev and Ir Amim, *Dangerous Liaison: The Dynamics of the Rise of the Temple Movements and Their Implications,* Y. Be'er, writer, trans. London Sappir (Jerusalem: Keshev and Ir Amim, March 1, 2013), esp. 41–42.

9. Temple Institute, *ha-Menorah* (Jerusalem: Temple Institute, 1999/2000), compact disc.

10. Arnon Segal, "Neḥbaim el ha-Kelim," *Makor Rishon,* October 3, 2014.

11. See https://www.youtube.com/watch?v=csXO9wQxtMA.

12. Babylonian Talmud, Ta'anit 26b.

13. See http://www.machonshilo.org/en/images/stories/files/Kina%20for%20Gush%20Katif.pdf.

Bibliographic Essays

The bibliographic essays that follow, together with the endnotes that accompany the text, guide you to the most important primary and secondary sources that undergird this project. The essays and the notes are not exhaustive, but selective. In every case, please refer to the bibliographies of the sources cited in order to access the primary sources and the history of scholarship—particularly note my own preparatory studies for this volume. On the various individuals, places, and primary sources mentioned, the most readily available and comprehensive resources are the *Encyclopedia Judaica* (Jerusalem: Keter, 1971, always preferable for its wealth of illustrations; 2nd ed., Detroit: Macmillan Reference USA, 2006); *The Oxford Classical Dictionary,* 4th ed., eds. Simon Hornblower and Anthony Spawforth (Oxford: Oxford University Press, 2012); and the *YIVO Encyclopedia of Jews in Eastern Europe* ed. Gershon D. Hundert (New Haven CT: Yale University Press, 2008, http://www.yivoencyclopedia.org). *Wikipedia,* useful in all of its languages, should be used with caution. I have tended to prefer sources in English where possible and worked to provide a mix of scholarly and more popular writings. Still, I have not hesitated to cite works in the broad range of languages and specializations in which this project "lives." Whether you are a student, a scholar, or a casual reader, these essays are an entrée into both the raw and the processed materials from which my narrative is built. They are an invitation for further study, contemplation, and perhaps even to experience some of the joy, exhilaration, and occasional sorrow that I have felt as these sources and the often long-dead people who produced them have become my intimates, friends, and occasional adversaries.

Introduction

It is often difficult to imagine the scope and range of ancient Rome, and there is no end to the number of basic introductions. Among my favorites is Christopher Kelly's *The Roman Empire: A Very Short Introduction* (Oxford: Oxford University Press, 2006), specifically because it sets the empire within an unsentimentally postimperial frame, includes the voices of ancient Jews, and explores the uses to which Rome has been put by modern empires—all in a mere 168 pages. Bernard Frischer's "Rome Reborn" (http://romereborn.frischerconsulting.com/) gives a very tactile virtual tour of Rome as it may have been. For the Jewish place in this world, including the Jewish War of 66–74 CE, I have brought together an array of materials on the Center for Online Jewish Studies curriculum on Jews and Judaism in the Greco-Roman World (http://cojs.org/jews_and_judaism_in_the_greco-roman_period/) that will certainly be of use. The most recent synthetic history of the Jewish War and its causes is Martin Goodman's *Rome and Jerusalem: The Clash of Ancient Civilizations* (New York: Alfred A. Knopf, 2007). All modern studies of the Arch of Titus are dependent upon Adriaan Reelant's magnificent *De Spolis templi Hierosolymitani in arcu Titiano conspicuis* (Trajecti ad Rhenum [Utrecht]: Gulielmi Broedelet, 1716). This slim volume, which includes all of the then-known primary literary sources, classical and rabbinic, and documents investigations of the arch menorah undertaken on behalf of Reelant by an English scholar in Rome, is the basis for all later research. It may be viewed at: https://archive.org/details/gri_hadrianirelaooreel. The exhaustive study of archaeological aspects of the Arch of Titus was prepared by Michael Pfanner, *Der Titusbogen* (Mainz am Rhein: P. v. Zabern, 1983). This should be read together with Leon Yarden's study, which focuses on the menorah panel: *The Spoils of Jerusalem on the Arch of Titus: A Re-Investigation* (Stockholm: Svenska Institutet i Rom, 1991). Yarden not only translates Reelant's report on the arch, giving new life to this Latin text, but pushed the boundaries of technology in his own time to create an important photographic record of the menorah panel. The most readable review of classical literature on the arch is still William Knight's *The Arch of Titus and the Spoils of the Temple* (London: Religious Tract Society, 1896), https://archive.org/details/archoftitusspoil1896knig. My recent Coursera course, "The Arch of Titus: Rome and the Menorah," which introduces the arch in a series of video conversations and learning activities, may be accessed at: https://www.coursera.org/learn/archoftitus. On the

Colosseum and its modern history, see Keith Hopkins and Mary Beard, *The Colosseum* (Cambridge, MA: Harvard University Press, 2005). Regarding the complexities surrounding Vespasian's ascension, see Gwyn Morgan, *69 A.D.: The Year of Four Emperors* (New York: Oxford University Press, 2007). For the history of the Roman triumphal parade, see Mary Beard, *The Roman Triumph* (Cambridge, MA: Harvard University Press, 2009), and for visual aspects, Ida Östenberg's outstanding *Staging the World: Spoils, Captives, and Representations in the Roman Triumphal Procession* (Oxford: Oxford University Press, 2009). Jewish and Roman coins that I discuss in this volume are collected by David Hendin, *Guide to Biblical Coins,* 5th ed. (Nyack, NY: Amphora, 2010). Freud's comment appears on a postcard sent to psychoanalyst Karl Abraham in Berlin during Freud's visit to Rome on September 13, 1913. The inscription, written below an image of the arch, reads, "Der Jude übersteht's! Herzlichen Gruss und Coraggio Kasimiro!," translated: "The Jew survives it! Cordial greetings and courage Kasimiro!" See Yosef Hayim Yerushalmi, *Freud's Moses: Judaism Terminable and Interminable* (New Haven, CT: Yale University Press 1993), figs. 8–9 and page 111; and Mary Bergstein, *Mirrors of Memory: Freud, Photography and the History of Art* (Ithaca, NY: Cornell University Press, 2012), 111–114.

On the polychromy of the Arch of Titus, see my "Menorahs in Color: Polychromy in Jewish Visual Culture of Roman Antiquity," *Images: A Journal of Jewish Art and Visual Culture* 6, no. 1 (2012): 3–25; and Heinrich Piening, "Examination Report: The Polychromy of the Arch of Titus Menorah Relief," in the same issue, 26–29. See also Steven Fine and Peter Schertz, "The Arch of Titus in Color: A Tentative Reconstruction of the Polychromy of the Menorah Panel," *Images: A Journal of Jewish Art and Visual Culture* 10 (2017); and our virtual reconstruction, produced together with Donald Sanders and his Institute for the Visualization of History, available at yu.edu/cis in December 2016. Renewed interest in polychromy in classical art has been spearheaded by Vinzenz Brinkmann and his team through a host of museum exhibitions and related catalogs. This work is reported in Brinkmann, Oliver Primavesi, and Max Hollein, *Circumlitio: The Polychromy of Antique and Mediaeval Sculpture* (Munich: Hirmer, 2010). Comparisons of the image of Titus in the writings of the Jewish/Roman historian Flavius Josephus, Suetonius's second-century *Lives of the Caesars,* and in Rabbinic sources of the fifth through seventh centuries provides a fascinating and complex image of an emperor in both Imperial literature and in the writings of the subdued—in Greek, Latin, Hebrew, and Aramaic.

Rabbinic sources, beginning with *Genesis Rabba* 10:7, are the focus of Joshua Levinson, " 'Tragedies Naturally Performed': Fatal Charades, Parodia Sacra, and the Death of Titus," *Jewish Culture and Society under the Christian Roman Empire,* ed. Seth Schwartz, Richard Kalmin (Leuven: Peeters, 2003), 349–382; and Galit Hasan-Rokem, "Rumors in Times of War and Cataclysm," in *Rumor Mills: The Social Impact of Rumor and Legend,* ed. Gary Alan Fine, Véronique Campion-Vincent, Chip Heath (New Brunswick, NJ: Aldine Transaction, 2005), 31–52.

Anthropologist Victor Turner popularized the concept of liminality in a range of publications, including his coauthored book with Edith Turner, *Image and Pilgrimage in Christian Culture* (New York: Columbia University Press, 1978). I became aware of its functionality for Jewish studies through Shlomo A. Deshen's "The Kol Nidre Enigma: An Anthropological View of the Day of Atonement Liturgy," *Ethnology* 18, no. 2 (1979): 121–133. A useful entry into Jung's work on symbols is Carl G. Jung and Marie-Luise Franz, *Man and His Symbols* (Garden City, NY: Doubleday, 1964). See also Mircea Eliade's deeply influential reflection on sacred space, *The Sacred and the Profane: The Nature of Religion* (New York: Harcourt, Brace and World, 1959). An excellent introduction to Goodenough's thought is the abridged edition of his *Jewish Symbols in the Greco Roman Period* prepared by Jacob Neusner, together with Neusner's introduction (Princeton, NJ: Princeton University Press, 1988). Dan Brown has described Joseph Campbell's influence on *The Da Vinci Code,* in particular *The Hero with a Thousand Faces* (Princeton, NJ: Princeton University Press, 1972) and *The Power of Myth* (with Bill D. Moyers, New York, 1988). See "Dan Brown: By the Book," *New York Times Sunday Book Review,* June 23, 2012, 8. See also my reflection on Goodenough and the interpretation of symbols in my *Art and Judaism in the Greco-Roman World: Toward a New Jewish Archaeology* (Cambridge: Cambridge University Press, 2005, rev. ed. 2010), 35–46; 137–173 and my *Art, History and the Historiography of Judaism in the Greco-Roman World* (Leiden: Brill, 2013), 161–180.

The work of Yael Zerubavel has been transformative for the study of modern Zionist culture and its search for ancient sources. See especially her *Recovered Roots: Collective Memory and the Making of Israeli National Tradition* (Chicago: University of Chicago Press, 1995). Alec Mishory has pioneered the study of Zionist and early Israeli visual culture, providing a baseline for further research. See his *Lo and Behold: Zionist Icons and Visual Symbols in Israeli Culture* (Tel Aviv: Am Oved, 2000, in Hebrew), the foundational study within this developing field. More generally, see the articles collected in *National Symbols, Fractured Identities: Contesting the National Narrative,* ed. Michael E. Geisler (Middlebury, VT: Middlebury College Press, 2005), especially Tamar Mayer, "National Symbols in Jewish Israel: Representations and Collective Memory," 3–34, and W. Scott Poole, "Lincoln in Hell: Class and Confederate Symbols in the American South," 121–48. Two major collections relating to the menorah have appeared in recent years, both of them accompaniments to museum exhibitions. See, most significantly, Yael Israeli's Israel Museum catalog, *In the Light of the Menorah: Story of a Symbol* (Jerusalem: The Israel Museum, 1999); and Raphael Gross's *Im Licht Der Menora: Jüdisches Leben in Der Römischen Provinz: Eine Ausstellung Des Jüdischen Museums Frankfurt in Kooperation Mit Der Römisch-Germanischen Kommission in Frankfurt Am Main: Jüdisches Museum Frankfurt, 11. Dezember 2014 Bis 10. Mai 2015* (Frankfurt Am Main: Jüdisches Museum Frankfurt, 2014).

Regarding the cultural history of symbols over the *longue durée,* I have been greatly encouraged by the work of Asher D. Biemann, *Dreaming of Michelangelo: Jewish Variations on a Modern Theme* (Stanford, CA: Stanford University Press, 2012); and Cristina Mazzoni, *She-wolf: The Story of a Roman Icon* (Cambridge: Cambridge University Press, 2010). Pierre Nora's studies of "places of memory" have been most significant in the framing of this work, particularly his edited collection *Realms of Memory: Rethinking the French Past,* tr. A. Goldhammer (New York: Columbia University Press, 1996); and his theoretical essay, "Between Memory and History: Les Lieux de Mémoire," *Memory and Counter-Memory* 26 (Spring 1989): 7–24. Within Jewish studies, Nora's work deeply influenced and was influenced by Yosef H. Yerushalmi, *Zakhor: Jewish History and Jewish Memory* (Seattle: University of Washington Press, 1982; 2nd ed.; 1996). Yerushalmi, with Nora, assumes a deep fissure between modern history writing/memory and premodern times. This notion of fissure is refuted by medievalist Amos Funkenstein, who in seminar and conversation at UCLA (1986) and in writing asserted considerable continuity between periods—and disagreement with Yerushalmi's modernist inclination to distinguish the recent past sharply from earlier periods (*Perceptions of Jewish History* [Berkeley: University of California Press, 1993], esp. 10–11). Thirty-four years after the initial publication of *Zakhor,* and deeply committed to postmodern approaches, I do not assert the level of modern distinctiveness that Nora and Yerushalmi lit upon. Still, as this study shows (and at the outset, much to my surprise), the modern history of the menorah is very different from what preceded it. My own approach sees disjunction even as it seeks out signs of continuity—thus this diachronic monograph.

Chapter 1

The basic study of Flavian architecture is R. H. Darwall-Smith's *Emperors and Architecture: A Study of Flavian Rome* (Brussels: Latomus, 1996). On the ideological underpinnings of the Temple of Peace, see Paul Zanker, "In Search of the Roman Viewer," *The Interpretation of Architectural Sculpture in Greece and Rome,* ed. D. Buitron-Oliver (Washington, DC: National Gallery of Art, 1997), 187; and Carlos F. Noreña, "Medium and Message in Vespasian's Templum Pacis," *Memoirs of the American Academy in Rome* 48 (2003): 25–43. Happily, the Temple of Peace has been excavated and published. See especially the articles and illustrations assembled by Roberto Meneghini and Rossella Rea, eds., *La Biblioteca Infinita: I Luoghi Del Sapere Nel Mondo Antico* (Milan: Electra, 2014), 241–340. On the invitation of defeated deities into Rome, see Emily A. Schmidt, "The Flavian Triumph and the Arch of Titus: The Jewish God in Flavian Rome," Ancient Borderlands Research Focus Group, UC Santa Barbara, March 31, 2010, https://escholarship.org/uc/item/9xwok5kh; and Jodi Magness, "The Arch of Titus and the Fate of the God of Israel," *Journal of Jewish Studies* 69 (2008): 201–217. On the Roman triumph as portrayed in literary and visual sources, see, most recently, Mary Beard, "The Triumph of Josephus," in *Flavian Rome: Culture, Image, Text,* (Leiden: Brill, 2003), 543–558; Mary Beard and her *The Roman Triumph* (Cambridge, MA: Harvard University Press, 2009); and Ida Östenberg, *Staging the World: Spoils, Captives, and Representations in the Roman Triumphal Procession* (Oxford: Oxford University Press, 2009). Rachel Hachlili conveniently catalogs all images of the menorah known at the time of publication and provides full bibliographical references. See her *The Menorah, the Ancient Seven-Armed Candelabrum: Origin, Form and Significance* (Leiden: Brill, 2001). On Roman marble candelabra, see Hans-Ulrich Cain, *Römische Marmorkandelaber* (Mainz: Zabern, 1985); and the marble candelabra retrieved from the Mahdia shipwreck, Hans-Ulrich Cain and Olaf Dräger, "Die Marmorkandelaber," in *Das Wrack. Der antike Schiffsfund von Mahdia,* ed. Gisela Hellenkemper Salies et al. (Bonn: Rheinisches Landesmuseums Bonn, 1994), 1:239–257. A wide variety of Roman domestic lampstands and other lighting devices were uncovered in Pompeii and Herculaneum. These are discussed and lavishly illustrated In Barbara Pettinau's "L'Illuminazione della Domus: Lucerne e Candelabri," in Lucia Pirzio Biroli Stefanelli, *Il Bronzo dei Romani: Arredo e Suppellettile,* exhibition catalog (Roma: "L'Erma" di Bretschneider, 1990), 81–101. The Magdala ashlar, with its menorah, has been the subject of considerable overinterpretation and hype, which I discuss in "The Magdala Ashlar: From Synagogue Furnishing to Media Event," *Symposium: Constructing and Deconstructing Jewish Art,* eds. Ilia Rodov, Mirjam Rajner, Sara Offenberg, forthcoming. See also R. Steven Notley, "Genesis Rabbah 98:17—'And Why Is It Called Genossar?' Recent Discoveries at Magdala and Jewish Life on the Plain of Genossar in the Early Roman Period," in *Talmuda de-Eretz Israel: Archaeology and the Rabbis in Late Antique Palestines,* eds. Steven Fine and Aaron Koller (Berlin: Walter de Gruyter, 2014), 141–157. On Greco-Roman period sources for the menorah, see Steven Fine, *Art and Judaism in the Greco-Roman World: Toward a New Jewish Archaeology* (Cambridge: Cambridge University Press, 2005; rev. ed. 2010), 146–163. Bezalel Narkiss's discussion of the Jewish Quarter menorah graffito appeared as "The Scheme of the Sanctuary from the Time of Herod," *Journal of Jewish Art* 1 (1974): 6–15. The most important discussions of the biblical menorahs are Carol L. Meyers, *The Tabernacle Menorah: A Synthetic Study of a Symbol from the Biblical Cult* (Missoula, MT: Scholar's Press, 1976, rep., with a new introduction, Piscataway, NJ: Gorgias Press, 2003); Carol L. Meyers, "Was There a Seven Branched Lampstand in Solomon's Temple?," *Biblical Archaeology Review* 5, no. 5 (1979): 46–57; Carol L. Meyers with Eric M. Meyers, *Haggai, Zechariah 1–8: A New Translation with Introduction and Commentary* (Garden City, NY: Doubleday, 1987); and Hachlili, *The Menorah,* 7–22. On Abraham J. Heschel's concept of "divine pathos," see his *The Prophets* (New York: Harper & Row, 1962). Corinthian bronze, is discussed by Dan Levene and Beno Rothenberg, *A Metallurgical Gemara: Metals in the Jewish Sources* (London: Institute for Archaeo-Metallurgical Studies, Institute of Archaeology, University College, 2007), 70–72. The tombstone of Samuel Senior Teixeira is discussed by Ellen S. Saltzman, "The Forbidden Image in Jewish Art," *Journal of Jewish Art* 8 (1981): 42–59, esp. 52–53. Saltzman describes a range of images that were used by Jews in the early modern period that one would not expect from the writings of the rabbinic leadership. Maximilian Kon's approach to the menorah base is closest to my own. See his "The Menorah of the Arch of Titus," *Palestine Exploration Quarterly* 82, no. 1 (1950): 25–30. Daniel Sperber surveys the relevant sources in "The History of the Menorah," *Journal of Jewish Studies* 16 (1965): 135–159. The Didyma column bases were redated to the early second century CE by Axel Filges, *Untersuchungen Zur Kaiserzeitlichen Bauornamentik Von Didyma* (Tübingen: E. Wasmuth, 1989), 17–46, esp. 40, 46. The implications of Adrienne Mayor's *The First Fossil Hunters: Dinosaurs, Mammoths, and Myth in Greek and Roman Times* (Princeton, NJ: Princeton University Press, 2011) have yet to be absorbed by scholars of rabbinic literature.

Chapter 2

I discuss Yannai's poem and its historical context in *Art and Judaism in the Greco-Roman World: Toward a New Jewish Archaeology* (Cambridge: Cambridge University Press, 2005; rev. ed. 2010), 161–163, and again in "Menorahs in Color: Polychromy in Jewish Visual Culture of Roman Antiquity," *Images: A Journal of Jewish Art and Visual Culture* 6, no. 1 (2012): 8–15. I discuss rabbinic sources for the presence of the Temple vessels in Rome in *Art, History and the Historiography of Judaism in the Greco-Roman World* (Leiden: Brill, 2013), 63–86, and in a more popular format as S. Fine, "The Temple Menorah: Where Is It?," *Biblical Archaeology Review* 31, no. 4 (2005): 18–25, 62–63. A number of scholars have approached these sources from differing perspectives in recent years: Fergus Millar, "Last Year in Jerusalem: Monuments of the Jewish War in Rome," *Flavius Josephus and Flavian Rome,* ed. J. Edmondson, S. Mason, J. B. Rives (Oxford: Oxford University Press, 2005), 101–128; David Noy, "*Rabbi Aqiba Comes to Rome:* A Jewish Pilgrimage in Reverse?," in *Pilgrimage in Graeco-Roman and Early Christian Antiquity: Seeing the Gods,* ed. J. Elsner and I. Rutherford (Oxford: Oxford University Press, 2005), 373–385; Mary Beard, *The Roman Triumph* (Cambridge, MA: Harvard University Press, 2009), esp. 151–153. The late antique/Byzantine contexts are discussed by Ra'anan S. Boustan, "The Spoils of the Jerusalem Temple at Rome and Constantinople: Jewish Counter-geography in a Christianizing Empire," in *Antiquity after Antiquity: Jewish and Christian Pasts in the Greco-Roman World,* ed. G. Gardner, K. L. Osterloh (Tübingen: Mohr Siebeck, 2008), 327–372; and Alexei M. Sivertsev, *Judaism and Imperial Ideology in Late Antiquity* (Cambridge: Cambridge University Press, 2011), 125–138; Steven D. Fraade, "The Temple as a Marker of Jewish Identity Before and After 70 CE: The Role of the Holy Vessels in Rabbinic Memory and Imagination," *Jewish Identi-*

ties in Antiquity: Studies in Memory of Menahem Stern, eds. Lee I. Levine and Daniel R. Schwartz (Tübingen: Mohr Siebeck, 2009), 237–265. On the Madaba mosaic map, see the Franciscan Archaeological Institute's volume, *The Madaba Map: 100 Years Since Its Discovery* (Madaba, Jordan: Franciscan Archaeological Institute, 2001). Shulamith Laderman surveys Jewish and Christian attitudes toward the Tabernacle and the Jerusalem Temple in general in her *Images of Cosmology in Jewish and Byzantine Art: God's Blueprint of Creation* (Leiden: Brill, 2013). Dan Barag convincingly identified the object set between the columns on Bar Kokhba tetradrachmae in his "The Showbread Table and the Facade of the Temple on Coins of the Bar-Kokhba Revolt," *Ancient Jerusalem Revealed,* ed. Hillel Geva (Jerusalem: Israel Exploration Society, 1994), 272–276. See also my "'Ark of the Covenant' or 'Table of the Showbread?': Bar Kokhba Tetradrachmae and their Interpreters," in *The Bar Kokhba Revolt Revisited,* ed. Menachem Mor, forthcoming. The palm tree served as a symbol for Judaea and Jews, as I discuss in *Art and Judaism,* 142–147.

My edited exhibition catalog, *Sacred Realm: The Emergence of the Synagogue in the Ancient World* (Oxford and New York: Oxford University Press and Yeshiva University Museum, 1996), introduces the archaeological and literary sources for the synagogue in antiquity, with relevant bibliography. Also see Lee I. Levine's encyclopedic *The Synagogue: The First Thousand Years* (New Haven, CT: Yale University Press, 2005). The deployment of Jews in late antique and Byzantine literature has been a major research area in recent years. To my mind the most significant studies are David Olster's *Roman Defeat, Christian Response, and the Literary Construction of the Jew* (Philadelphia: University of Pennsylvania Press, 1994); and Andrew S. Jacobs, *Remains of the Jews: The Holy Land and Christian Empire in Late Antiquity* (Stanford, CA: Stanford University Press, 2004). Byzantine imperial interest in Temple imagery is discussed through the refracting lens of the Church of St. Polyeuctus by R. M. Harrison, *A Temple for Byzantium: The Discovery and Excavation of Anicia Juliana's Palace-Church in Istanbul* (Austin: University of Texas Press, 1989). See also Nadine Schibille, *Hagia Sophia and the Byzantine Aesthetic Experience* (Farnham, UK: Ashgate, 2014), 73–74; and Laderman, *Images of Cosmology,* 47–49. On *Megillat Aḥima'az* and its response to Hagia Sophia, see Robert Bonfil, *History and Folklore in a Medieval Jewish Chronicle: The Family Chronicle of Aḥima'az Ben Paltiel* (Leiden: Brill, 2009), 154–156, 262–263. Gregorovius's comments are cited from *History of the City of Rome in the Middle Ages,* trans. Annie Hamilton (London: G. Bell, 1903), 1:211. They were given new—and disturbing—life under the Nazi regime as *Der ghetto und die Juden in Rom* (Berlin: Schocken, 1935); and postwar as *The Ghetto and the Jews of Rome,* trans. Moses Hadas (New York: Schocken, 1948). Hans Yohanan Lewy's influential essay appeared first in *Kedem: Studies in Jewish Archaeology* 2 (1945): 123–125, in Hebrew, and was collected posthumously in *Studies in Jewish Hellenism* (Jerusalem: Bialik Institute, 1969), 255–258. Samuel Krauss's analysis appeared in his *Studien zur byzantinisch-jüdischen Geschichte* (Leipzig: G. Fock, 1914), 107; and the comments of his teacher, David Kaufmann, appear in his foundational article, "Etudes d'archéologie juive. 1. La synagogue de Hamman-Lif," *Revue Etudes Juives* 13 (1886): 55. Byzantine terminology for the biblical lampstand is discussed by Jeffrey C. Anderson, *The Christian Topography of Kosmas Indikopleustes: Firenze, Biblioteca Medicea Laurenziana, Plut. 9.28= The Map of the Universe Redrawn in the Sixth Century: with a Contribution on the Slavic Recensions* (Rome: Edizioni di Storia e Letteratura, 2013), 50.

Little is remembered about Heinrich Strauss, a member of the leftist Berit Shalom Party, with its decidedly culturalist bent. His insightful "Jewish Art as a Minority Problem," *Journal of Jewish Sociology* 2 (1960): 147–171, was contrary to the national art paradigm regnant in early Israeli scholarship on Jewish art, and exemplified in the tradition of Sukenik as well as of Mordecai Narkiss and his son, Bezalel Narkiss. I discuss Strauss's achievement in *Art and Judaism,* 57. Strauss's essay on the menorah appeared in English as "The History and Form of the Seven-Branched Candlestick of the Hasmonean Kings," *Journal of the Warburg and Courtauld Institutes* 22 (1959): 6–16. For sources on the Christian destruction of synagogues, see *Art, Judaism,* 195–214. The discussion here of Jewish and Samaritan menorahs in late antiquity is based mainly upon *Art and Judaism,* 148–165, and my more recent study, which includes the Christian, Samaritan, and Muslim sources, " 'When Is a Menorah "Jewish?' On the Complexities of a Symbol under *Byzantium and Islam,*" *Age of Transition: Byzantine Culture in the Islamic World,* ed. Helen Evans (New York: Metropolitan Museum of Art, 2015), 38–53. On branched Christian candelabra, see Laskarina Boura and Maria G. Parani, *Lighting in Early Byzantium* (Washington, DC: Dumbarton Oaks, 2008), 6–11. The recently discovered synagogue mosaic from Horvat Kur shows oil lamps rather than glass cups. Its prompt initial debut appeared as "Magnificent Mosaic Menorah," *Biblical Archaeology Review* 42, no. 1 (2016): 10.

The Samaritan factor in the history of late antique Palestine has often been overlooked, an omission that became strikingly clear with recent discoveries in the West Bank. A notable exception is Hagith Sivan, *Palestine in Late Antiquity* (Oxford: Oxford University Press, 2008). For an illustrated and accessible overview of Samaritan synagogues, see Reinhold Pummer, "How to Tell a Samaritan Synagogue from a Jewish Synagogue," *Biblical Archeology Review* 24, no. 3 (1998): 24–35. On the Samaritans more generally, see his *The Samaritans: A Profile* (Grand Rapids, MI: Eerdmans, 2015). The small jugs from Jerusalem and environs from late antiquity bearing images of the menorah have usually been thought to have been used by Jews, and not intended for Christian use, as I have suggested. See the pivotal essays by Dan Barag, "Glass Pilgrim Vessels from Jerusalem, Part I," *Journal of Glass Studies* 12 (1970): 35–63; "Glass Pilgrim Vessels from Jerusalem, Parts II–III," *Journal of Glass Studies* 13 (1971): 45–63. Islamic "menorah" coins are also discussed by Barag, "The Islamic Candlestick Coins of Jerusalem," *Israel Numismatic Journal* 10 (1991): 40–48. I discuss the image of Bezalel as an artisan in late antique Jewish contexts in *Art and Judaism,* 99–103, and expand upon the Roman context with a focus upon elite Roman artisans through the refracting lens of Josephus's Bezalel (*Antiquities* 3.101–103) in *Art, History,* 21–36. I raised the connection between the *Targum Sheni to Esther* menorah description and Byzantine art in "The United Colors of the Menorah: Some Byzantine and Medieval Perspectives on the Biblical Lampstand," ed. Isaac Kalimi and P. J. Haas, *Biblical Interpretation in Judaism And Christianity* (London: T&T Clark, 2006), 112–113. See also *Art and Judaism,* 105–106, and now the exhaustive study of this motif by Allegra Iafrate, *The Wandering Throne of Solomon: Objects and Tales of Kingship in the Medieval Mediterranean* (Leiden: Brill, 2015), 137–139. Targum Onkelos, Rashi, Gersonides, and Naḥmanides on the Pentateuch are cited from *The Torat Chaim Chumash* (Jerusalem: Mossad Harav Kook, 1993), in Hebrew. On the neutering of late antique visual imagery by medieval scribes, note the fate of the Divine finger that is chronicled by Harry Fox, "'As If with a Finger'—The Text History of an Expression Avoiding Anthropomorphism," *Tarbiz* 49 (1980): 78–91, in Hebrew.

I discuss in considerable detail the shape of the menorah branches, particularly in medieval sources, in "Was the Lubavitcher Rebbe Right? On the Shape of the Menorah 'Branches' from the Bible to Menachem Mendel Schneerson," *Text, Tradition and the History of Second Temple and Rabbinic*

Judaism: Studies in Honor of Professor Lawrence H. Schiffman, ed. Stuart S. Miller et al. (Leiden: Brill, forthcoming). See also Yisrael Ariel, *Menorat Zahav Tahor* (Jerusalem: The Temple Institute, 2008), 61–62. On tefillin during the latter Second Temple period and in early rabbinic literature, see Yehudah Cohen, *Tangled up in Text: Tefillin and the Ancient World* (Atlanta, GA: Scholars Press, 2008); and Yonatan Adler, "Identifying Sectarian Characteristics in the Phylacteries from Qumran," *Revue de Qumran* 89 (2007): 79–92. The study of Rashi's drawings is still in its infancy. See, in the meantime, Mayer I. Gruber, "What Happened to Rashi's Pictures?," *Bodleian Library Record* 14, no. 2 (1992): 111–124. The relationship between Nicholas of Lyra's commentary on the Tabernacle vessels, Rashi, and Jewish visual tradition is discussed by Bernice M. Kaczynski, "Illustrations of Tabernacle and Temple Implements in the 'Postilla in Testamentum Vetus' of Nicolaus De Lyra," *Yale University Library Gazette* 48, no. 1 (1973): 1–11. On Rashi's use of the word *nieller,* see Mordecai Narkiss, "Niello: Pereq be-yedi'at ha-tekhniqah shel Rashi," *Sefer Rashi,* ed. J. L. Maimon (Jerusalem: Mossad Harav Kook, 1956), 538–542, in Hebrew; Fine, "The United Colors of the Menorah," 111–112. Peter Bloch's pivotal studies of medieval Christian menorahs appeared as "Siebenarmige Leuchter in christlichen Kirchen," *Wallraf-Richartz-Jahrbuch* 23 (1961): 55–190. An abbreviated version was prepared as "Seven-Branched Candelabra in Christian Churches," *Journal of Jewish Art* 1 (1974): 44–49, and served as the basis for Bianca Kühnel, "The Menorah and the Cross: The Seven-Branched Candelabrum in the Church," in *In the Light of the Menorah: Story of a Symbol,* ed. Yael Israeli (Jerusalem: The Israel Museum, 1999), 117–121. For a survey of images of menorahs in medieval Hebrew manuscripts, see Bezalel Narkiss, "The Menorah in Illuminated Hebrew Manuscripts of the Middle Ages," in the same volume, 81–86. The Samaritan curtain is in Herman Glaser, "Die Samaritaner," *Menorah: Jüdisches Familienblatt für Wissenschaft, Kunst und Literatur* (December 20, 1923): 7; and discussed by L. A. Mayer, "A Sixteenth Century Samaritan Hanging," *Bulletin of the Jewish Palestine Exploration Society* 13, nos. 3–4 (1939): 169–70, pl. 5, in Hebrew.

Art historical sources for the seven-branched lampstand in Renaissance art are surveyed admirably by Avraham Ronen, "The Menorah in Renaissance Art," in *In the Light of the Menorah,* 122–125. The lampstand of Santa Maria in Vulturella is first discussed by Attilio Rossi, *Santa Maria in Vulturella (Tivoli): ricerche di storia e d'arte* (Rome, 1905), 91, and subsequently by Bloch and Kühnel. On Jews at the Arch of Titus during papal installations, see Amnon Linder, "'The Jews too were not absent . . . carrying Moses's law on their shoulders': The Ritual Encounter of Pope and Jews from the Middle Ages to Modern Times," *Jewish Quarterly Review* 99, no. 3 (2009): 323–395; and Daniela Di Castro, *Et Ecce Gaudium: The Roman Jews and the Investiture of the Popes* (Rome: Museo Ebraico di Roma, 2010), 22–36. Di Castro's volume pointedly commemorates an exhibition created at the Jewish Museum in Rome for the visit of Pope Benedict XVI on January 17, 2010. On the medal of Urban VII, see Nathan T. Whitman and John L. Varriano, *Roma Resurgens: Papal Medals from the Age of the Baroque* (Ann Arbor: University of Michigan Museum of Art, 1983), 49; of Benedict XIII: Walter Miselli, *Il Papato Dal 1700 Al 1730: Attraverso Le Medaglie* (Torino: Il Centauro, 1997), 173, 183. On Bosio and his discovery of Jewish catacombs, see *Art and Judaism,* 154–155. The Scola Catalana in Rome is discussed by Bice Migliau, "Nuove prospettive di studio sulle Cinque Scole del ghetto di Roma: l'identifijicazione ed il recupero dell'arón di Scola Catalana," *Henoch* 12, no. 2 (1990): 191–205. The stele at St. John of the Lateran is illustrated by Daniela Di Castro, *Arte Ebraica a Roma e nel Lazio* (Rome: Museo Ebraico di Roma, 1994), 122. On standing Hanukkah menorahs, see Mordecai Narkiss, *The Hanukkah Lamp* (Jerusalem: Bney Bezalel, 1939), 71–81, in Hebrew; and Susan L. Braunstein, *Five Centuries of Hanukkah Lamps from the Jewish Museum: A Catalogue Raisonné* (New York: The Jewish Museum, 2004), 12, 18–19, 117–120. On two-headed eagles in Eastern European synagogues, with an emphasis upon lamps, see Ilya Rodov, "The Eagle, Its Twin Heads and Many Faces: Synagogue Chandeliers Surmounted by Double-Headed Eagles," *Jewish Ceremonial Objects in Transcultural Context* (*Studia Rosenthaliana,* 37 [2004]): 77–129. Messianism at the time of Ibn Yahya is discussed by Moti Benmelech, "History, Politics, and Messianism: David Ha-Reuveni's Origin and Mission," *AJS Review* 35 (2001): 35–60. *The Chronicle of Josippon,* its distribution, and particularly its long-term influence on the Zionist movement are admirably traced by Steven Bowman, "'Yosippon' and Jewish Nationalism," *Proceedings of the American Academy for Jewish Research* 61 (1995): 23–51. I treat Moses Mendelssohn and his fascinating discussion of the arch menorah more fully in "Jerusalem in Rome: Moses Mendelssohn on the Arch of Titus Menorah," *Lema'an Ziony: A Festschrift in Honor of Ziony Zevit,* ed. Frederick Greenspoon and Gary Rendsburg (Eugene, OR: Wipf and Stock, forthcoming). The finest and most readable introductions to synagogue architecture and its transitions in the nineteenth and twentieth centuries are still Rachel Wischnitzer, *Synagogue Architecture in the United States* (Philadelphia: Jewish Publication Society, 1955); and *The Architecture of European Synagogues* (Philadelphia: Jewish Publication Society, 1964). On the ideological creation of the modern Western synagogue, see Michael A. Meyer, "'How Awesome Is This Place!' The Reconceptualization of the Synagogue in Nineteenth-Century Germany," *Leo Baeck Institute Yearbook* 41, no. 1 (1996): 51–63. On the Staglieno Cemetery in Genoa, see Giovanni Grasso and Graziella Pellicci, *Staglieno* (Genoa: Sagep, 1974). On the London Oratory, the most comprehensive source is still Henry Sebastian Bowden's *Guide to the Oratory, South Kensington* (London: The London Oratory, 1897). C. W. Wilshere's collection of gold glass is discussed by Susan Walker, "The Wilshere Collection of Late Roman Gold-Glass at the Ashmolean Museum, University of Oxford," in *Neighbours and Successors of Rome: Traditions of Glass Production and Use in Europe and the Middle East in the Later 1st Millennium AD*, eds. Daniel Keller, J. Price, and Caroline M. Jackson (Oxford: Oxbow, 2014), 68–72; and Walker's *Saints and Salvation: Charles Wilshere's Collection of Late Roman Gold-Glass, Sarcophagi and Inscriptions* (Oxford: Ashmolean Museum, forthcoming).

Chapter 3

Many of the early Zionist sources presented in this chapter are discussed in detail in my "Who Is Carrying the Temple Menorah? Jewish Counter-Memory and the Arch of Titus Spolia Panel," *Images: A Journal of Jewish Art and Visual Culture* 9 (2016). On the Wilshire Boulevard Temple and the Warner Murals by Hugo Ballin, see Edgar F. Magnin, *The Warner Murals in the Wilshire Boulevard Temple, Los Angeles, California* (Los Angeles: Wilshire Boulevard Temple, 1974). See also the exquisite photography in Tom Teicholz, Ann Lucke, and Tom Bonner, *Wilshire Boulevard Temple and the Warner Murals: Celebrating 150 Years* (Los Angeles: Wilshire Boulevard Temple, 2013). Documents confirming both Magnin's masonic membership and Dubin's participation in the Jewish Legion are housed in the Wilshire Boulevard Temple archives.

The ritualization of Jewish visitation to Rome is a subject unto itself. Biemann's *Dreaming of Michelangelo* is an important step toward fully conceptualizing this pilgrimage, and here I allude to elements of it as related to this volume. I will return to this form of modern pilgrimage in more detail in a forthcoming article. Wolfson's archives are at Harvard University. Alas, the Hebrew original of his poem is not preserved there. While

Jews described themselves as Maccabees, Zealots, and the warriors of Bar Kokhba, British soldiers in Palestine used Crusader metaphors for themselves. See Elizabeth Siberry, "Images of the Crusades in the Nineteenth and Twentieth Centuries," in *Oxford Illustrated History of the Crusades,* ed. Jonathan Riley-Smith (Oxford: Oxford University Press, 1995), 383–384.

The most recent study of the Jewish Legion, and my personal favorite, is Michael Keren and Shlomit Keren, *We Are Coming, Unafraid: The Jewish Legions and the Promised Land in the First World War* (Lanham, MD: Rowman & Littlefield, 2010). The *Yehuda Mistraḥreret* ("Judaea frees herself") medals are not widely known. See Eliezer Morav, *Iudaea Capta* (Israel: self-published, 2014), 50–51, in Hebrew; and my "Who Is Carrying the Temple Menorah? Jewish Counter-Memory and the Arch of Titus Spolia Panel." On the Bezalel School and Schatz, the best general treatment in English is by Margaret Olin, *The Nation without Art: Examining Modern Discourses on Jewish Art* (Lincoln: University of Nebraska Press, 2001), 33–70. Jess Olson contextualizes Schatz's novel in his "'Jerusalem Rebuilt': The Temple in the Fin-de-siècle Zionist Imagination," in *The Temple of Jerusalem: From Moses to the Messiah: In Honor of Professor Louis H. Feldman,* ed. Steven Fine (Leiden: Brill, 2011), 329–348. Shmuel Werses, in *S. Y. Agnon Literally: Studies of His Writings* (Jerusalem, 2000), 264–290, in Hebrew, details the background for Agnon's presentation of Schatz in *Tmol Shilshom,* providing a vivid image of Jerusalem Zionist culture and Agnon's place in it.

The broad subject of Jewish Freemasonry, the Independent Order of B'nai B'rith, and related groups, so important for the process of Jewish Westernization, is still understudied. See Jacob Katz, *Jews and Freemasons in Europe, 1723–1939* (Cambridge, MA: Cambridge University Press, 1971); Daniel Soyer, "Entering the 'Tent of Abraham': Fraternal Ritual and American-Jewish identity, 1880–1920," *Religion and American Culture: A Journal of Interpretation* 9, no. 2 (1999): 159–182; Cornelia Wilhelm, *The Independent Orders of B'nai B'rith and True Sisters: Pioneers of a New Jewish Identity, 1843–1914* (Detroit, MI: Wayne State University Press, 2011); Alice M. Greenwald, "The Masonic Mizraḥ and Lamp: Jewish Ritual Art as a Reflection of Cultural Assimilation," *Journal of Jewish Art* 10 (1984): 87–101; Nir Ortal, "Finding Freemasonry in Jerusalem," *Segulah* (June–July 2010): 60–70; Steven Fine, *Art, History and the Historiography of Judaism in the Greco-Roman World* (Leiden: Brill, 2013), 183–184. On Charles Warren, see Robert Morris, *Freemasonry in the Holy Land: Or, Handmarks of Hiram's Builders; Embracing Notes Made During a Series of Masonic*

Researches, in 1868, in Asia Minor, Syria, Palestine, Egypt and Europe, and the Results of Much Correspondence with Freemasons in Those Countries (London: Robert Morris, 1872), esp. 431. On the art of Ze'ev Raban, see Batsheva Goldman Ida's foundational *Ze'ev Raban: A Hebrew Symbolist* (Tel Aviv: Tel Aviv Museum of Art, 2001), in Hebrew, and Ida's earlier English exhibition catalog, *Raban Remembered: Jerusalem's Forgotten Master: Essays and Catalogue of an Exhibition at the Yeshiva University Museum, December 1982–June 1983* (New York: Yeshiva University Museum, 1983). Many thanks to Dr. Ida for pointing out to me the breadth of Masonic imagery in Raban's oeuvre. On the Jewish Lads' Brigade, see Emil Lehman, *The Tents of Michael: The Life and Times of Colonel Albert Williamson Goldsmid* (Lanham, MD: University Press of America, 1996). Jess Olson, *Nathan Birnbaum and Jewish Modernity: Architect of Zionism, Yiddishism, and Orthodoxy* (Stanford, CA: Stanford University Press, 2013), 24–66, discusses the early history of the Kadimah Society. For Jabotinsky's use of the logo *kadimah,* see Hillel Halkin's excellent biography, *Jabotinsky: A Life* (New Haven, CT: Yale University Press, 2014), 54. Jabotinsky's letter of June 17, 1919, to Edward G. Derby is preserved at the Jabotinsky Institute, letter number 3394, Reference Code: A 1–2/9. On Rabbi Leib Isaac Falk as a Mason, see Raymond Apple, "Masonic Ministers in Australia," *Journal of the Australian Jewish Historical Society* 20, no. 4 (2012): 566–579. The disturbances of 1929 were discussed most comprehensively by Hillel Cohen in his *Year Zero of the Arab-Israeli Conflict 1929* (Waltham, MA: Brandeis University Press, 2015), which should be read together with Benny Morris's 2013 review of the Hebrew edition, http://mida.org.il/2013/11/22/ביקורת-ספר-תרפט-שנת-האפס-בסכסוך-היהו. On Jabotinsky's role, see Cohen, 221–222.

Joseph Tischler's urban planning projects in Tel Aviv were highlighted in Baruch Ravid's 2008 exhibition, the catalog to which was published as *Yosef Tishler: Architect and Town Planner in Tel Aviv* (Tel-Aviv: Bauhaus Center, 2008), in Hebrew. See also Nathan Harpaz, *Zionist Architecture and Town Planning: The Building of Tel Aviv (1919–1929)* (West Lafayette: Indiana University Press, 2013), 199–201. On Hareuveni and his menorah plant, see the essays collected by Tamar Manor-Friedman, *The Botanist's Brush: Shmuel Charuvi's Drawings for the Hareuveni Flora Treasury of the Land of Israel* (Jerusalem: The Israel Museum, 2006); Ephraim Hareuveni, "The Knobs of the Menorah and the Cretian Apples," *Leshonenu* 1 (1928): 49–52, in Hebrew; and Noga Hareuveni, " 'Knob and Flower' in the Design of the Menorah," in *In the Light of the Menorah: Story of a Symbol*, ed. Yael Israeli (Jerusalem: The Israel Museum, 1999), 39–42. The continuing power of Hareuveni's unconventional scholarship is such that as late as 1999 this essay opens this catalog, and still inspires contemporary artists. See, for example, Noa Raz Melammed, "Capsule," exhibited at the Jerusalem Artists' House in 2015, and the catalog to this exhibition, *Gatherer/Nonfunctional Display*, text by Tali Ben Nun, trans. Daria Kassovsky (Jerusalem: The Jerusalem Artists House, 2015), 50–51, 56.

I discuss the synagogue of the Jewish Hospital of Philadelphia (now the Einstein Medical Center) and the history of early Zionist archaeology, with special emphasis upon Slouschz and Sukenik, in *Art and Judaism in the Greco-Roman World: Toward a New Jewish Archaeology* (Cambridge: Cambridge University Press, 2005; rev. ed. 2010), 12–34. Weizmann's visit to Rome and the menorah presentation is moderated by Wiley Feinstein, *The Civilization of the Holocaust in Italy: Poets, Artists, Saints, Anti-Semites* (Madison, NJ: Farleigh Dickinson University Press, 2003), 183–184. My translation of the accompanying dedication is based upon the primary Italian-language document, housed in archives of Yad Chaim Weizmann, Rehovot. See also *American Addresses of Dr. Chaim Weizmann* (New York: Palestine Foundation Fund, 1923), 24–25. On the Menora Masonic Temple, see http://www.nycago.org/Organs/Bkln/html/MenoraMasonicTemple.html. The Ochs menorah has been thoroughly investigated by my student, Yitzchak Schwartz, "A Gift from One of the Jewish Faith: The Menorahs at John the Divine Cathedral and Liberal Religion in Interwar America," *Images: A Journal of Jewish Art and Visual Culture* 8 (2015): 25–45. The magnificent gates produced by Samuel Yellin for the Jewish Theological Seminary, now removed (and the menorah lost), are discussed in *Dedication of the Seminary Gates, September 26, 1934* (New York: Jewish Theological Seminary, 1934), unpaginated (6). Nahum Gutman's poster is discussed somewhat differently than I have by Batia Donner, "The Zionist Perspective in Keren Hayesod Posters," *Keren Hayesod Sows—The Jewish People Reap: Keren Hayesod Posters 1920–2010*, ed. D. Tartakover (Jerusalem: Keren Hayesod, 2010), 31, in Hebrew. On Gutman's meeting with Klausner in Rome, see Joseph Klausner, *My Path to Rebirth and Redemption: Autobiography (1874–1944)* (Tel Aviv: Masada, 1946), 265, in Hebrew. Fascist architecture and symbolism in Italy is discussed by Aristotle A. Kallis, *The Third Rome, 1922–1943: The Making of the Fascist Capital* (New York: Palgrave Macmillan, 2014). Regarding Morbiducci's bas-relief, see 264–265.

The protest at the arch on July 2, 1946, is reported by Jewish Telegraphic Agency, "Jews in Italy Hold Mass Demonstrations and Fast Protesting Palestine Raids, Arrests," (July 3, 1946); "Italian Jews Protest," *Palestine Post,* July 3, 1946, 7. A model of the destroyed embassy is exhibited at the Museum of the Irgun Tzvai Leumi—Etzel in Tel Aviv. On the Arch of Titus and its strong ideological connection to the 1946 bombing of the British Embassy among Irgun members and sympathizers, see Jacob Weinshall's historical novel, *In the Shadow of the Arch of Titus: A Story Set in the Explosion of the British Embassy by Soldiers of the Irgun* (Tel Aviv: Shalaḥ, 1952), in Hebrew. Weinshall was deeply involved in Revisionist culture of his day, and it is sometimes difficult to know what in his writings reflects otherwise undocumented fact and what is fiction.

The December 2, 1947, demonstration was covered by a wide range of news outlets. See, for example, "Jews Hail New Jewish State under Arch of Titus, Erected to Mark Destruction of Judea," *Jewish Telegraphic Agency,* December 3, 1947. The unanimity of the assembled survivors, is of course, rhetorical. In an oral history preserved at the U.S. Holocaust Museum, Eliezer Lidovski, a Jewish Partisan leader who participated in the protest, describes his embarrassment "before the world" at overt tensions between Revisionists and the Socialist "Hashomer ha-Tsair with their red flags" (RG-50.120*0092, 18:11:36ff., my translation). This event is well known in Israel, as film of it appears as a high point of the Israel Broadcasting Authority's documentary series *Pillar of Fire* (1981).

Chapter 4

The development of the Israel state emblem is detailed by Alec Mishory, *Lo and Behold: Zionist Icons and Visual Symbols in Israeli Culture* (Tel Aviv: Am Oved, 2000), in Hebrew, 138–164, and summarized as "The Menorah and the Olive Branches: The Design Process of the National Emblem of the State of Israel," *In the Light of the Menorah: Story of a Symbol,* ed. Yael Israeli (Jerusalem: The Israel Museum, 1999), 16–23. I have relied heavily upon documents preserved in the Israel State Archives, in the files of *Va'adat ha-Semel ve-ha-Degel shel Moetzet ha-Medinah* (the Committee on the State Symbol of the State Council) 19.7.48–9.2.49, 395/1-ג. A website dedicated to the Shamir brothers (http://www.shamir-brothers.com) contains significant additional documents of this process. On the Indian national emblem, see the brief comments of Nayanjot Lahiri, *Ashoka in Ancient India* (Cambridge, MA: Harvard University Press, 2015), 14. Arundhati Virmani's *A National Flag for India: Rituals, Nationalism and the Politics of Sentiment* (Ranikhet, India: Permanent Black, 2008) is a valuable study of a parallel and interrelated development. Rabbi Herzog's response to the choice of the Arch of Titus menorah as the state emblem appeared in print a number of times and seems to have been part of a concerted, if unsuccessful, campaign. In addition to his "The Shape of the Menorah in the Arch of Titus," *Scritti in memoria di Sally Mayer* (Jerusalem: Fondazione Sally Mayer; Milan: Scuola superiore di Studi Ebraici, 1956), 95–98, in Hebrew, see Menachem Barash, "ha-Rav [Yehoshua] Hutner Nilḥam al Shinui Semel ha-Medinah," *Yediot Aḥaronot,* January 23, 1958, 5. Herzog's part in the acceptance of the Beno Elkin menorah by the Knesset is discussed by Mishory, *Lo and Behold,* 180–181. Herzog's position is discussed by Tovia Preschel, "ha-Temunah she-ba-Keshet Titus be-Roma," *ha-Doar* 53 (1974): 579–580. On the term *semel,* "symbol," see the *Historical Dictionary Project* of the *Academy of the Hebrew Language,* s.v. *semel,* http://maagarim.hebrew-academy.org.il/Pages/PMain.aspx. For the pig as a symbol in Israeli civil religion, see Daphne Barak-Erez, *Outlawed Pigs: Law, Religion, and Culture in Israel* (Madison: University of Wisconsin Press, 2007; exp. Hebrew ed., Jerusalem: Keter and Ramat Gan: Bar Ilan University Press, 2015). On the notion of Zionist/Israeli secularism, see Amnon Raz-Krakotzkin, "Between 'Beret Shalom' and the Temple: The Dialectics of Redemption and Messianism Following Gershon Scholem," *Theory and Criticism* 20 (2002): 87–112; and his well-titled essay, "Ein Elohim Aval Hu Natan Lanu et ha-Aretz" (There is no God, but he gave us the Land), *Mita'am* 3 (2005): 71–76, both in Hebrew. The classic application of the sociological term "civil religion" to Israeli culture is Charles S. Liebman and Eliezer Don-Yehiya, *Civil Religion in Israel: Traditional Judaism and Popular Culture in the Jewish State* (Berkeley: University of California Press, 1983), esp. 107–112.

On Shlomo Sakolsky's "Menorat Yisrael," see Leah Hovev, "Yom ha-Atsma'ut be-Shirat Yeladim" (Independence day in children's poetry), *Derekh Efrata* 8 (1999): 37–38. On David Hillman and his window projects, see Leonard Fertleman, *The Splendours of the Central Synagogue, London: A Pictorial Study of the Stained Glass Windows by David Hillman* (London: Central Synagogue, 2010). The ritualization of Israel Independence Day is discussed by Aaron Ahrend, *Israel's Independence Day—Research Studies* (Ramat Gan: Bar Ilan University Press, 1998), 38–39, 71; and Levin Kipnis, *Haggadah shel Atsma'ut* (Tel Aviv: Karni, 1973). Mishory, *Lo and Behold,*

174–175, 197–199, assembles images of Jews bearing the menorah in Israeli art. On Rapoport, see James Edward Young, *The Texture of Memory: Holocaust Memorials and Meaning* (New Haven, CT: Yale University Press, 1993), 219–224; Batia Donner, *Nathan Rapoport: A Jewish Artist* (Jerusalem: Yad Izhak Ben Zvi Institute, 2014), 303–304, 328–330, in Hebrew. Jacob Birnbaum and the Hanukkah March are well documented in the archives of the "Student Struggle for Soviet Jewry Records 1956–2006," Yeshiva University Archives, Box 2, folder 10.

The rich culture of early Israeli reflection on the state "symbol" is exemplified mainly in ephemera and small objects, which have only recently begun to be collected, exhibited, and published. Among my favorites is the *Israel Liberata* series of commemorative medals and the related advertising materials. These are published by collector Eliezer Morav, *Iudaea Capta* (Israel: self-published, 2014). On the Arch of Titus Hanukkah lamp and other forms of historicizing craftsmanship in early Israel, see Nurith Canaan-Kedar, *Modern Creations from an Ancient Land: Metal Craft and Design in the First Two Decades of Israel's Independence from the Collection of Vicky Ben-Zimri* (Tel Aviv: Eretz Israel Museum; and Jerusalem: Yad Izhak Ben Zvi, 2006), 33–35, 95, in Hebrew and English. On the national symbol in newspaper cartoons, see Daniela Gardosh and Yoram A. Shamir, eds., *Lo Raq Semel: Semel ha-Medinah be-Karikaturah* (Holon: Israeli Cartoon Museum, 2011).

The visual context of Schneerson's menorah project is detailed by Maya Balakirsky Katz, *The Visual Culture of Chabad* (Cambridge: Cambridge University Press, 2011), 135–137. For a full discussion of the Qafiḥ/Schneerson hypothesis, see Steven Fine, "Was the Lubavitcher Rebbe Right? On the Shape of the Menorah 'Branches' from the Bible to Menachem Mendel Schneerson," *Text, Tradition and the History of Second Temple and Rabbinic Judaism: Studies in Honor of Professor Lawrence H. Schiffman,* ed. Stuart S. Miller et al. (Leiden: Brill, forthcoming). The menorah campaign is discussed by Sue Fishkoff in *The Rebbe's Army: Inside the World of Chabad Lubavitch* (New York: Schocken, 2003), 285–300. The comment cited by David Berger is part of a larger Modern Orthodox polemic against Chabad messianism after the death of Rabbi Schneerson in 1994. See his *The Rebbe, the Messiah, and the Scandal of Orthodox Indifference* (London: Littman Library of Jewish Civilization, 2001), 62. On the *Magen David,* see Gershom Scholem, "The Star of David: History of a Symbol," *The Messianic Idea in Judaism and Other Essays on Jewish Spirituality* (New York: Schocken, 1978), 257–281. This essential reflection should be read with my review of the slightly updated Hebrew version (ed. Avraham Shapira, trans. and ed. Galit Hazan-Rokem [Ein Harod, Israel: Mishkan Leomanut, 2008]), which contextualizes the essay within Scholem's wider project. It was published in *Images: A Journal of Jewish Art and Visual Culture* 5 (2011): 128–130.

Chapter 5

Scholars have begun to discuss the culture of television documentaries, related media, and the ways that this genre is affecting both scholarship and the broader culture. See, for example, Ryan Byrne and Bernadette McNary-Zak, *Resurrecting the Brother of Jesus: The James Ossuary Controversy and the Quest for Religious Relics* (Chapel Hill: University of North Carolina Press, 2009); and Lawrence H. Schiffman, "Inverting Reality: The Dead Sea Scrolls in the Popular Media," *Dead Sea Discoveries* 12, no. 1 (2005): 24–37. As a kind of remedy, a traveling exhibition organized by the National Geographic Society, *Indiana Jones and the Adventure of Archaeology*, http://www.indianajonestheexhibition.com/, is a well-crafted use of the Indiana Jones franchise to teach the history and craft of archaeology.

A range of scholars have dealt with urban myths of the Holy Grail, the Ark of the Covenant, and the "Ten Lost Tribes." See, in particular, Juliette Wood, *The Holy Grail: History and Legend* (Cardiff: University of Wales Press, 2012); Tudor Parfitt, *The Lost Tribes of Israel: The History of a Myth* (London: Weidenfeld & Nicolson, 2002); Parfitt, *The Lost Ark of the Covenant: Solving the 2,500 Year Old Mystery of the Fabled Biblical Ark* (New York: HarperOne, 2008); Zvi Ben-Dor Benite, *The Ten Lost Tribes: A World History* (Oxford: Oxford University Press, 2009); and Moti Benmelech, "The Ten Lost Tribes of Israel in Early Modern Jewish Eyes," *Zion* 77 (2012): 491–527, in Hebrew. The Samaritan redeemer, the *Taheb,* is discussed by Reinhold Pummer, *The Samaritans: A Profile* (Grand Rapids, MI: Eerdmans, 2015), s.v. *Taheb.* For a brief survey of biblical and later literature on the lost Temple vessels, with a focus upon *Kelim,* see James R. Davila, "The Treatise of the Vessels (*Massekhet Kelim*): A New Translation and Introduction," in *Old Testament Pseudepigrapha: More Noncanonical Scriptures,* ed. Richard Bauckham, James R. Davila, and Alexander Panayotov (Grand Rapids, MI: Eerdmans, 2013), 393–402. On the tiles from Kfar al-Kafil that include parts of this text, see Józef Tadeusz Milik, "Notes d'épigraphie et de topographie palestiniennes," *Revue Biblique* 66 (1959): 567–575. See also Chaim Milikowsky, "Where Is the Lost Ark of the

Covenant? The True History (of the Ancient Traditions)," in *Tradition, Transmission, and Transformation from Second Temple Literature through Judaism and Christianity in Late Antiquity,* ed. M. Kister, H. I. Newman, M. Segal, R. A. Clements (Leiden: Brill, 2015), 208–229.

Regarding Benjamin of Tudela, see Steven Fine, *Art, History and the Historiography of Judaism in the Greco-Roman World* (Leiden: Brill, 2013), 85. For the medieval Christian context, I have relied upon the foundational work of Marie Thérèse Champagne, *The Relationship between the Papacy and the Jews in Twelfth-Century Rome: Papal Attitudes toward Biblical Judaism and Contemporary European Jewry* (Ph.D. dissertation, Louisiana State University, 2005); and her "Treasures of the Temple: The Jewish Heritage of Papal Rome in the Twelfth Century," *Aspects of Power and Authority in the Middle Ages,* ed. Brenda M. Bolton and Christine E. Meek (Turnhout, Belgium: Brepols, 2007), 107–118. See also Champagne's essay with Ra'anan Boustan, which also discusses Benjamin of Tudela: "Walking in the Shadows of the Past: The Jewish Experience of Rome in the Twelfth Century," *Medieval Encounters* 17 (2011): 462–492.

Midrash Bereshith Rabbati, ed. Ch. Albeck (Jerusalem: Mekitse Nirdamim, 1940), is discussed in Fine, *Art, History,* 79–80, and extensively by Armin Lange, "The Severus Scroll Variant List in Light of the Dead Sea Scrolls," in Kister et al., *Tradition, Transmission, and Transformation,* 179–207. For John Allegro's popular presentation of the Copper Scroll, see his *The Treasure of the Copper Scroll: The Opening and Decipherment of the Most Mysterious of the Dead Sea Scrolls, a Unique Inventory of Buried Treasure* (Garden City, NY: Doubleday, 1960). The comprehensive discussion of the Copper Scroll is by Judah K. Lefkovits, *The Copper Scroll—3Q15: A Reevaluation: A New Reading, Translation, and Commentary* (Leiden: Brill, 1999). Since that date, see the following studies on the Copper Scroll: Philip R. Davies, "On John Allegro and the Copper Scroll," in *Copper Scroll Studies,* ed. George J. Brooke and Philip R. Davies (London: T&T Clark, 2002), 25–36; Steven Weitzman, "Myth, History, and Mystery in the Copper Scroll," in *The Idea of Biblical Interpretation: Essays in Honor of James L. Kugel,* ed. Hindy Najman and Judith H. Newman (Leiden: Brill, 2004), 239–255; Hanan Eshel, "What Treasures Are Listed in the 'Copper Scroll,'" in *Exploring the Dead Sea Scrolls: Archaeology and Literature of the Qumran Caves,* ed. Shani Tzoref Barnea Levi Selavan and Hanan Eshel (Göttingen: Vandenhoeck & Ruprecht, 2015), 113–130. The documentary *Ancient Refuge in the Holy Land* presents the process of scholarly evaluation and paradigm formation. It was aired November 23, 2004, on PBS, and is mounted at: http://www.pbs.org/wgbh/nova/ancient/ancient-refuge-holy-land.html.

J. D. Eisenstein's excited discovery appears as "The Fate of the Temple Vessels," *The Menorah: A Monthly Magazine for the Jewish Home* 31 (1901): 169–178. In his voluminous publications, Eisenstein never mentions this "discovery" again. I discuss his pilgrimage to the Arch of Titus in "Who Is Carrying the Temple Menorah? Jewish Counter-Memory and the Arch of Titus Spolia Panel," *Images: A Journal of Jewish Art and Visual Culture* 9 (2016). On the process of nineteenth-century "discovery" and its larger implications, see Neil Asher Silberman, *Digging for God and Country: Exploration, Archeology, and the Secret Struggle for the Holy Land, 1799–1917* (New York: Knopf, 1982), esp. 181–188.

On the ashlar at the Jewish Museum, Rome, see Daniela Di Castro, *From Jerusalem to Rome and Back: The Journey of the Menorah from Fact to Myth* (Rome: Museo Ebraico di Roma, 2008), 1–2; and her *Treasures of the Jewish Museum of Rome: Guide to the Museum and Its Collections* (Rome: Museo Ebraico di Roma, 2010), 40. Hawthorne's comments appear in his *The Marble Faun: Or, the Romance of Monte Beni,* (Boston: James R. Osgood, 1876), 1:200–201. The report of a menorah discovery in the Tiber appears in *Israel: The Jewish Magazine* 3 (1900): 72.

On the historical context for Agnon's "The Tale of the Menorah," see Shmuel Werses, *S. Y. Agnon Literally: Studies of His Writings* (Jerusalem, 2000), 254–255. The Israel Museum example was donated to the museum by "Arthur Lejwa, a native of Kielce, in memory of the Jewish community of Kielce, annihilated in the gas chambers in 1942." See Chaya Benjamin, "A Hanukkah Lamp from Poland," in *The Arthur and Madeleine Chalette Lejwa Collection in the Israel Museum,* ed. Ruth Apter-Gabriel (Jerusalem: The Israel Museum, 2005), 48–49. I discuss in this context just a few of the newer and older novels centered on the lost menorah. The list grows almost yearly.

Chapter 6

I first approached the issue of the menorah at the Vatican in "The Temple Menorah: Where Is It?," *Biblical Archaeology Review* 31, no. 4 (2005): 18–25, 62–63; and returned to it briefly in *Art, History and the Historiography of Judaism in the Greco-Roman World* (Leiden: Brill, 2013), 62–68. See especially Ronen Bergman, "The Pope's Jewish Treasures," *Musaf Haaretz,* May 15, 1996, 18–20, 22, in Hebrew; and Lisa Palmieri-Billig, "Shetreet:

Pope Likely To Visit Next Year," *The Jerusalem Post,* January 18, 1996, 1. On Yudl Rosenberg, see Ira Robinson, "Literary Forgery and Hasidic Judaism: The Case of Rabbi Yudel Rosenberg," *Judaism* 40, no. 1 (1991): 61–78; and Robinson's forthcoming biography of Rosenberg; Shnayer Z. Leiman, "The Adventure of the Maharal of Prague in London: R. Yudl Rosenberg and the Golem of Prague," *Tradition* 36, no. 1 (2002): 26–58. On Rosenberg as a fiction author, see Curt Leviant's introduction to Rosenberg's *The Golem and the Wondrous Deeds of the Maharal of Prague* (New Haven, CT: Yale University Press, 2007), xvii–xiv. For Hasidic attitudes toward holy objects, see Batsheva Goldman Ida's *Hasidic Art and the Kabbalah* (Boston: Brill, forthcoming).

Herzog's dissertation on the "royal blue" was published as *The Royal Purple and the Biblical Blue: Argaman and Tekhelet: The Study of Chief Rabbi Dr. Isaac Herzog on the Dye Industries in Ancient Israel and Recent Scientific Contributions,* ed. Ehud Spanier (Jerusalem: Keter, 1987), 17–147. Herzog discusses Gershon Henoch Leiner's project on pages 114–118. I first heard the legend of Herzog seeing the Temple vessels at the Vatican in 2000 from an Anglo-American immigrant to Israel. It is referenced in a long and fascinating interview with Rabbi Menachem Borstein: Shimon Cohen, "Az Eifo Nimtsaim Klei ha-Miqdash?," *Arutz Sheva,* July 29, 2012, http://www.inn.co.il/News/News.aspx/241786. Michael R. Marrus discusses Isaac Herzog's actual visits to the Vatican in "The Vatican and the Custody of Jewish Child Survivors after the Holocaust," *Holocaust and Genocide Studies* 21, no. 3 (2007): 390–394. Leiner's "visit" to Rome is noted in his Wikipedia entry: "Legend has it that on one of the Rebbe's visits to Rome; he succeeded in persuading the Vatican to allow him a quick glimpse of the Holy Vessels of the Beis HaMikdosh, to match his findings with the techeiles [blue dye] on the priestly garments," https://en.wikipedia.org/wiki/Gershon_Henoch_Leiner. On Yitzḥak Ḥai Bokovza and his relationship with Victor Emmanuel III, see Yosef Gion (Gi'on) ben David, "Rabbi Yitzḥak Ḥai Bokovza, z"l," *Ada* 116 (2010): 13–17, in Hebrew.

I have collected two recordings of Oscar Goldman discussing his Vatican trip: one provided by Joseph Frager and a second provided anonymously. On Moshe Blau, see http://crownheights.info/blogs/380656/our-heroes-rabbi-moshe-yehuda-hakohen-blau-1913-2003/; and the parallel Chabadpedia article, http://chabadpedia.co.il/index.php/חיים_משה יהודה_בלוי. See an article by Rabbi Blau's grandson, Menachem Mendel Elishevitz, and Chaim Eliezer Halevy Haber, "In the Footsteps of the Lost Vessels,"

KFAR CHABAD Weekly Magazine, n.d., 16–22, in Hebrew. The tale of Tannenbaum at the arch is recounted by Hershel Friedman, *Sefer me-Afelah le-Or Gadol: Nes Hatzolah fun Rebin z.y.ʿa. 21 Kislev 5705* (Kiryas Joel, NY: Di Idishe pene, 2001), 228–232, in Yiddish. Fulvo Cervini's essay on the lampstand in Prato was published as "La "menorah" secondo gli umanisti. I candelabri di Maso di Bartolommeo a Prato e Pistoia," *Artista* (1997): 114–125. This article was located by Yaakov Fine. Nissan Sherefi's claims appeared in an article by Yitzhak Qaqon, "The Temple Vessels Are Stored in the Vatican Vaults," *Yom le-Yom,* December 28, 2006, 3, in Hebrew. The story appeared in the general press in Gilad Shinhav's "Following the Temple Treasure," December 28, 2006, *MaarivNRG,* in Hebrew, http://www.nrg.co.il/online/1/ART1/523/773.html.

Yonatan Shtencel and his project is described, and the letter from the Papal Nuncio is reproduced in Nesanel Gantz, "Vanished Vessels of the Beis Hamikdash: Vatican Responds to Claim that the Church has our Holy Kelim in Its Possession," *Ami Magazine,* November 27, 2013, 119–126. Introductions to the modern history of papal relations with the Jewish community include David I. Kertzer, *The Popes against the Jews: The Vatican's Role in the Rise of Modern Anti-Semitism* (New York: Alfred A. Knopf, 2001); John Connelly, *From Enemy to Brother: The Revolution in Catholic Teaching on the Jews, 1933–1965* (Cambridge, MA: Harvard University Press, 2012).

Chapter 7

A recording of the Moldova event appears on YouTube. See http://www.jpost.com/Jewish-World/Priest-leads-attack-on-Moldova-menorah. The anti-Semitic venom of many of the responses that appear on this and other sites give pause. The Moldova menorah incident is cited from Elana Kirsh of the Associated Press, "Priest Leads Attack on Moldova Menorah," December 14, 2009, http://www.jpost.com/Jewish-World/Priest-leads-attack-on-Moldova-menorah/. These are supplemented with documents made available by Wikileaks, https://wikileaks.org/plusd/cables/10CHISINAU23_a.html and by correspondence with the Moldovan Foreign Ministry, which was facilitated by the Embassy of the Republic of Moldova in Washington, DC.

On the Temple Institute and its founder, Yisrael Ariel, see, first of all, www.temple institute.org, which provides a wealth of sources, including an extensive record of its activities on YouTube. See also the 2014 menorah lighting, with the participation of current Ashkenazi Chief Rabbi David Lau, https://www.youtube.com/watch?v=TLiXwN4F3TI. https://www.youtube.com/watch?v=xmI2yL7XKMo. The most significant secondary studies of the Temple movements, which include the Temple Institute, include: Aviezer Ravitzky, *Messianism, Zionism, and Jewish Religious Radicalism,* trans. Michael Swirsky and Jonathan Chipman (Chicago, IL: University of Chicago Press, 1996); Israel Shahak and Norton Mezvinsky, *Jewish Fundamentalism in Israel* (London: Pluto, 1999); Gershom Gorenberg, *The End of Days: Fundamentalism and the Struggle for the Temple Mount* (New York: Free Press, 2000); Motti Inbari, *Jewish Fundamentalism and the Temple Mount: Who Will Build the Third Temple?* (Albany, NY: SUNY Press, 2009); Sarina Chen, "Between Poetics and Politics—Vision and Praxis in Current Activity to Construct the Third Temple" (Ph.D. dissertation, Hebrew University of Jerusalem, 2007), in Hebrew, especially 39, 93–96, 183; Keshav and Ir Amim, *Dangerous Liaison: The Dynamics of the Rise of the Temple Movements and Their Implications,* Y. Be'er, writer, trans. London Sappir (Jerusalem: Keshav and Ir Amim, March 1, 2013), http://www.ir-amim.org.il/sites/default/files/Dangerous%20Liaison-Dynamics%20of%20the%20Temple%20Movements.pdf. On the Temple Institute menorah, see Yisrael Ariel, *Menorat Zahav Tahor* (Jerusalem: Temple Institute, 2008); and Temple Institute, *ha-Menorah* (Jerusalem: Temple Institute, 1999/2000), compact disc. For the "Holy Land Experience" and related phenomena, see Annabel Jane Wharton, *Selling Jerusalem: Relics, Replicas, Theme Parks* (Chicago, IL: University of Chicago Press, 2006), esp. 189–232; Joan Branham, "The Temple That Won't Quit: Constructing Sacred Space in Florida Theme Parks," *Harvard Divinity Bulletin* 36, no. 3 (2008): 18–31. For funding of the Temple Institute, see Keshev and Ir Amim, *Dangerous Liaison,* 55; Inbari, *Jewish Fundamentalism,* 31–32; Yotam Berger, "ha-Medinah Memamenet Amutot ha-Poalot le-Veniyat Beit ha-Miqdash," *Galei Tsahal,* August 4, 2013, http://glz.co.il/1064-23925-HE/Galatz.aspx. For the relationship between the Temple Institute and Koren Publishers, see https://www.facebook.com/media/set/?set=a.10150464990244969.1073741896.227386849688&type=3. For conflicting claims that the menorah is at the Vatican and its rebuttal by Temple Institute staff, see Mordechai Parser, "Eduyot Ḥadashot al Klei ha-Miqdash ba-Roma," *Nofim: Shevu'on le-Nadlan, Batim ve-Hitlahavut,* no. 17 (August 22, 2014), https://www.jerusalem-temple.com/Heb/?CategoryID=1046&ArticleID

=3448; Arnon Segal, "Neḥbaim el ha-Kelim," *Makor Rishon,* October 3, 2014, http://the--temple.blogspot.com/2014/10/blog-post_29.html.

The removal of the synagogue menorah from Netzarim may be viewed at https://www.youtube.com/watch?v=csXO9wQxtMA. On Hirszenberg's *Exile,* see Richard I. Cohen and Mirjam Rainer, "Invoking Samuel Hirszenberg's Artistic Legacy—Encountering *Exile,*" *Images: A Journal of Jewish Art and Visual Culture* 8 (2015): 46–65. Aaron Shevo's work appears on his professional website, http://shevo.com/pictures/default.asp?lang=eng. I discuss Shevo, the Netzarim evacuation, and the relationship between his poster and the work of David Tartikover in more detail in "Who Is Carrying the Temple Menorah? Jewish Counter-Memory and the Arch of Titus Spolia Panel," *Images: A Journal of Jewish Art and Visual Culture* 9 (2016). See also Dror Eydar, "The Door's Keepers: About 'Exclusion' and the Politicization of the Aesthetic in the Discourse of Israeli Art," *Protocols: History and Theory* 10 (2008), in Hebrew.

Conclusion

Yehuda Amichai's "I Feel Good in My Pants" appears in his *Shalvah Gedolah: She'elot u-Teshuvot* (Jerusalem: Schocken, 1980), 95, and in *The Selected Poetry Of Yehuda Amichai,* ed. C. Bloch and S. Mitchell, trans. S. Mitchell (Berkeley: University of California Press, 2013), 135. My translation varies at points. The Manado menorah was reported on by Norimitsu Onishi in "In Sliver of Indonesia, Public Embrace of Judaism," *New York Times,* November 23, 2010, A4. The Cosenza menorah display and the new myth of the menorah there were reported on by Rossella Tercatin in "Italian Town's Arab Street Decked with Menorahs for Xmas," *Times of Israel,* December 19, 2014, http://www.timesofisrael.com/italian-towns-arab-street-decked-with-menorahs-for-xmas/. This legend is presented, based upon Procopius and secondary reading, in a trade book by Daniel Costa, *The Lost Gold of Rome: The Hunt for Alaric's Treasure* (Stroud, England: Sutton, 2007), 182–188. The Arch of Titus *tableau vivant* appears at minute 11:24 of Yael Bartana's *Inferno.* On the film, its sources, and the Universal Church of the Kingdom of God in São Paulo, see *Yael Bartana: Inferno,* with text by Benjamin Seroussi and Eyal Danon (New York: Petzel, 2015), esp. 48. On contemporary Samaritan menorahs, see my *Art and Judaism in the Greco-Roman World: Toward a New Jewish Archaeology* (Cambridge: Cambridge University Press, 2005; rev. ed. 2010), 139–140.

Index

Index

Index

Index

Index